GREECE

Welcome to Greece

John and Shirley Harrison

GW00708394

Collins
Glasgow and London

Cover photographs
Brian Dicks (top: Thissio, Athens)
Derek Porteous (btm: Pithagorio, Samos)

Photographs
British Museum, Trustees of the
p. 12

Brian Dicks
pp. 38 (col. 2: 3rd, btm rt), 47, 51, 55, 62, 93 (l.), 96,
109 (top), 122

National Tourist Organization of Greece
pp. 38 (col. 1: 2nd, btm; col. 2: top, 2nd), 52, 73, 81,
82, 102

Van Phillips
pp.38 (col. 1: top, 3rd), 66, 71, 78, 90, 92, 93 (rt), 95,
97, 99, 101, 103, 104, 116, 118

Derek Porteous
pp. 38 (col. 2: 4th, btm l.), 67, 108, 109 (btm), 110,
124

Regional maps
Mike Shand

Town plans
M. and R. Piggott

Ground plans
Collins Companion Guides

Illustration
pp. 6–7 Peter Joyce

First published 1981
Copyright © John and Shirley Harrison 1981
Published by William Collins Sons and Company Limited
Printed in Great Britain

ISBN 0 00 447310 8

HOW TO USE THIS BOOK

The contents page of this book shows how the country is divided up into tourist regions. The book is in two sections; general information and gazetteer. The latter is arranged in the tourist regions with an introduction and a regional map (detail below left). There are also plans of the main towns (detail below right) and certain sites. All the towns in the gazetteer are shown on the regional maps. Places to visit and leisure facilities available in each region and town are indicated by symbols. Main roads, railways and airports are shown on the maps and plans.

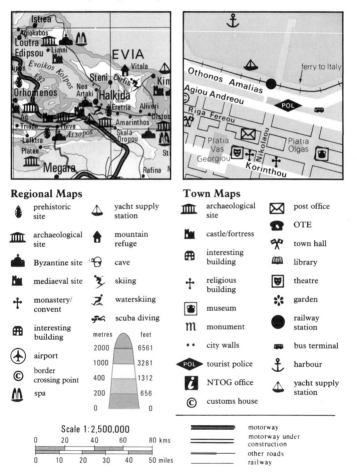

Regional Maps

💧	prehistoric site
🏛	archaeological site
⛪	Byzantine site
🏰	mediaeval site
✝	monastery/convent
🏢	interesting building
✈	airport
©	border crossing point
♨	spa

⛵	yacht supply station
🏠	mountain refuge
🕳	cave
🎿	skiing
🚤	waterskiing
🤿	scuba diving

metres	feet
2000	6561
1000	3281
400	1312
200	656
0	0

Scale 1:2,500,000

| 0 | 20 | 40 | 60 | 80 kms |
| 0 | 10 | 20 | 30 | 40 | 50 miles |

Town Maps

🏛	archaeological site
🏰	castle/fortress
🏛	interesting building
✝	religious building
🏛	museum
m	monument
••	city walls
POL	tourist police
𝑖	NTOG office
©	customs house

✉	post office
☎	OTE
✂	town hall
📖	library
🎭	theatre
❀	garden
●	railway station
🚌	bus terminal
⚓	harbour
⛵	yacht supply station

▬▬▬	motorway
═══	motorway under construction
▬▬▬	other roads
────	railway

Every effort has been made to give you an up-to-date text but changes are constantly occurring and we will be grateful for any information about changes you may notice while travelling.

CONTENTS

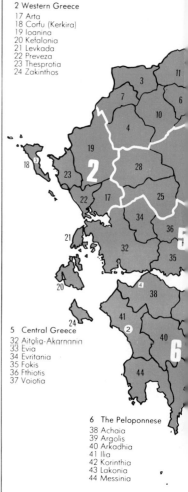

2 Western Greece
17 Arta
18 Corfu (Kerkira)
19 Ioanina
20 Kefalonia
21 Levkada
22 Preveza
23 Thesprotia
24 Zakinthos

5 Central Greece
32 Aitolia-Akarnania
33 Evia
34 Evritania
35 Fokis
36 Fthiotis
37 Voiotia

6 The Peloponnese
38 Achaia
39 Argolis
40 Arkadhia
41 Ilia
42 Korinthia
43 Lakonia
44 Messinia

1 Northern Greece
1 Drama
2 Evros
3 Florina
4 Grevena

5 Halkidiki
6 Imathia
7 Kastoria
8 Kavala
9 Kilkis

10 Kozani
11 Pela
12 Pieria

13 Rodopi
14 Seres
15 Thessaloniki
16 Xanthi

3 Thessaly and the Sporades
25 Karditsa
26 Larissa
27 Magnesia
28 Trikala

4 North-East Aegean Islands
29 Hios
30 Lesvos
31 Samos

8 The Cyclades
48 The Cyclades

7 Athens, Attica and the Argo-Saronic Islands
45 Attica
46 Pireas
47 Greater Athens

9 The Dodecanese
49 The Dodecanese

10 Crete
50 Hania
51 Iraklio
52 Lassithi
53 Rethimno

GREECE

The Greece of the travel brochures is real – sparkling seas, clear bright light, temples and olive groves, the free happy life of the *tavernas*. Alongside this however is Greece of the perpetual earthquake – half-built or half-collapsed, indifferent to food, revelling in disorder. Accept these contrasts within the country, and enjoy a warmth of welcome that will draw you back again and again.

This duality runs throughout Greece. It has endured 4000 years of history – periods of greatness and neglect, marvel and squalor, expansion and invasion – yet acts like a land with no past. Look at Greece and the East is before you; talk to Greeks and they see only the West. Last year's plastic greenhouse blows in shreds between next year's bold new crops.

The area of Greece, 131,944sq km/ 50,944sq mi, makes it just 1554sq km/ 600sq mi larger than England and almost exactly the same size as the state of Alabama. There are over 2500 islands accounting for one fifth of that area. A third of the total population of 9½ million lives in Athens while the mountains and islands suffer depopulation. Only one quarter of the land is arable, the rest is rough grazing or bare hillside.

On the islands, and to less extent on the mainland, the old clan ways persist. Just how long they can continue is a question that worries thinking Greeks. The girls are rigorously shielded until marriage, and while marriage is not exactly arranged, the girl is presented with a small number of suitable young men to choose from. The young man openly enquires about the size of the dowry before making his proposal. The young people accept the ancient ways not because the family is a tyrant but because it is the great protector. Nevertheless the Athens papers are full of advertisements from divorced parties willing to try again.

When Greeks leave their family, they enter the bigger family of the nation. They are intensely patriotic, with a strong sense of being all Greeks together. Their common enemies are the Turk and the rich Greek. Greek society is not classless, but class distinction is based only on outward signs of wealth. Greeks are strongly conservative, but the political initials you see everywhere are the KKE (communist) and PA.SOK (socialist).

The form of government has been subject to sudden change, but currently it is a democratic republic with a single-chamber parliament. Government is strongly centralized with most decisions taken by a Ministry in Athens. For administration the country is divided into 55 'nomes', but these are not units of local government like an English county – the nome is nearer to a French *département*, under a government-appointed nomarch. The nomes are grouped into larger units called provinces, which have strong historical associations but play little part in the day-to-day running of the country.

Each province has its own very different character, and in this book we have followed the provincial divisions in presenting ten tourist regions. These are: **Northern Greece,** the Balkan provinces of Makedonia and Thraki which were joined to Greece only 70 years ago; **Western Greece,** the ancient land of Epiros with its deep gorges and mountain villages, together with the soft Ionian Islands; **Thessaly,** a hot agricultural plain shut in by lovely mountains, together with a group of rather neglected islands, the **Sporades; Central Greece** which physically and in mood is a bridge between the more sombre north and the clear-aired south but is itself made up of three quite different areas; **Attica,** essentially the vast sprawl of modern Athens and its surrounding playground, including the islands of the Argo-Saronic Gulf; the **Peloponnese,** which with Attica makes the Greece of antiquity; the **North-East Aegean Islands,** nearest to the Turkish coast but with the deepest hostility to Turkey; the **Cyclades,** archetypal model of a Greek island now threatening to become a holiday camp for fugitives from holiday camps; the **Dodecanese,** an Italianate version of the Cyclades with a

soft winter climate; and **Crete**, home of civilization and legend, a country in itself.

More people are engaged in agriculture than in any other occupation. One of the banes of Greek agriculture is the system of dividing the land equally on inheritance amongst all the sons. Plots have become so small and dispersed that a farmer can spend half his time walking from one tiny field to another. This may explain the curiously disjointed landscape of the plains, with a tiny orchard in a wheat-field, or a few lines of tobacco across scrubby pasture. Where the peasants have been persuaded to exchange and consolidate their holdings, the land – away from the mountains – becomes intensely productive. The main crops are wheat (2 million tons a year, mainly from Thessaly), cotton (120,000 tons, concentrated in Makedonia), tobacco (80,000 tons officially, mainly in Thraki, but you can see little strips of tobacco anywhere), and olives (1 million tons, everywhere). The symbolism of the olive should not be forgotten – its oil is not only for food, but lights the lamps and heals wounds, its branches make the fire and even its centuries-old, gnarled trunk forms the coffin. The government is encouraging production of citrus fruits with some success.

Industry has overtaken agriculture as a money-spinner. Bauxite is the main mineral, used now in the aluminium smelter near Delfi, and deposits of lignite (brown coal) fuel the power stations and factories. Petrochemicals, shipbuilding and textiles, and a small steel industry based on local iron/nickel ores are scattered near the Aegean coast. Most industry, and nearly all agriculture, is small-scale, private enterprise, and the role of the government is to provide development loans.

Unextended loans are blamed for the state of Greek towns. On the outskirts there are just two styles of building – reinforced concrete piles with a cladding of red brick, and reinforced concrete piles with no cladding at all. In the centre there is no heart, for the towns have not grown up, they have been put up. The untidy dereliction that is a modern Greek town has one peculiar property – it is invisible to Greeks.

This ability to live in one of these towns and daily add to the disorder tells you something about the Greek character, though it is hard to say what. The light encourages them to look outward and beyond, to see an ideal world. Perhaps they see through the grey concrete to their friends inside, for social contact with neighbours is the essence of Greek life. Part of the Greek character is an interest in politics – politics are still a more popular pastime than television – and another part is the need for the approval of others. Praise is treasured; pride is easily wounded; nothing is impractical, it just doesn't get done; nothing is impossible, it just isn't attempted. Underneath the apparently dreamy exterior, Greeks are realists – centuries of natural disasters and wars have discouraged idealists. At a time of real crisis the impossible can be achieved.

One side of this complex personality is the extreme friendliness shown to foreign visitors. Don't be surprised when drinks arrive at your table, but find out who sent them and raise your glass – buying back is not the custom. If Nikos at the next table has paid for your meal, there's not much you can do but assure him he has a kind heart. In business, when your associate says 'We've finished, now let's talk', he really wants to talk and not fish for better terms.

In the gazetteer of this book the towns are in alphabetical order within each region, as centres from which to explore their surroundings. Most towns have a museum that is worth visiting if you're interested in antiquities, and an ancient church for the lover of architecture. The true appeal of Greece is found outside the towns – mountain villages, roadside and seaside *tavernas*, wild scenery and pastoral landscapes, limestone hills behind a palm-fringed cove, spiky cypress trees above a red-roofed church, oleanders, sheep, tomatoes, and the eternal twisted olive. Then there are the archaeological sites – the Glory that was Greece. Visit them, even if only out of duty.

The weather in summer is undeniably hot, but only inland is it airless. On the eastern coasts there can be a refreshing breeze in the afternoon; the west coasts can have sudden downpours, but the sun soon dries up everything. Winter in the north is miserable – rain and damp mist, and snow over the mountains; further south winter is mild but unexciting, and this is an ideal time to visit the antiquities – before the hordes of tourists appear. For many visitors the best time of all is probably spring, when temperatures are bearable, the ground is fresh and alive with flowers, and the air is clear.

THE PAST

For Americans, there are barely 300 years of history, and even for the English the world seems to have begun abruptly in 1066; to them, Greek history is some sort of vague memory from schooldays. Greeks may be a bit cynical about the glories of the past, dinned into them by Colonels and romantics, but they are aware that the history of their land stretches back continuously for 4000 years. It is worthwhile for the visitor to know something of that history to recognize the names you see and have some understanding of why Greece is the way it is today.

The Mycenaeans The original Greek speakers arrived in the Aegean some time before 2000 BC. This was the first of a 3000-year-long series of invasions by northern tribes into the more civilized Mediterranean. Initially they were dominated by the Minoans of Crete, but around 1500 BC the effects of a volcanic eruption on the island of Thira (Santorini) so weakened Minoan society that mainland Greeks took over the palace at Knossos. Their name for themselves was Achaeans, but archaeologists call the period Mycenaean, after their chief city, Mikines, where tourists now flock to see the ruined citadel and the tombs of the chiefs. It was Greeks of the later Mycenaean period who banded together for the war with Troy.

The Dorians and Dark Ages The next invaders came around 1000 BC – the Dorians, not just a conquering aristocracy like the Achaeans, but a whole nation. They remain the great mystery in the development of Greek culture. To Pharaoh's Egypt they were the People of the Sea – senseless savage raiders like the Vikings of a later age – but to some Greeks their coming was the Return of the Sons of Heracles. Did they smash the Mycenaean world and delay

its turning into classical Greece, or were they the vital spark that led to classical Greece?

The 300 years or so after the Dorians are the Dark Ages – dark because we know nothing about them.

Archaic and Classical Greece 800–350 BC From the Dark Ages there emerged hundreds of small, independent communities, each going its own way, all going roughly the same way. Some were quite large towns, others were no more than villages; these were the city states (*polis* in Greek). They were immensely creative continually inventing new forms of government – benevolent monarchy, tyranny (rule by a revolutionary leader, whose only claim to power was that he held it), rule by small cliques, democracy of the 'worthy citizen', democracy of the 'sailor rabble', dictatorship. They created the ways of thinking which, for good or ill, are accepted as the ideal for the modern world – moderation, a belief in reason, tolerance of others; plus a pursuit of 'wholeness' – every man an athlete, a warrior, a farmer or sailor, a poet and a politician. Their cultural achievements are touched on in the next chapter.

The Great Wars In 490 BC the city states saw their independence threatened by Persia, which was a huge, centralized empire, with everybody subject to the Great King – the opposite of the Greek ideal. However, they could not unite in self-defence. Many of the cities 'medized' – they invited the Persians in, preferring life under an idle satrap to bickering with their neighbours. Only Athens fought continuously, beating off a reconnaissance in force at the Battle of Marathons in 490 and then, after Spartan help to delay the Persians at Thermopiles, smashing the invading fleet at Salamina in 480.

Athens finally defeated Persia, again with Spartan help, at Platee in 479. In the next forty years, the 'Golden Age', classical Greece reached the peak of its achievements. During this time the temples on the Acropolis were built, and most of the temples on the islands – ruins now, but still beautiful.

Eventually, Athenian pride led to the futile war with Sparta – thirty years of high hopes, defeat and despair. These times are described in Thucydides' *History of the Peloponnesian Wars* and if ever you feel depressed at the modern world, read that. The war ended with the total defeat of Athens in 404 BC. Within ten years Athens had fully recovered and seemed more alive, more prosperous than ever, but the classical age was finished.

The Conquerors While the Greeks were fighting each other, Philip of Macedon was raising an army and plotting their ruin. In 338 BC he defeated a coalition of rivals at Heronia (page 74) and the Greek cities were finally united under the rule of a half-Greek barbarian. Philip's son Alexander the Great led the combined Macedonian and Greek armies to conquer Egypt, Persia and India. His empire split up when he died, leaving Ptolemy in Egypt, Seleuces in Syria, and chaos in Greece. Another 150 years of warring disunity ended when Roman legions defeated the last Macedonian phalanx at Pydna in 168 BC. The Greek cities, conquered separately, were united as the Roman province of Achaea.

While Greece became subject to these outsiders politically, the outsiders were dominated by Greek culture. All over the eastern Mediterranean Greek ideas, language, art and science were adopted by the rulers and some of the population. The style was not so strong and original as the pure Hellenic culture of the classical period, but clearly derived from it, so it is called Hellenistic. Alexandria, not Athens, was the centre of Athenian culture of the Hellenistic period. Later, when the Greek ideals of harmony joined with the Roman will to impose, the style is called Greco-Roman.

Byzantium The Roman Empire grew too big to be manageable, and in AD 286 was divided into a western part and an eastern part. Rome in the west survived another 200 years; in the east a new capital was built at Byzantium, which in AD 330 the Emperor Constantine re-named Constantinople (now Istanbul). Constantine was the first Christian emperor, and the first Byzantine emperor. He set the example of religious preoccupation, sumptuous ritual, intrigue, and brave defence of the Empire, which meant 'Byzantine' for the next thousand years.

Successive emperors fought off invading Goths, Serbs, Avars, Albanians and Bulgars, and tried to fight off Arabs and Seljuk Turks who posed a greater threat to the Orthodox religion – the unifying force of the Greek east.

The Great Betrayal In 1204 an army of Frankish barons, on their way to recover Jerusalem for Christ in the fourth Crusade, paused in Constantinople and stole the Byzantine Empire for themselves. Little Frankish kingdoms and dukedoms were set up in Greece and you can still see their remains as ruined castles on the hilltops. The Franks did not last. Others came for the pickings – Venetians, Catalans – until a new dynasty of Emperors, the Palaeologi, recovered the throne and partly restored the Empire.

Turkish Rule In 1453 the Ottoman Turks captured Constantinople, and most of Greece quickly fell to the Turks. Some of the islands remained under Venice for two hundred years but were then overrun. Only the western islands remained a haven of freedom. Over three hundred years passed but the Turks left almost no trace – a few hump-backed bridges, some pretty merchants' houses in the north, and a lively hatred of the Turks in the Greek people today. The Greeks preserved their language and religion, and developed a national consciousness – something which had eluded the classical age.

The War of Independence In 1821 the Greeks revolted against Turkish rule, and after eight years of courage, betrayal, massacre, love of country and love of gold, freedom of a sort was won. (See Pilos page 84 and Messolongi page 74.) The end of the war was a compromise dictated by the Great Powers to stop Russian expansion into the Balkans. Southern Greece became a republic, the north remained under Turkey. The first Greek president, Capodistrias, was assassinated after only three years, and so the Great Powers imposed a king – Otho, Prince of Bavaria.

The Great Idea Otho became king in 1833 at the age of 17. His Bavarian architects built mock classical style palaces which you can see in Athens today. In front of one of them he was forced to grant a constitution, in the square which is now the centre of Athens – Sintagma (Constitution) Square. Finally he was deposed.

Otho was replaced by another 17-year-old prince, George William of Denmark. In 1863 he took the title, 'George, King of the Hellenes', asserting that he was king not just of a few scraps of land at the foot of the Balkan peninsula, but of all Greeks. This coincided with the birth of the Great Idea, the theme that dominated Greek politics into the 20th century. For some, the Great Idea was the impossible dream of restoring the Byzantine Empire, others dreamed only of political union for all Greeks. A start was made: George William brought with him as a dowry from Britain the Ionian Islands; Thessaly and part of Epiros were recaptured in 1881; Crete came under a Greek governor in 1897; and in the Balkan wars of 1912 the dream was nearly realized. Greece ganged up with Serbia and Bulgaria to chase the Turks out of Europe, and then Greece relieved the Bulgarians of Makedonia.

The Great War and Smyrna At the start of the 20th century a Cretan patriot, Venizelos, became the leading Greek politician. His name is recalled now by a street or square in almost every town in Greece. His driving passions were the Great Idea and the ideals of classical Greece, including the establishment of a free democracy. It was he who brought Greece into the world war of 1914 on the side of the Western Allies, although King Constantine was pro-German. Greek and British troops fought a long, hard campaign against the Bulgarians and Germans; over much of eastern Makedonia are memorials to the fallen – a smaller version of the cemeteries of the Western Front.

At the end of the war, Greece took all of Thraki almost to the walls of Constantinople, and the Great Idea was nearly complete. There remained the Greek communities of Asia Minor – 1½ million people, prosperous Christians in a Muslim sea. To assert control over them too, the Greek army attacked the Turks at Smyrna (Izmir) in 1922 and was torn to pieces. Lloyd George, the British prime minister who had encouraged the Greeks and then deserted them, lost his job; three former Greek prime ministers and the commander-in-chief were executed. Turkey recovered Thraki as far as the River Evros, and all the Greeks living in Turkey were expelled – nearly one Greek in three was a refugee. The Great Idea was fulfilled.

The Second World War Somehow the Greeks managed to absorb the refugees while trying to build a modern country. Kings came and went. In 1935 the monarchy was restored; General Metaxas became prime minister in 1936 and then dictator. Under him the army was ready for the next great day. On 28 October, 1940, Metaxas answered just 'OXI' (No) to Mussolini's demand for passage through Greece, and since then it has been a national holiday – Οχι Day. The Italians were defeated, but then German troops were diverted from the attack on Russia to force a way through Yugoslavia and help the Italians. Greece was under Nazi rule until 1944 and suffered more than any other occupied country – 10 percent of Athens' population died of starvation.

As soon as the Germans left, civil war started between Communists and Royalists, lasting until 1949. At first British, and then American, support kept Greece on the western side of the Iron Curtain. Then with massive American subsidies, Greece began again to try to become a modern nation.

The Colonels Greece had an educated, cultured people, was the founder member of the club of 'Western' nations, and yet was as abjectly poor as almost any undeveloped country. The strain was too much and in 1967 a military junta took over, to restore Greece, home of democracy, with a spell of Fascism. In 1974 the colonels were removed, and Greece became a democratic republic again.

Every age has left its monuments. The Mycenaean tombs, classical temples, Frankish castles, Venetian palaces, Byzantine churches – each tells you something of Greece's history. The Colonels have left tourist hotels.

The EEC In May 1979 Greece signed the Treaty of Rome, becoming the tenth full member of the European Economic Community, effective from 1st January, 1981.

THE ARTS

In art as in life, the ideal for classical Greece was 'the true, the good and the beautiful', with nothing to excess. Byzantine art was wholly religious in purpose. Modern Greek art expresses the suffering of the recent past.

Architecture

The **Greek temples** were built to house the gods – worship of the gods was at an altar outside. Most of them are now ruined, but the ideal of the Greek temple survives as the standard for serenity and balance in architecture. The effect of a ruined temple today is due more to its setting than to the architecture, and why not – from the beginning the site was conceived as part of the building.

The ruins are made more interesting if you know what to look for and can follow the names in guide-books. The two main types of temple are the austere Doric and the more decorated Ionic which became popular after the Golden Age. The best-preserved Doric temple is the 'Thesseion' in Athens. Other lovely ruins are at Vasses in the mountains, Cape Sounio overlooking the sea, Egina, Delfi and Olympia. The most beautiful ruins of all must be on the Acropolis; besides the Parthenon, the Propylaea is a mixture of Doric and Ionic, while the little Temple of Athena is pure and delightful Ionic. The chamber tombs of the Macedonian kings, as at Vergina and Pela, look like miniature Ionic temples. (See page 37.)

Byzantine churches are found all over Greece, but especially in the north. See the 11th-century monasteries of Dafni (page 101), Ossios Loukas (page 70) and Nea Moni (Hios, page 63), and the many churches of Thessaloniki. The basic plan of a Byzantine church is a cube, capped by a dome, with equal arms projecting from the sides of the cube to make the square Greek cross. This creates a tremendous sense of space within small dimensions. The exuberant decoration makes it easy to imagine that a Byzantine interior is a recurrence of Minoan rather than Hellenic taste.

The cubic style of **Cycladic houses** (see page 108) led Le Corbusier, our most influential modern architect, to regard the aim of his own work as 'the masterly, correct and magnificent play of masses brought together in light'.

Literature

When the Greek alphabet was devised around 750 BC, it was used at once to write poetry which was meant to be sung. **Epic poems** recalled the heroes of the recent past. Homer wrote the *Iliad*, describing a few weeks in the war with Troy, and the *Odyssey*, the adventures of one of the returning warriors. The works are probably a collection of ballads sung by the Achaeans when they were driven by invading Dorians to settle in Troy. Hesiod was the other famous epic poet. **Lyric poetry** was the chief creation of Sappho (6th cent. BC) who wrote love poems to her Lesbian friends (see page 65). The fables of Aesop, a contemporary of Sappho, and the works of Solon (c 639–559 BC) show the developing Greek taste for drawing moral conclusions in poetry. Pindar (c 522–442 BC) wrote choral odes honouring the victors of the Olympic Games.

Drama was developed by Aeschylus (524–456 BC) whose trilogy *The Oresteia*, still attracts modern audiences; Euripides (c 480–406 BC) whose interest was in human ideas and emotions; and above all Sophocles (c 496–406 BC) whose *Antigone* and *Electra* have inspired many modern playwrights. Sophocles was concerned with human destiny and inexorable fate. His *Oedipus Rex* (see page 70) is perhaps the most intense play ever written, more moving now than when it was first performed. Aristophanes (c 448–388 BC) wrote Old Comedy – political satire which with

little effort you can apply to the modern world. Menander (c 342–292 BC) wrote New Comedy – biting comment on the degenerate manners of his age.

The father of **history** was Herodotus (c 484–424 BC), who not only tried to document events but to arrive at judgements. Thucydides (c 460–400 BC) looked rationally for the causes and origins of the wars he lived through and described. Xenophon (c 430–355 BC) gives an account of the return from Asia of an army of Greek mercenaries which matches any modern adventure tale. Plutarch (c AD 46–120) wrote biographies. Pausanias (2nd century AD) wrote a guide-book, *Description of Greece*.

The New Testament was written in Greek (apart perhaps from Matthew) and it is interesting to speculate how Christianity would have differed if it had originally been written in Latin. Byzantine literature was religious, historical or biographical, and is hardly read today.

The following is a sample of some of the well-known names in modern literature: Dionysios Solomos (1798–1857) *The Free Besieged*; Kostis Palamas (1859–1943) *The Twelve Words of the Gipsy*; Andreas Karkavitsas (1866–1923) *The Beggar*; Nikos Kazantzakis (1885–1957) *Zorba, the Greek*; George Seferis (born 1900) *The King of Asine and Other Poems*; Odysseus Elytis (born 1911) *Orientations*.

Pictorial Art

Classical Greek painting was renowned and highly praised by later ages. Unfortunately it has nearly all disappeared. Agatharkos discovered perspective but the technique was lost again until the Italian Renaissance. To see the development of the Greek view of life, compare the different examples of painted vases in a museum. In the archaic period **black-figure pottery** was highly prized, and a principal source of income for Athens. It was replaced by the **red-figure** work which struggled to become more naturalistic (see page 12). By the classical age, the difficulty of painting on an earthenware vessel led to a decline in artistic quality, and the pottery of the Hellenistic period is less admired by artists than reproduced for tourists.

The Byzantine period produced many paintings – large scale **frescos and murals,** and small **ikons** which look you straight in the face so that you get the full force of the saintly power. **Mosaics** and above all **book illustrations** show Byzantine art at its best.

Some of El Greco's (Domenikos Theotokopoulos) paintings (1541–1614) show a strong Byzantine influence. The most famous of Greek painters, he was born in Crete but spent most of his life in Spain.

Modern art (see the Museum thereof in Athens) is in two streams – naive pictures by peasant artists who remain genuine peasants, and the more celebrated 'names'. Look out for Gounaro (the effects of light in distorting the senses), Kondoglou (modern ikons), Hadzikyriakos known as Ghika (landscapes), and Tsarouhis (a cross between Manet and Lowry).

Black and red-figure pottery

Philosophy and Science

Science and philosophy were a single activity for the Greeks – an attempt to understand the world, not to change it. Modern science is based on experiment, but the Greeks looked down on *technike* and left it to the Romans to develop engineering and to the Arabs and Indians to provide the numbers that made modern mathematics possible.

Thales and Anaximander in the 7th century BC looked for unity in the universe. Pythagoras (c 582–507 BC) not only established his famous theorem, he also made discoveries in acoustics that later scientists could build on. Heraclitus (c 540–480 BC) opposed Pythagoras, and put forward an early version of the theory of relativity. Archimedes (287–212 BC) discovered, and put to use, several fundamental principles of modern physics. Euclid (c 300 BC) rationalized all the geometry of his predecessors, to baffle the Pharaoh of Egypt

and torment generations of schoolboys. Heron of Alexandria (1st century AD) invented the steam engine and used it as a toy.

Greek **medicine** was justly renowned. Hippocrates (c 460–377 BC) was the 'father of medicine', insisting on observation, intuition and care for the patient in equal measure. Hippias (5th century BC) was the first exponent of self-sufficiency, in the Golden Age of Athens. Galen (AD 130–200) made discoveries about the working of the body, eg the nerves, which were too far ahead of his time. It was only in the 19th century that they were understood. Plato (427–347 BC) tried to formulate a view of the world from first principles; he founded and taught in the Academy – an early school of philosophy. Aristotle (384–322 BC) was one of his students. He sought to assemble all the scientific knowledge of his time, however inaccurate, and proceed from that to universal law, however subjective.

Later philosophers adopted the maxim 'Man is the measure of all things'. Epicurus (341–270 BC) taught that the way to happiness was through virtue and peace; Zeno (c 320–250 BC) preferred submission to the law and destiny, in order to make misery bearable. His followers were called Stoics and included the Roman Emperor Marcus Aurelius.

Sculpture

Carvings on temples, especially scenes on the pediment, and statues of the human body, are the best known types of Greek sculpture. The early figures were rather rigid, grimacing with the 'archaic smile', but by the Golden Age statuary was almost alive; it lives on as the ideal for many sculptors. There were three very famous sculptors. The work of two of them – Phidias (c 500–432 BC) and his contemporary Polyclitus – can be seen only in later copies. Fortunately some of the work of Praxiteles (4th century BC) survives, eg the famous statue of *Hermes* at Olympia. Phidias carved, or directed the carving of, the famous friezes of the Parthenon.

Much of the best classical sculpture is now in foreign museums, especially in London, Paris, the Vatican and Naples, but in Greece you should not miss: *Poseidon* and Praxiteles' *Marathon Youth* in the National Archaeological Museum; the bronze *Charioteer*, and *Agias* at Delfi; the frieze from the Siphnian Treasury at Delfi; and *Apollo* from the pediment of the Temple of Zeus at Olympia.

PAPERWORK

Passports

A passport is needed (i) on entry into Greece, (ii) when changing cash in a bank or a travellers' check anywhere, (iii) on checking into a hotel (by law, you must register in any accommodation whatever), (iv) on booking into a campsite, when your passport will be retained until you leave.

For details of how to obtain a passport, get a passport application form at any post office. A British Visitor's Passport (lasting one year only), obtainable from a post office, is valid for entry into Greece; regulations say it is not valid for passage through Yugoslavia, but at the frontier it is accepted.

No visa or vaccination certificate is needed for nationals of the following countries: Australia, Canada, Eire, New Zealand, South Africa, UK, USA.

Visitors from Australia, Canada, New Zealand, South Africa and USA are permitted to stay up to three months. For a longer stay, you must apply to the Aliens Bureau or to the police. There are no restrictions for citizens of the UK and Eire as members of the EEC.

Health and Insurance

If you have an accident or fall ill, you can contact a hospital in most main towns (Tel: 166). Otherwise, consult a doctor, though in country regions you may have difficulty finding one. There are nearly ten times as many doctors in Athens (per head of pop.) as in rural districts. In principle, you have to pay for any medical treatment but in practice minor emergency treatment is likely to be gratis at a hospital. A doctor's consultation fee is very modest by North American standards (say 500 dr), and may well be waived.

Citizens of the UK and Eire, being members of the EEC, are entitled to the same treatment from the National Health Service as Greek citizens. However, the range of this treatment is much less comprehensive than in Britain and so personal medical insurance is advisable. For non EEC visitors, it is even more important to have medical insurance; you don't want to spend all your holiday money on medical treatment. If you already have medical insurance, you should be able fairly cheaply to extend it to cover you in Greece. Medical insurance bought just for your holiday is limited in amount of cover, and fairly expensive if you balance the cover against the risk; it is cheaper to combine medical insurance with baggage insurance (see below). Most insurance schemes require that you pay for treatment at the time, and claim the money from the insurer when you return home.

The Association for Medical Assistance to Travellers in New York provides a list of English-speaking doctors and an on-the-spot payment scheme. Europ-Assistance Ltd of Croydon, Surrey provides medical insurance backed by a 24-hour answering service that will tell you the name of a doctor and guarantee payment; they also provide a 'get-you-home' service.

If you lose any of your baggage, report it to the Police or Tourist Police. In Greece, lost property is more likely to be handed in than in some other countries; a few days' patience and you may be pleasantly surprised. However, bags 'fall overboard', or can even 'leap out of a locked car', and to have to replace all your clothes suddenly could spell disaster for a holiday. You can get short-term luggage insurance (specify expensive items like cameras) through any insurance broker, travel agent, or more expensively from a machine at an airport. A policy which combines medical with baggage insurance gives better value, because much of the cost is in administration, not in cover.

For insurance when motoring, see page 19. The motoring organizations (AA, RAC, AAA) offer a 'get-you-home' scheme. Read the literature carefully to judge whether it is worth having, because the schemes are loaded in favour of cars that are very unlikely to break down, and even then are quite limited in what they offer.

CUSTOMS

(For currency regulations see page 16.)

Import into Greece

Visitors with goods to declare at Customs move through the RED channel; with nothing to declare, through the GREEN channel. You are allowed to import duty-free: personal belongings; food and beverages up to 10 kg; one litre of spirits (hard liquor); 200 cigarettes or equivalent tobacco; 50 cigars; one still camera and one cine camera with film; binoculars; record player; typewriter; radio; tape recorder; sports equipment; bicycle; shotgun, but it is supposed to be registered on entry and you must re-export it; personal jewellery; gifts up to $150 (approx. £75) in

Duty-free allowances for UK residents *subject to change*		Goods bought in a duty-free shop	Goods bought (tax paid) in Greece
Tobacco	Cigarettes or	200	300
	Cigars *small* or	100	150
	Cigars *large* or	50	75
	Pipe tobacco	250gm	400gm
Alcohol	Spirits *over 38.8° proof* or	1 litre	1½ litres
	Fortified or sparkling wine plus	2 litres	3 litres
	Table wine	2 litres	4 litres
Perfume		50gm	75gm
Toilet water		250cc	375cc
Other goods		£28	£120

value. Customs officials are normally very lenient, but many imported goods, *eg* film, electronic equipment, are heavily taxed and if you take so many it looks as though you intend to sell them, you will be in trouble.

Small domestic pets may be imported with a certificate of freedom from contagious disease authorized by a vet in the country of origin. Dogs must have had an anti-rabies injection in the previous 12 months.

Export from Greece

You can take out what you like (apart from currency, page 16) with the important exception of antiquities and works of art found in Greece. If these are exported without a permit, the articles are confiscated and the offender is then prosecuted. Permits from the Archaeological Service, 13 Polygnotou Street, Athens. A fee may be levied for permission to export antiquities; if permission is refused, the article is acquired for half its value by the State.

Duty-free goods when returning home
Canada: gifts up to $50 in value, plus 50 cigars or 200 cigarettes, for any Canadian resident. Two Canadian pints of wine or liquor, or 24 pints of beer, for persons over 18 or 19 years old (according to place of entry).

United Kingdom: see table at the top of the page.

United States of America: personal purchases up to $300 in value, 100 cigars per person, one US quart (in effect, one litre) of liquor per person over 21 if allowed by State law at place of entry.

Animals The UK totally prohibits the importation of animals (including domestic pets) except under licence. One of the conditions of the licence is that the animals are retained in approved quarantine premises for up to six months. No exemptions are made for animals that have been vaccinated against rabies. Penalties for smuggling involve imprisonment, unlimited fines and the destruction of the animal.

For details apply to the Ministry of Agriculture (Animal Health Division), Hook Rise South, Tolworth, Surbiton, Surrey KT6 7NF.

Any animal being imported into the US must have a valid certificate of vaccination against rabies.

CURRENCY

Keep a supply of two or three days' spending money in US dollars, German marks or British pounds; these are most readily negotiable if you run out of Greek currency over a week-end.

The unit of currency is the drachma (δραχμα) – abbreviated to dr (Δρ) – worth roughly one penny (British) or two cents (US). Called 'drax' among English-speakers, but not by Greeks.

Notes are issued in denominations of 50, 100, 500 and 1000 drachmai. The current coins are 1 and 2 dr (bronze) and 5, 10 and 20 dr (nickel); a 50-dr coin is proposed.

The drachma was formerly divided into 100 smaller units (lepta). There is still in circulation a 50-lepta (half-drachma) coin which is almost valueless. Coins of smaller denomination have vanished entirely.

Older coins which are not of the same size as those shown in the illustration, and nickel coins of 1 and 2 dr which look like a nickel 5-dr piece, are still in circulation.

Banks

The sign for a bank is ΤΡΑΠΕΖΑ. Banking hours Mon-Fri are 0800–1330 in winter. They are the same in summer but there is also early evening opening (around 1800 hrs – it varies) in main tourist centres. Saturday morning opening has ended except at a few main tourist centres in summer. Bank closures for strikes or local saints' days are not infrequent; strikes are more predictable. Banks will change currency and travellers' checks but will not give cash for credit cards. Personal checks backed by a Eurocheque guarantee card can be cashed in almost any branch of the Bank of Greece (Τραπεζα τις Ελλαδος) and in other banks displaying the EC sign. However, in a large town with many banks you may be directed to a central branch for personal checks.

The rate of exchange is no worse than the prevailing rate for buying Greek currency at home (unlike most countries for which it is better to buy foreign currency before leaving), and is the same in all banks. There is a small commission (currently 50 dr) on each transaction. You will need your passport for any exchange in a bank.

Hotels

Most hotels will change travellers' checks or foreign currency; international hotels will take credit cards for payment; only the largest will take personal checks.

Travel Agencies

You can pay for tickets with foreign cash or travellers' checks; credit cards are refused nearly as often as accepted; personal checks are rarely accepted.

Shops

Shops which clearly cater for tourists will take foreign currency or travellers' checks when you buy something, and give you the change in drachmai. Usually they will change cash or travellers' checks at a discount of 2 or 3 percent.

Greek Customs Regulations

You can *import* foreign currency or gold up to any amount you please, but no more than 1500 dr in Greek currency. You can *export* up to 500 US dollars or equivalent in other foreign currency; and no more than 1500 dr in Greek currency. You can exchange Greek for foreign currency at a main bank (but not at the airport) on production of the bank-slips showing where you purchased the drachmai. Gold, and foreign currency in excess of $500 (approx. £250), may be exported only if it was declared on entry and a voucher obtained.

HOW TO GET THERE

Package Tours

A package tour ('charter-inclusive tour' to the trade) provides a return flight, transport if necessary between Greek airport and holiday centre, and either accommodation, or a rented car, or a boat. The package can also include a coach tour (*eg* of the main classical sites) or cater for a special interest like painting, sports, golf, botany, island-hopping, early Christianity. There are approximately 50 firms offering package tours from the USA, and over 150 from the UK. A list of the firms, arranged by name, destination, and special interest can be had from your national office of the NTOG (page 33).

A package tour is usually between 10 and 25 percent more expensive than the cost of organizing the same holiday yourself, provided you get a charter plane fare (see below). Immediately before or after the peak period, the large package tour operators' prices can be as cheap as arranging it yourself. The small operators offer competitive prices for facilities like car rental or yacht cruising.

The chief advantage of a package tour is that you don't have the bother of organizing all the different aspects; the disadvantage is the loss of freedom. If you want to stay in one seaside town and have a busy but relaxing time in the sun with no hassle, a standard British package tour is the answer. Book early. US packages tend to be tours of the classical sites.

Scheduled Airlines

There are direct flights to Greece from London (British Airways), New York (TWA) and Montreal (CPA). Flying time from: London 3½ hrs; New York and Montreal 10½ hrs. Frequency in winter: London/Athens 2-3 daily; London/Thessaloniki 2 weekly; New York/Athens 4 daily; Montreal/Athens 1 weekly. Frequency in summer: London/Athens 6-7 daily; London/Thessaloniki 4 weekly, also London/Corfu, Rodos, Crete; New York/Athens 4 daily; Montreal/Athens 1 weekly.

If you are travelling in Europe, the most frequent flights to Athens are from Frankfurt and Rome.

The full scheduled fare is very expensive; discount schemes bring it down to about 50 percent more than a charter fare, but they are accompanied by some restrictions on minimum length of stay or advance booking. From the UK, the discount scheme is APEX (advance purchase excursion); USA and Canada have APEX and ABC (advance booking charter). Currently the cheapest way to Greece from North America is by Skytrain to London and then charter flight.

Charter Airlines

Charter flights to Athens are sold openly in the UK; they cost only a pound or so more than a package tour operator has to pay. There are more restrictions on charter flights; for example, the return is on a specified date, usually two or three weeks after departure. In theory a charter flight has to be sold with accommodation, but you're meant not to ask where the accommodation is. Availability of charter flights is advertised especially in the Sunday papers, at the offices of operators, and to a limited extent with travel agents.

By Bus

The bus journey from London to Athens takes 3½ days, and most tourists would find it arduous. It can be fun for the young. The return fare is not much less than a cheap charter air fare, but you are not tied to any return date. (Most tickets are sold one-way.) Europabus enquiries to Victoria Coach Station, Buckingham Palace Road, London SW1; there are about ten other companies with a bus service to Athens – advertisements in the weekly magazine *Time Out*. In Athens, bus services back to western Europe are advertised in shops in Omonia Square.

By Car or Trailer

The cost of taking a car with three adults from London to Athens and back is roughly the same as three adult return air fares by charter flight. It is however a lot cheaper than flying to a rented car, and allows you to take your sports gear and similar necessities, and bring back all your purchases. But it is a very long drive – out of the question for a two or even three week holiday.

From London to Athens is just on 3200 km, say 2000 mi, and that means about 40 hours at the wheel. Forceful driving and a fast car make little difference to the journey time – any reasonable car can make good time on the motorway, and no car can cut the time down across Yugoslavia. How you add to those 40 hours with pit-stops and sleep is up to you – less than three days' travelling cuts into safety, few people take more than six days unless they are looking for diversion.

The Channel ports that can be used are: Calais (British Rail and Townsend Thoresen ferry, British Rail and Hoverlloyd hovercraft), Dunkerque (British and French Rail ferry), and Oostende (British or Belgian Rail ferry). The quickest total journey is Calais – Liège – München (Munich), then either Villach – Ljubljana – Zagreb or Klagenfurt – Maribor – Zagreb. From Zagreb via Beograd (Belgrade), Nis and Skopje (by-pass) to the frontier at Gevgelija (Yugoslavia)/Evzoni (Greece) is very boring; one way to lessen this is to drive continuously for 18-20 hours, stopping only to fuel the car and passengers, and to change drivers.

The alternative frontier crossing is at Niki, reached from Skopje or, a long way round, via Dubrovnik; this is used only if you're sightseeing on the way. Evzoni to Athens via Thessaloniki is 550km/342mi, Niki to Athens via Florina is 600km/373mi. There are frontier crossings at Promahonas for Bulgaria, at Kipi and Kastanies for Turkey, none for Albania.

More agreeable, though more expensive than driving across Yugoslavia, is the 'Sea Bridge' from an Italian (Adriatic) port to a Greek port (Igoumenitsa, page 51 or Patra, page 83). Car fares are modest, passenger fares are not. Sleeping on deck is more pleasant in summer than a reclining seat in a smoky saloon. In summer, it is advisable to book – peak periods are sold out months in advance. You can turn up at the port without a booking and probably get a crossing within a couple of days. Bookings through a travel agent; or contact the Greek or Italian tourist office, or write direct to the ferry company. Addresses: Achaic Line (from Brindisi), 15 Hadzikyriakou, Pireas; Adriatica (from Venice to Pireas, expensive), 19 Akti Miaouli, Pireas; Epirus (from Bari), Galaxias Building, 6 Skouze Street, Pireas; Fragline (from Brindisi), 5a Rethimnou Street, Athens; Ionian (from Brindisi), 4 Marni Street, Athens; Karageorgis (from Ancona), Akti Kondyli, Pireas; Hellenic-Mediterranean (from Brindisi), Electric Railway Building, Box 57, Pireas; Libra Maritime Co. (from Brindisi), 4 Plateia Ludovikou, Pireas; Strintzis Line jointly with Linee Canguro (from Ancona), 38 Akti Possidonos, Pireas.

By Train

There is nothing to recommend the train unless you're a railway fanatic, or have a free pass. The single fare is as high as a return charter air fare; the time – three days – makes it nearly as long as the bus journey. However, with a train ticket you can stop off where you like and as long as you like on the way. The Athens Express (Paris-Milano-Beograd (Belgrade)) and the Hellas Express (Amsterdam-München (Munich)-Beograd) both provide wagons-lit and reclining seats. Details from British Rail and Hellenic Railways.

By Ship

In addition to the services from Italian ports mentioned above, you can take a ship to Pireas or Patra from the major ports of the eastern United States, and from London or Southampton. Sailings are infrequent and the journey long.

Several operators run cruises of the eastern Mediterranean taking in Greece, Turkey, possibly Egypt or Italy. The cruises change every year. You fly out, join the cruise ship for two or three weeks, and fly home. Your travel agent may be less well informed about cruises than the NTOG, write to them (page 33), or get the *Key Travel Guide* or *Greek Travel Pages* (see below).

INTERNAL TRAVEL

Timetables are generally difficult to obtain. For any extensive do-it-yourself travel, get the *Key Travel Guide*, published monthly from 6 Kriezotou Street, Athens 134 and available from BAS Overseas Publications, 45 Sheen Lane, London, SW14 or *Greek Travel Pages*, published monthly from 4 Voukourestiou Street, Athens 133. Both available from kiosks in Athens.

Domestic Air Services

All internal flights are by Olympic Airways. Athens to: Alexandroupoli, Ioanina, Kalamata, Kastoria, Kavala, Kozani, Sparti, Thessaloniki, on the mainland; and to Corfu, Crete (Hania and Iraklio), Hios, Kefalonia, Kos, Kythira, Limnos, Milos, Mikonos, Lesvos (Mitilini), Rodos, Samos, Skiathos, Thira (Santorini) and Zakinthos. There are connections to Andravida, Agrinio and Preveza occasionally.

The only other services are Thessaloniki-Limnos; Rodos-Kos; Rodos-Karpathos, Rodos-Iraklio. New airports are opening up gradually.

Flights linking mainland towns only cost between two and three times the bus fare.

Railways

There are two railway lines in Greece. The *Peloponnese Line* serves Athens-Korinthos (branch to Tripoli and Kalamata) – Patra-Olympia-Kalamata. The *Northern Line* serves Athens-Larissa (branch to Volos and Kalambaka)-Thessaloniki (branch to Kozani and Florina)-Alexandroupoli (for Istanbul).

Trains are slow but cheap. A return ticket costs 20% less than two singles. Children of 14, or under, get tickets at half price.

Buses

The main towns are connected by an excellent network of long-distance buses, which are reasonably fast, and keep remarkably well to the timetable. They become crowded at the terminus where they start, and usually do not pick up passengers on the way (a) because they are full and (b) because they have left the nome (county) from which they started and are not allowed to steal the traffic of the next nome. If the bus is stopped, it is never too full to take just one more passenger. The buses are often air-conditioned. Canned music is continuous and loud. At the terminus you get a ticket before boarding the bus; pay the driver if you are collected en route.

The two bus organizations are the State Railways (OSE), which connect Athens to most places on the railway line, and the KTEL. The KTEL is a pool of coach owners, who have agreed not to poach each other's trade. A timetable of KTEL buses to and from Athens is published in the *Key Guide*, but if you are planning to go across country by bus, other than direct to Athens, you can only get information from the bus station in the capital of the nome you are starting from. No general timetable exists for provincial buses.

Local buses, connecting villages to larger towns or the capital of the nome, provide a good service once a day – often leaving very early in the morning. They will stop by the roadside if you raise your hand.

Ferries

There are about 200 ports in the Greek islands and 50 ports on the mainland with scheduled sea connections. As a general rule, take it that there is a ferry to any island you want to get to from the nearest port on the mainland, and to about half the islands direct from Pireas. In addition, the towns along coastal stretches such as the eastern Peloponnese and Ipiros, where roads are not too good, may be connected by ferries.

The frequency of ferries varies from one hundred a day (Rio-Antirio) to one a week (Patra-Paxi and Corfu-Paxi). There is no central information agency, and timetables must be sought locally. In Pireas, contact the Pireas Port Authority (Tel: 4511-311). A collection of the main ferry timetables, incomplete but helpful, appears in the *Key Guide* (see page 17).

Taxis

For Athens' taxis, see page 97. Nearly all other towns have taxis in the main square, and even in a small village motorized transport will be found if you ask in a café for a taxi. For short local journeys you pay by the kilometre. For long excursions, ask the fare in advance – don't understand the reply, so the figures have to be written down. There is then less chance of a misunderstanding afterwards.

Taxis are plentiful in towns, cheaper than in western Europe, and used frequently for quite long journeys. Waiting time is considerably cheaper. If a one-way trip costs 65 dr, the same trip out and back should be 100 dr.

Excursions

Several Greek companies offer coach tours of Athens, Attica and Greece generally. Most prominent is probably CHAT Tours, 4 Stadiou, Athens. (Information from Seagull Holidays, 46 Maddox Street, London W1). Others: Key Tours, 2 Ermou, Athens, American Express (see page 34), ABC, 47 Stadiou, Athens and Hellenic Express 17 Filellinon, Athens.

Car Rental

The NTOG provides a list of car rental firms, and you can also get details from the English-language papers in Athens, or from the London or New York offices of international firms. The rates quoted often don't include the various taxes, which add another 20%. Car rental is usually by the day with 'kilometrage' extra (minimum 100km/62mi), or by the week with unlimited 'kilometrage'. Car rental is roughly twice as expensive as in the UK because of taxes. You can often negotiate a substantial reduction (one quarter), if business is slack, and if you are a skilful negotiator. You are more likely to succeed out of season. Do examine the condition of the car before taking it.

If you are considering rental for a long period, it may be considerably cheaper to buy a car with a guarantee of re-sale subject to the car's condition. The international car rental firms deal in this way, and several of the firms in Syngrou, Athens.

For licences, see below.

Hitch-hiking

This is much easier than elsewhere in Europe. Do try to learn enough Greek to say who you are, where you're going, what you like about Greece and where you've come from.

MOTORING

Citizens of the UK and Eire can drive in Greece with their national driving licence. Citizens of Australia, Canada, New Zealand, South Africa and the USA need an international driving licence, which can be obtained from your national motoring organization or in Greece from the Greek Automobile and Touring Club (ELPA), see page 33.

Own Car

Third party insurance (against damage you may do to another car) is compulsory in Greece; comprehensive insurance (against damage somebody else may do to your car and not pay for) is strongly recommended. You can buy temporary insurance at a frontier post, and extend it to longer-term insurance on application to the Motor Insurance Bureau, 10 Yenofontos Street, Athens (Tel: 3236–733). It is much cheaper and simpler to obtain an international motor insurance certificate (Green Card) from your insurers at home, extending your cover to Greece. Under EEC regulations the car insurance valid in any member state (*eg* UK and Eire) gives cover in any other member state (*eg* Greece) so strictly speaking no Green Card is needed. However, this

extension of cover gives only the *minimum* required by the law of the host country – for comprehensive cover you need a Green Card.

It is not compulsory to carry your vehicle registration documents, but a useful precaution. Greek regulations say you must have either a *carnet de passage* issued by your national motoring organization, or a 'free-use' card issued by Customs on entry, against a passport entry. In practice, cars are allowed to enter without satisfying these regulations.

Car Rental

See page 18 for details.

Fuel

'Super' petrol (gasoline) is 96 octane, and should be used for all modern engines. 'Regular' petrol is allegedly 90–92 octane, which is barely adequate for a modern low-compression engine, but can be as low as 88 octane, which causes pinking. In order to limit consumption, Greek petrol is the most expensive in Europe – roughly 50% higher than UK prices. Diesel fuel is about half the price of petrol. Engine oil is expensive and it is sensible to take cans of oil with you to Greece.

There are plenty of service stations around the main towns, but in country districts they can be further apart than a spare can will take you. Don't let your tank get less than one quarter full. Service stations are liable to close early on holidays and early at night, but you can usually get someone to find the proprietor of a country service station in an emergency. Government regulations, part of the energy-saving programme, are shortening opening hours.

Some garages will advertise for years to come that they accept petrol coupons, which formerly provided reduced-price petrol for foreign tourists. The issue of petrol coupons ceased in March 1979.

Rules of the Road

Keep to the right; overtake on the left; priority at cross-roads as indicated by standard international signs; at unsigned cross-roads, priority to the right. Don't expect other drivers to observe these rules, especially out of town.

Use of the horn in town is not permitted except as an unavoidable warning; Greek drivers tend to ignore this. If you hesitate for a fraction of a second before moving off at traffic lights, expect a blast from the driver behind you, especially a taxi.

Headlamps should be dipped to the right when facing oncoming traffic. To convert British cars to right-hand dip, use a displacer strip to deflect the beam on a modern car with a patterned headlamp lens, and a continental bulb on an older car.

It is compulsory to wear seat belts in a car and a crash helmet on a motorbike or moped. The police enforce the law (1000 dr fine) but so far the only penalty for foreigners is a ticking off.

The speed limit in towns is 50kph/31mph; in practice speeds are much less than that. There are no indications of the speed limit on entering a town. Elsewhere the speed limit is 110kph/68mph – faster than most traffic can travel.

Parking is difficult in most towns and gets impossible at night. Restrictions are much the same as in other western European countries and are indicated by conventional signs. They are disregarded by Greek motorists and Greek police to a greater extent than anywhere else, but the pace of westernization is fast. There are unwritten codes of parking behaviour in most towns – copy the next driver, but try to set an example of considerate parking.

Roads and Road-signs

For a poor country with a lot of road per head of pop., road surfaces are surprisingly good. There are still plenty of dirt roads in country districts, but on all the main tourist routes the road surfaces are metalled. On dirt roads no harm will come to your vehicle if you keep your speed down; if there is a stream across the road, go very slowly – it may conceal a deep pothole.

The highway from the frontier at Evzoni to Thessaloniki is a free motorway; from Thessaloniki to Athens is a toll motorway with three pay-stages (total cost in 1980 – 110 dr); from Athens to Patra via Korinthos is a toll motorway with two pay-stages (total cost in 1980 – 70 dr). 'Motorway' is an exaggerated description by the standards of western Europe, but the road is more than adequate for the traffic.

Road signs are given in Greek characters, and on all main roads and many minor roads the name of the next town is repeated, 50m/164ft after the Greek sign, in Latin characters. There is, to put it mildly, variation in the Latin spellings. On main roads where the signs are erected by the NTOG, the spelling is almost identical to that used on NTOG maps (as followed in this book – see page 34). On smaller roads

the local authority erects the sign, and the smaller the road, the more original the spelling.

There is a road classification system (first class, good, motorable, poor) but it tends to be misleading. Roads are being improved so quickly that published information is generally out-of-date. A road numbering system exists but is not used. Traffic symbols are those used internationally but you may come across the following written signs:

ΕΞΟΔΟΣ	exit
ΕΙΣΟΔΟΣ	entrance
ΚΙΝΔΥΝΟΣ	danger
ΑΡΓΑ	slow
ΑΠΟΓΟΡΕΥΕΤΑΙ Η ΣΤΑΘΜΕΥΣΙΣ	no parking
ΑΠΟΓΟΡΕΥΕΤΑΙ Η ΕΙΣΟΔΟΣ	keep out

Alcohol

Drivers suspected of drunkenness may be stopped by the police, and made to take an Alcotest (blood test, administered by trained officers). If you refuse to undergo the test it is an admission of guilt. An alcohol content in the blood above 50mg/ml (the British limit is 80mg/ml) is an offence punishable by up to six months imprisonment, plus a fine up to 5000 dr, plus up to six months disqualification. Enforcement of the law tends to be lax, but less so each year. You may get favourable treatment as a tourist but expect to be treated like a Greek.

Breakdown

It is not obligatory to carry a warning triangle, but it is a wise precaution. Place it 50m/164ft behind the car if you break down.

If you are within 60km/37mi of the five principal mainland towns (Athens, Thessaloniki, Patra, Lamia, Larissa) telephone 104 (answers in English) for the ELPA road assistance service. There are 28 other towns outwith these areas which have correspondents of the ELPA – list available from the ELPA or ask the police. A charge is made for answering a call, and for a tow to a garage.

In most large towns, there is one area where the garages for different makes of car are congregated. Someone will direct you to the garage you want. Imported spares are expensive, labour is fairly cheap. If your car develops serious trouble, limp into a large town or pay to be towed there rather than rely on a small country garage. Local engineers are moderately skilled, very ingenious and tremendously confident.

Carry your vehicle's handbook – the pictures can be a vital means of communication, and at least the simplest spares, *eg* fan belt, radiator hose. Motoring organizations will rent out a more extensive set of basic spares, and you get your money back if they are unused.

WHERE TO STAY

Finding Accommodation

The unfailing recommendation for a tourist who has not booked a bed is 'consult the Tourist Police'. Greece has town police (αστινομια from *asti*, town and *nomos*, law) and out-of-town it has the gendarmerie (χοριορυλετε from *hora*, country and *filax*, watchman). The Tourist Police are either *astinomia* or *horiofilete*, and wear the same uniforms but with a shoulder flash saying ΤΟΥΡΙΣΤΙΚΕ. They have the same power and duties as the regular police, but in addition they have a special brief to help tourists and have had a rudimentary training in foreign languages. It is their job to know where accommodation exists and help you find it – it is not their job to provide accommodation where none exists.

In the out-of-the-way places there are no Tourist Police, indeed no police at all. For help then, go to the café clutching your phrase book.

Publicity leaflets on each region are given out by the National Tourist Organization. They give addresses and grades of hotels down to C grade, and addresses of NTOG campsites. You can pick the leaflets up at airports, border posts, travel agencies and big hotels.

Sleeping Out

For the greatest freedom in seeing Greece you don't want to book in advance, but to move around, finding accommodation as you go. The price of this freedom is to be prepared to sleep out – you may never need to.

If you do arrive in a place where all beds are taken, it is quite bearable to just lie down and sleep under the stars – it's never far to get out of town. Under these conditions the Tourist Police turn a blind eye to the breach of regulations, or direct you where to sleep.

Camping

The law on camping is quite clear – camping is prohibited everywhere except on a government-approved campsite. There are government-run (NTOG) campsites at about 18 of the most-visited centres on the mainland, six on the islands, and about 200 approved campsites run privately. The NTOG campsites offer a very high standard of amenities but are rather regimented – addresses on NTOG leaflets for each region (see above). Private campsites are more individual, and all are well above minimum standard; rather uninformative lists are available from the NTOG, but it is better to ask the Tourist Police on the spot.

The reason for the uncompromising law on free-lance camping is hygiene. In addition, campers have abused Greek hospitality, with tents on beaches and in parks. Enforcement of the law is at the discretion of the police, and the law tends to be enforced more strictly every year. In practice you can camp with the permission of the landowner, and overnight camping is tolerated if you're well away from habitation. You can certainly camp out in the wilds because nobody knows that you're there – the difficulty may be to find somewhere flat.

Look out for ant trails, especially if you camp near pines, and take insect repellent for mosquitoes.

Hostels

There are YMCA hostels in Athens and Thessaloniki; and YWCA hostels in Athens, Thessaloniki and Rethimno. There are youth hostels of the Greek YHA (Organosis Xenonon Neotitas Ellados) in or near Athens (five), in Crete (Ag. Nikolaos, Hania, Ierapetra, Iraklio, Malia, Rethimno, Sitia), Corfu (two), Delfi, Kallidromo (Lamia), Hoziakos (Trikala), Litohoro, Mikines, Nafplio, Olympia, Pireas, Thessaloniki (three), and Thira. (Details in the International Youth Hostels Association handbook.)

Private Houses

A room in a private house is by far the best way to get to know Greeks. In principle, all rooms are subject to official inspection for suitability and to price control by the Tourist Police. Accommodation is simple, but is most unlikely to be bad and will not be over-priced.

The Tourist Police have the names of householders with rooms to let. Otherwise, on the islands you are greeted off the ferry by housewives with rooms to offer, and on many islands there is a local 'godfather' at the port (the police will direct you to him) who has a list of rooming houses. In villages, you can recognize rooms for rent by the sign ΔΩΜΑΤΙΟ.

Rooms are not booked in advance unless you have a personal contact. It is only at the height of summer on some islands that you might not find a room.

Tavernas and Low-grade Hotels

A *taverna* is first of all an eating house, and incidentally may have a few rooms to rent. It's not the place to stay for quiet and early nights, but can be much more lively and friendly than a hotel. Tavernas are graded using the same classification as hotels (see below) and are usually D or E grade, sometimes C grade. Prices are determined according to the grade and must be displayed inside the room. If you stay in a taverna, you are expected to eat there.

D and E grade hotels are clean and can be comfortable and entertaining, but on the whole they are the older hotels and may be very small, stuffy in summer and with limited facilities. There are no centrally available lists of D and E grade hotels; the Tourist Police will direct you. Look at the outside and use your judgement. Package tour operators do not use these hotels.

In addition to D and E hotels there are 'guest houses' and 'student hostels' in the Plaka district of Athens; these cost about half as much as a cheap C grade hotel. They are clean but sometimes have interesting toilet facilities.

Hotels

All hotels are graded by the NTOG on a classification L (luxury), A, B, C, D down to E. The names and addresses of L to C hotels are listed on NTOG leaflets for each region, and are also available from the NTOG in Athens. Reservations can be made (i) in writing, to the hotels directly or with the Chamber of Hotels of Greece, 6 Aristidou Street, Athens, (Tel: 3233–501); (ii) in person, at 2 Karagiorgi Servias Street, Athens, (Tel: 3237–193) or at the Athens Main Airport (East), (Tel: 9009 –437).

The classification is based on objective factors, namely: materials of construction, size of bedrooms, width of corridors, proportion of private bathrooms, number of public rooms. There is no direct relationship between the classification of a hotel and its quality, *ie* location, bedding, whether the manager knows his job, and the staff like theirs. D and E grade hotels and many C grade hotels are run by the proprietor. Some package tour operators grade their hotels (as seen in their prices) according to their own view of how much people will like it. Their grading is often very different from the official classification.

All hotel rooms are subject to maximum prices according to classification and the price must be displayed inside the room. This displayed price excludes: turnover, revenue and municipal taxes (say 6%); surcharge for a stay of one or two days (10% – often not added); surcharge for heating or cooling from a central air-conditioning installation (up to 75 dr); surcharge during Carnival and Trade Fairs (20%); rebate out of season (up to 40% rebate in winter, up to 20% in October, April and May). In an A or B class hotel, you are unlikely to get the rebate unless you ask – don't hesitate. C class hotels may well give no discount.

The *Key Guide* and *Greek Travel Pages* (see page 17) give lists of hotels, with current prices and pictures of many of them.

Under the Colonels (1967–74), interest-free loans were handed out fairly freely to build hotels. These are now used mainly by package-tour operators and are centres for a static holiday. They do not encourage passing trade. However, tour operators reserve blocks of accommodation, but don't make firm bookings unless they have a customer. You can therefore book in at a package tour hotel if you find one that you like which has unoccupied rooms. The hotelier may not be interested in a stay of one or two nights only.

Xenias

These are government-owned hotels, built to ensure adequate accommodation at key tourist sites. They are classified on the same basis as any other hotel, and priced accordingly, but tend to be much better than the classification, *eg* C grade, would suggest. Many Xenia hotels are now being leased to private operators, but retain the name Xenia because it has become a mark of quality.

Traditional Settlements

The NTOG has a programme to restore and preserve rural buildings in the old Greek style. Some of them are beautiful by any standards; all are more delightful than modern accommodation, but not luxurious. The object is preservation of a tradition, not for tourists but for Greeks. However in some cases the houses can be let to visitors, in other cases they are still lived in but will receive visitors. Traditional settlements geared to tourism are at Ia on Thira; Makrinitsa in the Pelion (17km/11mi from Volos); Vizitsa in the Pelion (39km/24mi from Volos); Vathia in the Mani (35km/22mi from Areopoli) and Fiskardo (Kefalonia).

Villas

'Villa' is a tour-operator's term for a flat or small house where you can do your own catering. A villa is available only for a period of a week or more, and you are not likely to find one available on the spot. The only way to get a booking in advance seems to be through a tour operator.

EATING AND DRINKING

Nearly all Greek eating-places, even quite expensive tourist restaurants, are informal – there's no getting dressed for dinner. Even if the menu is in English, you are as well to go to the kitchen to see what is available.

Usually the day's dishes are kept in large pans on a hotplate either at the entrance to the restaurant, or in a cooking area at the back. Salads and sweets are also on display. Be warned that even food that you would expect to be hot – cooked vegetables, moussaka, spaghetti or chips – will very often be almost cold when it arrives. If you persuade the kitchen to make it hot, the waiter will find a cold plate to put it on.

Service is prompt in cheap places; in smart places you can, as the brochures say, 'linger over a leisurely meal'. Helpings are very generous. If you're in a party, it is sound practice to have one different dish each, and then share. You can always have more if you find something you particularly like. It's quite usual to have just one course.

If you order everything at once, it will arrive all at once – soup, salad, main course and sweet. Excellent bread is served as soon as you sit down – don't eat too much or you will spoil your appetite.

In a fish-taverna (ΨΑΡΙΟΤΑΒΕΡΝΑ) you will be asked to choose the fish you want from the ice-tray, and it will arrive freshly cooked at your table with a little slip showing the weight – you pay according to the weight.

Two prices are marked for each item on the menu – the first without service, the second with service. You will automatically be charged the second price. In an ordinary restaurant, prices are low enough that you don't need to count up the cost before ordering. You're not expected to tip on top of the service charge, but give some small coins to the assistant-waiter. It is normal for the proprietor to come and sit at your table when you ask for the bill, and ask what you had before adding up. Don't worry about forgetting something – he will know. Don't be afraid to query an item you haven't had – he may make a mistake.

Greek Food

Greek holidays and Greek food are based on the three 'S's – sea, sun and sand, and salad, souvlakia and stew.

A **salad** is chopped cabbage in winter, sliced tomato and sliced cucumber in summer; both are dressed with olive oil and a squeeze of lemon juice. A **Greek salad** (χωριατικο *ie* country salad) is summer salad plus a couple of other vegetables like green pepper, grated carrot, and raw onion, plus olives, plus goat's cheese (*feta*). If you're away from civilization and find the local offerings unappetizing, live off Greek salad. Keep some bread to mop up the juice.

Souvlakia are little cubes of lamb or pork, sometimes interspersed with kidney, mushrooms or onion, cooked on a skewer over a charcoal grill. If you have 'small' souvlakia, take three or four skewers; a 'large' souvlakia, a single skewer, usually served with some salad and maybe a few chips, is a meal in itself.

'Stew' is a tourist's word for the basic main course in Greece – pieces of meat cooked slowly with a single vegetable. Each dish has its own name, but the description means nothing and you must go and look at the pan. Most meat is tough and badly butchered, and needs this long, slow cooking to make it edible. It is cooked with its vegetable – aubergines(eggplant), peas, courgettes (zucchini), potatoes, beans, lady's fingers (okra) – and kept warm. 'Stew' may look unappetizing and oily, but the fat is only olive oil and the meat should be very tender.

'Stew' may well be the only dish in an eating-place in a provincial town or inland village, but in the bigger places you will find the Greek dishes that have been made famous by Greek restaurants abroad. All the following are very good. *Taramosalata* is pinkish fish roe, made into a paste with olive oil; the most common starter. Another good starter is *tzatsiki* – raw onion in a biting white yoghurt-like sauce. Soup is uncommon, but don't miss bean soup when you see it. *Moussaka* is the best-known main dish – a mixture of minced meat and rice, covered with aubergines, dressed with a cheesy sauce, and cooked in the oven. Other ingredients like tomato and onion can be added at the discretion of the chef. *Dolmades* are a saucy mixture of meat and rice wrapped in a vine leaf or sometimes a cabbage leaf. Almost invariably good. Tomatoes and peppers stuffed with a meat-and-rice mixture are also reliable.

Meat when not stewed is 'roasted' on a spit. The battery-chicken industry is only just beginning in Greece, and roasted chicken in a Greek restaurant is very good indeed – though the portion may be too large. Lamb or huge pork chops, cooked while you wait (listed on the menu under *Tis Oras*, 'of the hour') are best when flamed on the charcoal grill, but are very good fried with a sprinkling of herbs. *Bifteki* are a sort of hamburger; *soutzoukakia* are meat balls in tomato sauce; *keftedes* are very spicy meat balls.

Fish is not plentiful in Greek waters; the big fleshy fish are uncommon and expensive, but delicious; the small fish are much cheaper and good when fresh. The redder the gills, the fresher the fish. Expect it to be served complete with head and eyes, see page 23.

Spaghetti (not *pasta*) is usually served without a sauce, and cooled. *Pasta* is anything cooked with pastry, including pizzas.

Tost is a sandwich of sliced bread containing a meat or cheese filling, toasted to perfection in a good establishment. Unfortunately it can also be old rusks filled with leathery salami.

Sweets Cakes and pastries tend to be very sweet, usually with honey rather than sugar, and flavoured with almonds. You must try *halvas* (a flaky sesame seed block – not too sweet – an unopened 2½ kg block is little more expensive to bring home than half a block), *baklava* (pastry with chopped nuts and raisins dripping in honey), *kataifi* (a sort of *baklava* covered in shredded wheat), and *bougatsa* (the famous or notorious custard pie).

Coffee *Kafe* without qualification means Greek coffee. Finely ground beans are boiled with water to a coffee 'soup' and served black in a minute cup. Allow time for the grounds to settle. It will come sickly-sweet unless you ask for it *metrio* (semi-sweet) or *sketo* (no sugar). For European coffee, ask for *Nes*. This is a powdered coffee, which may or may not be Nescafé, and

will come as a cup of black coffee or as a sachet or spoonful of powder with a jug of warm water. If you want milk specify *me gala* and without sugar *ohi zaharo*.

Frappe is instant coffee made with cold water and shaken to make it frothy – better than it sounds on a hot day. Only very expensive places provide European coffee made from beans.

Many restaurants and *tavernas* do not serve coffee; Greeks do not take coffee to complete a meal, but to start the afternoon after a siesta.

Where to Eat

There are three main types of eating-house in Greece – the *taverna* (ΤΑΒΕΡΝΑ), the restaurant (ΕΣΤΙΑΤΟΡΙΟ) and the rotisserie (ΨΥΣΤΕΡΙΑ). In provincial towns especially, there is no real difference between them – a *taverna* tends to open only in the evening, a restaurant may have a waiter with a tie, and a rotisserie has a glass outhouse for the charcoal grill. The food is much the same in all of them – salad or souvlakia or 'stew' – and this is the reason why Greek food has such a poor reputation.

In Thessaloniki and Patra, in the smart suburbs and Plaka district of Athens, and in package-tour hotels and *tavernas* in the main holiday centres, there is a greater differentiation, and the food improves. The *taverna* is essentially family-run and is a place for a complete evening out; service begins about 2000 and goes on as long as energy-saving regulations permit; it is in the *tavernas* that you find impromptu dancing as the evening wears on, and plate smashing (every plate goes on the bill). The *taverna* serves Greek food. The restaurant serves Greek food also, but adapted to western tastes; the more pretentious it is, the more likely it is to serve 'international' foods. Quite simple places that rely mainly on tourists also have an internationalized Greek cuisine. A good rotisserie serves excellent flamed chops, and produces 'steak' (strips of veal) so attractively garnished you may not notice it is tough. In short, if you're not too demanding, you can eat fairly well, and if you're not silly you can eat quite cheaply.

In addition to the *taverna*, restaurant and rotisserie, 'fast-food' places are developing in a vaguely American style. The big stores in Athens serve excellent Greek food.

A *kaffeneinon* is the true Greek café, which usually serves only Greek coffee; in the village, men sit here all day long over a cup of coffee, and in the towns they sit for an hour or so to play cards or backgammon. A *kaffeneinon* is by custom out-of-bounds to women, but women are usually welcome in one that is not full, and can always sit outside for coffee. Its characteristic appearance at night is a vast cavern, lit by a dim blue glow from an under-voltaged neon strip obscured by tobacco smoke.

A café-bar (ΚΑΦΕ-ΜΠΑΡ) is basically a *kaffeneinon* which also serves alcoholic drink. You are much more likely to get ordinary coffee here than in a *kaffeneinon*.

A patisserie (ΖΑΧΑΡΟΠΛΑΣΤΕΙΟ) sells Greek pastries and chocolates, and also has a few tables where you can have pastries and coffee.

Drink

The ordinary bottle of Greek wine like Demestica is usually quite drinkable, certainly as drinkable as its counterpart in France. The more expensive bottled wines are better, but not much better. Noted reds are Naoussa, Nemea, Romeiko (from Crete), Mavroudi (from Delfi) Ropa (from Corfu). The wines which Greeks praise like Mavrodaphne tend to be sweet. Wine from the barrel can be just rough, or rough but likeable. Wine bought in bulk from a roadside stall is very young but fruity. A real red wine is *mavro* (black) and the more usual light red or rosé is *kokino* (red); white is *lefkos*; dry is *xiros*.

The white wine of Attica is normally dosed with pine resin during fermentation, to produce a distinctly flavoured wine called *retsina*; served in restaurants in a metal jug. It is worth getting to like *retsina* – six glasses are enough to decide whether you can. Drink it cold. There is a red *retsina*, rare, but it ought to be prohibited.

Wine is sold by weight. A normal bottle holds 640–680gm, and usually contains about 67cl, *ie* rather less than the standard French bottle.

Native spirits are *ouzo* (very cheap) and brandy (fairly cheap). Imported spirits are expensive. Metaxa brandy has a sweetish flavour to cover the roughness; Otrys brandy is paler and smoother but without depth of flavour. *Ouzo* is a colourless spirit flavoured with aniseed. It is always served with a glass of cold water, and you can mix the two to make a long drink – ideal for a hot summer day. By tradition ouzo is served with *mezes* – a plate with a few mouthfuls of food: olives, fried octopus, *feta* – but they are disappearing where the main customers are tourists.

Greek beer is a lager type, a good thirst quencher on a hot day. Fix or Hellas are about the same price as wine; foreign beers made in Greece are notably more expensive.

Fruit drinks, both concentrated and fizzy, are strongly recommended – a non-synthetic fruity taste and not too much sweetening. Water from a mains supply is wholesome in all the towns.

SPORTS

Beach Sports

There are nearly 20 NTOG public beaches and most of them are miniature sports centres. Facilities include: swimming pools, canoes, pedalos, games fields, tennis courts, volley- and basketball courts, playgrounds for the children; they have patisseries, snack bars, restaurants, shops and discos. There is a charge for entry. The NTOG beaches of Attica are open all the year round, elsewhere only from April to October. Around the main holiday centres there are plenty of beaches with a choice of beach/sea sports provided by private operators.

Swimming

Swimming is possible throughout Greece (sea temperature above 17°C) from May to the end of October, and in the southern islands all the year round. The water is unpolluted, except near Pireas, and very clear because there is no river big enough to disturb it. There are no life-guards on Greek beaches, but no tides to worry about. In late summer the wind gets up in the afternoon especially along eastern coasts and the sea can become very rough.

The biggest problem for the swimmer is jellyfish, which just look like floating transparent plastic bags. Their sting can be extremely painful, and the jellyfish with a red core can induce partial paralysis of an arm lasting a week. To relieve the pain or swelling apply calamine lotion or a weak solution of ammonia. Sea urchins can also be a problem if you scramble about the rocks, and plastic shoes are the answer.

Nude bathing is no longer prohibited in many places on the islands – out of courtesy check first.

For enthusiasts: the Hellenic Athletic Swimming Federation, 2 Nikodimou, Athens, (Tel: 3227–318).

Snorkelling and Underwater Swimming

These (but not scuba diving) are permitted everywhere. Snorkels may be bought, and sometimes rented inexpensively, in most seaside villages. Underwater fishing with a speargun is also permitted. Fish under 150gm/4oz may not be killed. The Ionian Islands are probably best if this is your great love.

Scuba Diving

Diving with breathing apparatus is only allowed in some of the Halkidiki peninsula, and at Mikonos, Corfu, Paxi, Lefkada, Kefalonia, Zakinthos. It is forbidden in areas known to contain antiquities; they can sometimes be seen littering the sea bed and 'explorers' are asked to report sightings.

Depressurizing chambers are available at: the Hellenic Federation of Underwater Activities (Tel: Athens 9819–961); The Naval Hospital, 66 Akti Moutsopoulo, Pireas (Tel: 4512–466); Souda Bay Naval Base, Hania, Crete; Melioglou School, Thessaloniki; The Barracuda Club, Corfu.

There are compressed air service stations at the Hellenic Federation of Underwater Activities (see above); at the Kartelia School, 3 Karagiorgi Servias Street, Kastella, Pireas (Tel: 4122–047); at the Barracuda Club, Corfu; at Corfu Yachting Club (Tel: 0661–30470); Naval Athletic Club of Kalamaria (Tel: Thessaloniki 031–412068).

Waterskiing

Available all round Greece though it is expensive. There are many training centres, often with a variety of other sea sport facilities. In smaller villages there may well be private instructors available for lessons.

For information on individuals and on training centres the Water Ski Federation, 32 Stournara Street, Athens (Tel: 5231–875). Significant waterskiing at: Hania, Elounda (Lassithi), Gerakini and Kalithea (Halkidiki), Halkida, Ioanina, Kithira, Mitilini (Lesvos), Poros, Porto Heli, Rodos, Skiathos, Spetses, Thes/niki, Volos.

Wind-surfing

Becoming increasingly popular and offered as part of the programme of some tour operators. There are facilities at 50 or more of the popular beaches. Wind-surfing championships are held at Ermioni (see page 85). For information on this sport ask at the nearest NTOG office.

Sailing

Many villages, off-shore islets and caves can be reached only by boat, and dinghy hire is growing fast. Sailing regattas are organized by various clubs, detailed information available from the Hellenic Yacht Club, 1 Phillellion Street, Athens (Tel: 3230–330). Motor caiques may be rented in most large island villages for picnics at sea or exploring deserted islands.

The seas can look calm and deceptively safe in the morning sunshine but, especially in August and at the end of the summer, the afternoon wind can whip up a nasty swell. Take the advice of local authorities before embarkation. Information from the Hellenic Sailing Federation, 15a Xenophontos Street, Athens.

Cruising

Probably many people's dream way of seeing Greece and not always as expensive as you might think. Fly-cruise packages have made the idea cheaper and easier since you join your boat at a convenient port; there are now many tour operators and private companies that specialize in this type of holiday – lists from NTOG, some advertise in Sunday papers. You can choose engine-power or sail; sail solo or cruise in company with other boats ('flotilla cruising'). Some companies offer a cook and crew, others provide a boat and skipper for you to crew, while with others you are on your own. Whatever you choose, you have the freedom of hundreds of miles of superbly romantic coastline, warm seas with dolphins and unforgettable sunsets over the water. There are 85 yacht supply stations.

The NTOG brochure – *Greece for the Yachtsman* – tells you all you need to know if you bring your own craft. Useful addresses: B. Koutsoukellis, 3 Stadiou, Athens; T. A. Hermes, 4 Stadiou, Athens; the Marine Corner, Tourkolimano, Pireas, which also rents fishing, skin diving and waterskiing equipment.

Walking and Climbing

Walking can be hot work in Greece which is why mules are still popular! Walking is a necessity not a sport to the Greeks. However, there are rambling holidays organized from abroad and a few hiking and mountaineering clubs on the mainland and the islands. In the spring or autumn the mountains are idyllic with flowers.

Women walking alone are generally quite safe. There are few of the hazards that beset them elsewhere in Europe as the Greek, though friendly, is rarely familiar. For climbers, there are refuge huts throughout the mountains of Greece but for information on routes and equipment, and renting pack animals contact the Greek Skiing and Alpine Association, 7 Karagiorgi Servias Street, Athens (Tel: 3234–555), the Greek Ramblers Association, the Greek Touring Club, 12 Polytechniou Street, Athens (Tel: 5248–601), The Federation of Excursion Clubs of Greece, 4 Dragatsaniou Street, Athens (Tel: 3234–107).

Cave Exploring
Most of Greece is porous limestone and so far 6200 caves and underground waterways have been discovered – 3200 in Crete, and 420 in Attica. Very few are safe without a guide but those that have been equipped with tourist facilities are amongst the finest in the world. For information on caves contact the NTOG. Always take a torch.

Caves equipped for visits at: Pramanta and Perama (Ipiros); Sami (Kefalonia); Milopotamos (Kithira); Andiparos; Diros (see Areopoli page 78); Peania (Attica).

Skiing
From December to March there is skiing on many mainland mountains and on Crete and Evia, at altitudes above 1800m/5900ft. (Olympus, Pindos and Parnassos are suitable to the end of May.) There are ski centres served by chair lifts at Mt Vermio, Metsovo, Mt Pilio and Mt Parnassos. Information from the Greek Skiing and Alpine Association, 7 Karagiorgi Servias Street, Athens.

Riding
There is very little riding outside the expensive riding clubs in Attica and at Thessaloniki. Mules and donkeys are available in many villages for mountain treks but are not cheap. Information: The Hellenic Riding Club, 18 Paradissou Street, Maroussi (Tel: 6812-508).

Tennis
NTOG public beaches usually have tennis courts, as do many campsites and hotels. Public courts are rare, equipment is not usually provided.

Golf
This is new to Greece and there are still only four courses: Glifada in Attica, Rodos, Corfu, and a new one in Halkidiki. They are set amongst superb scenery; pines, olives and sandy beaches. More are planned. In summer international tournaments are held in which you may participate. Details from the local NTOG office.

Fishing
In summer and autumn, sea fishing is ideal and boats and tackle can be rented everywhere. Licences are not required and *taverna* chefs will probably cook your catch. Information from the Amateur Anglers and Maritime Sports Club, Akti Moutsopoulou, Pireas (Tel: 4515–731). River and lake fishing are very limited. Trout, carp, eel and crayfish can be found in the lakes, with trout in some rivers. No licence needed. Information available from Ministry of Agriculture, 3–5 Ipocratsus Street, Athens.

Hunting
Permitted on all open country for a fee. There are no game reserves or private estates. Shotguns may be imported if the number is on your passport. Mountain goats and the stags of Rodos are protected. The shooting season is August-March; hare, quail, partridge, water fowl, woodcock, wild boar and duck. For information: Ministry of Agriculture, 3–5 Ipocratsus Street, Athens and the Confederation of Greek Shooting Clubs, 2 Kouri, Athens 132.

Spectator Sports
Football is by far the most popular spectator sport. In recent years over 40 sports stadiums have been built to improve athletics and encourage international contests. The Acropolis Rally attracts motor-racing enthusiasts and there is speed racing on some of the islands. The only horse-racing course is in Athens.

ENTERTAINMENT
Music and Dance
The *bouzouki* really belongs to the town. (This most 'Greek-sounding' instrument was in fact imported in the 1920's by refugees from Asia Minor.) Greek village music is played on bagpipes (*tsamtouna*), the clarinet (*klarino*) and the violin. The lyre is peculiar to Crete.

If you want to hear authentic city music in Athens, wait till November when the tourist shows and discos close down. To hear folk music you should explore villages and go to festivals and weddings – often on a Sunday evening. Usually after a while everyone joins in and though there's now a law against *spasimo* – plate breaking – it is often forgotten in the enthusiasm of the dance.

If you want to watch Greek dancing there are professional companies in

Athens, Corfu and Rodos, but if you would rather try it yourself – much more fun – go to the tavernas or the *bouzoukia* (nightclubs) in the towns. The best known dance is the *staetria*, done in a circle with hands on shoulders. The circle is incomplete and everyone follows the leader's speed and steps. The *syrto* is slow and graceful; the *kalamatiano* is a difficult dance with 12 steps; the *tsiphte teli* is a belly dance; and the *zeybekiko* is for men only. If you are interested or want to learn the steps before you go, get Theodore Petrides' book on Greek folk dances.

Theatre

In addition to the unforgettable productions at Epidavros (see p. 78) there is a festival of ancient drama, music, opera and ballet in Athens, July-September – artists from all over the world perform at the Herod Atticus Odeon. Theatrical performances also take place in the ancient theatres of Dodoni, Thassos and Filipi – usually in July and August – and throughout the summer in Athens at the theatre on Likavitos (Lycabettus) Hill and the Odeon.

Greece has two National Theatre companies – in Athens and Thessaloniki. In summer they present NTOG festival programmes, reverting in winter to their own choice of notable international drama. There are over 40 theatres in Athens, many of them 'fringe' and 'experimental', about half in production at any one time.

Opera is to be heard sung by the *Lymki Skini* at the Olympia Theatre, 59 Acadimias Street, Athens.

The International Trade Fair in Thessaloniki is the occasion of two big festivals in October – The Film Festival and the Festival of Light Song. The Demetria Festival which is part of the broader programme of the trade fair includes drama, music, ballet and opera.

From April to October, *Son et Lumière* performances are given at the Acropolis, Athens; in Corfu town; and in the Palace of the Grand Masters, Rodos.

Wine Festivals

Every summer the NTOG organizes three lively wine festivals. There's no charge for wine-tasting, and several *tavernas* offer a wide variety of Greek food specialities. Dances and contests for the visitor. Festivals at Dafni (11km/9mi out of Athens) from July 9 – September 11; Alexandroupoli at the NTOG campsite July 2 – August 15;

Rodos at Rodini Park July 2 – September 4. There are also festivals in Samos in August and September.

Nightlife

There are discos (canned Western and Greek pop music, and somewhere to dance) in most holiday centres, but almost nowhere else. More sophisticated nightlife (nightclubs, casinos and theatres) is only found in the main towns. Floor shows with a singer and live *bouzouki* music are tourist-oriented but are patronized by Greeks.

WHAT YOU NEED TO KNOW

Electricity

The standard supply is 220 volts AC. A few remote areas are on 110 volts AC, so a check should be made before plugging in electric shavers, hair dryers, *etc*. Razors may need an adaptor for continental plugs.

Festivals

Local Festivals On most of the islands, 'festivals' are held mainly in summer and are called *panayieria*. Each village has its festival to which the people of surrounding villages go; good, plain food is often provided for anybody who appears – rice, vegetables, fruit, and sometimes a suckling pig or a goat. In principle the festival is held on a fixed date, which is usually the saint's day of the local church, and we have tried to list in the regions when the festivals are held and the saint's name. In practice local festivals are held when somebody wants to hold one – rather like an English village fete. There can be no guarantee that festivals will be held when stated, or at all, and free food is not guaranteed. August is generally a popular month for festivals.

On most of the islands, the young people who have left to work on the mainland or abroad return for several weeks in summer; the more 'traditional' the island they have left, the stronger the urge to return. Festivals are for them – they move from one village to the next, meeting old friends and making new ones. Visitors may tag along if there are not too many of them.

National Holidays and Festivals 1 Jan., Feast of St Basil, public holiday; **6 Jan.**, Epiphany, public holiday – blessing of the water (both the sea and the springs), notable ceremonies in Pireas and Crete; Carnival is the **three weeks**

before Lent (remember that the Greek Easter is fixed according to the Julian calendar, and may be later than in the west) and is a time of fun and dancing nearly everywhere; **25 March,** Independence Day, public holiday; Easter (see above) is celebrated more in Greece than in western Europe – the deep hold of the Orthodox religion is then seen most forcibly. 1st day of Lent, Good Friday, Easter Monday and Whit Monday are public holidays. **23 April,** St George's day, is celebrated in many mainland villages; **30 April,** the day before the start of summer, is an occasion for house-decoration and jollification in the streets; **1 May,** May Day, public holiday; **17 July,** St Marina's day, the first grapes are ready for cutting; **20 July,** Festival of Profitis Elias (Prophet Elijah), whose name seems to be the name of two or three villages on each island of the Cyclades; **15 Aug.,** Assumption of the Virgin, public holiday – a religious occasion rather than a festival, but it turns into merry-making; **29 Aug.,** Martyrdom of John the Baptist, also the occasion of a feast in many villages, especially if the church is named for John; **26 Oct.,** Feast of St Demetrius, the new wine should be ready for tasting; **28 Oct.,** Ohi Day, a national holiday; **6 Dec.,** St Nicholas' day, celebrated especially on the islands and in towns with seafaring connections; **25 Dec.,** Christmas Day, public holiday; **26 Dec.,** St Stephen's Day,

public holiday.
Others throughout the summer, organized festivals (mainly for the benefit of tourists) are put on in the main towns. These vary in timing and place from year to year, and a fairly comprehensive list of that year's programme can be obtained from the NTOG. For the main wine festivals and festivals of drama, *etc,* see page 28.

Maps

To supplement the maps in this book, you can get the maps given out by the NTOG (1:1,000,000) or use those printed in their regional leaflets. Maps by the Greek Survey at 1:200,000 can be bought from the Ethniki Statistiki Yperesia tis Ellados (National Statistical Service of Greece), 14 Likourgou, Athens, or from Stanfords' of Long Acre, in London.

Opening Times

Museums and sites If you are on a tight schedule, check opening times first with the NTOG. Sometimes opening hours are restricted to the more popular times, but the major museums and archaeological sites do stick to the advertised times, and in small local museums you can often get the custodian to let you in out of hours, if you are seriously interested. The opening hours were re-organized in 1980, and the pattern is likely to remain stable for some years.

Opening hours of museums and archaeological sites

Season	Major museums (1)	Major sites (2)	Others (3)
Winter Nov. 1–March 31	0930–1630	0900–1700	0930–1600
Spring April 1–May 15	0900–1800	0900–1830	0900–1330 1600–1800
Summer May 16–Sept. 15	0900–1900	0800–1900	0830–1230 1600–1800
Fall Sept. 16–Oct. 31	0900–1730	0900–1800	0900–1300 1530–1730

Sundays and public holidays: admission free, open 1000–1630 all year round.
Tuesdays: closed (may be Mondays in minor museums).
(1) Athens: National Archaeological; Byzantine, Acropolis, Agora; Delfi; Epidavros: Hios; Komotini; Korinthos; Limnos; Lesvos; Mistras; Olympia; Samothraki.
(2) Athens; Acropolis, Agora; Delfi; Epidavros; Korinthos; Mikines; Mistras; Olympia; Samothraki.
(3) All other museums and sites.

Shops Small village shops tend to open for 12 hours or more a day, but are liable to be closed 1300–1500 (when all good customers are asleep), after midday on Sunday, and on local saints' days. (Often open for a couple of hours in the morning on saints' days and public holidays.) Shops in towns follow a more regular pattern: open Monday, Wednesday, Saturday – 0800–1430; Tuesday, Thursday, Friday – 0800–1300 and 1700–2030. Most shops are closed on Sundays, but the Monistiraki district of Athens, and many gift shops in tourist areas, open on Sunday morning. Long after the markets are closed, food shops around market areas may stay open especially on a Saturday night.

Post

Post office buildings are marked ΤΑΧΥΔΡΟΜΕΙΟΝ: a letter or telegram is γραμμα and a stamp is γραμμα τοστημα. Post office opening hours vary. Use 0800 to 1300 as a guide. Stamps can be bought at post offices, or from kiosks and shops which sell postcards. Post boxes are painted yellow – if there is a choice, ΕΣΟΤΕΡΙΚΟΥ means inland and ΕΞΟΤΕΡΙΚΟΥ means abroad. Mail can be sent to you for collection at the post office of any town – make sure it's marked *Poste Restante*; you need a passport when collecting it. Parcels are not delivered but must be collected from the post office.

Shopping

Gifts At the top of the list of good buys are textiles, leather goods, furs and metal-work. 'Greek art' which may look mere tourist bait when you see it in serried ranks in a shop, can also be pleasing as a single piece at home.

Textiles are the best value: gaily-coloured and traditional-patterned rugs, light blankets, and the fleecy coverings called *floccates*. You will find these in shops in mountain villages all over the mainland; many of them are made locally, many more come from the cottage industries of Livadia or Edessa, but you can't distinguish them by appearance or by price. Arahova is a good place to buy. Clothing is a more doubtful matter; clothes can be well-made and very cheap, or cheap but ready to fall apart. You can get a good suit made in Rodos quickly and cheaply (duty-free). Leather work is found throughout the north of Greece – try the western outskirts of Thessaloniki. Furs come mainly from western Makedonia, especially Kastoria, though you are likely to find greater choice under one roof in Athens. The tradition of making finely-worked copper and filigree silver goods (from Turkish times) is still strong in the north, especially Ioanina. Sandals have unusual designs and are good value; shoes may be cheap but are nothing special.

Tourist shops are often crammed with plastic Spartans and Parthenon-decorated plates – whether this represents tremendous demand or over-production is a mystery. However, alongside the junk, you can very often find attractive paintings and pottery. Some of the items may appear to be overpriced, but look carefully at the quality. You can get vases which are a direct copy of works of antiquity or are in an antique style; modern works with a line and delicacy inspired by antiquity; and determinedly modern pieces – nearly all of them show skill and sensitive craftsmanship. They turn up in gift shops in quite unlikely places, so just keep your eyes open from the day you arrive.

All of these local products can be bought in Athens – handicrafts especially in the Monastiraki area, the more expensive items between Monastiraki and Panepistimiou. Athens' prices tend to be a little dearer. In a store, where you're served by an assistant, the marked price is final, but in small shops it is just an indication of what you may have to pay. Out-of-season you may be offered a 10 percent discount just for pausing by the shop. If you would like to haggle, two good openers are 'Can you help me with the price?' and 'I like it but it's too expensive'; if the price is negotiable, this will bring the boss. If you're asked to name a price, suggest a bit less than you're willing to pay rather than guess what the price will come down to. If no price is marked, the first price quoted is open to negotiation. Don't waste time over something you're not really interested in. You will get a better price (if you ask) by buying all your blankets in one place. If a store is busy, a reduction is less likely because everybody will want one.

Basic shopping If you're self-catering, be prepared to change your habits and enjoy what is available. The three biggest towns, of course, have department stores – comprehensive but unexciting – and about a third of the towns of any size have a 'supermarket' (ΣΟΥΠΕΡΜΑΡΚΕΤ). A supermarket is a fairly well stocked self-service food store with laden shelves and queues at

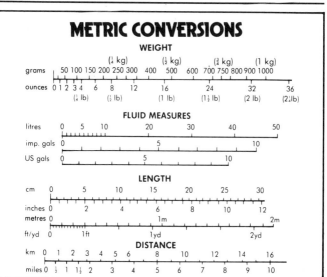

the checkout, just like home; uninteresting perhaps but reliable if you have to feed a family.

Thereafter, it's Greek-style shopping. Shops tend to be highly specialized – you may find a hardware store, for example, but it offers just miles and miles of plastic tubing, along with a few steel bars for reinforcing concrete. A food shop may look well-stocked with canned goods but on inspection there are only three different brands of green beans. If you explain what you want, however, with phrase book or pictures, you may be invited into a storeroom crammed with necessities they don't bother to sell. Many shops have no shop-front or window. There may be an open counter, or you may need to venture into a gloomy interior to discover if the shop sells shoes or paraffin.

A village store is liable to offer just two packing cases – one containing a few batteries, toothpaste, cans of milk, and a pack of needles, and another loaded with furry tomatoes, hard rolls and soft potatoes. The compensation for this is the availability of fresh food. You may find a greengrocer for vegetables, but that is rare and it is more usual to buy from a travelling shopkeeper/grower. Usually he has a Japanese pick-up, or sometimes a small Italian scooter attached to a large trailer. His vehicle is marked ΑΓΡΟΤΙΚΟΝ

and he will weigh out any amount you want. Greek housewives buy in huge quantities, but don't be afraid to get only a little – there is difficulty keeping food fresh in the heat. Choice may be limited but quality is excellent.

In a town find the market for fresh food – they all have a produce market (αγορα) somewhere. In Athens, there is an agora in every district but the most central is off Ermou Street, just south of Omonia, and on the Kolonos side of the station.

Meat from a butcher's shop is cut across the grain and tends to be tough unless it is stewed; chops are safer than 'steak'. Bread (ψωμι) is superb. White bread is basically a good British loaf with the savour of French bread. Brown bread is likeable and keeps well. If you buy a tub of margarine make sure it is not the blotchy grease sometimes sold under the same name, and highly prized by Greeks.

Best treat of all for self-caterers is fresh food from peasants in remote villages. There will be a fairly limited choice – eggs, honey, goat's cheese, fruit, sometimes bread – but if you're offered perfection, why worry?

Telegrams

These can be sent either from a main post office or from an OTE office (see over).

Telephones

Telephones are run not by the post office but by the OTE (Greek Telecommunications Organization). In main towns there are no telephones in post offices, they are at the OTE offices which have separate booths for long-distance and for local calls (distinguished by the word LOCAL). You fight your way to the counter and will then be directed to an empty booth. If you can find a slack period, the staff will help you make a call. In small towns there are telephone booths in post offices where the staff are usually less busy and can help you.

Most public telephones are in use all the time, because long-distance calls from anywhere but Athens somehow don't get through, and people just keep on trying.

In principle there is direct dialling from any telephone to anywhere in the world on the trunk dialling system. In a booth, you dial the call yourself and then pay at the desk. Most hotels and many restaurants have telephones with a meter, which you can use even if you're not staying there.

Dialling codes:

Australia	0061
Canada	001
Ireland	0044
New Zealand	0064
South Africa	0027
UK	0044
USA	001

Standard services:

Directory enquiries	131
Provincial enquiries	132
General information	134
Time	141
Medical care	166
City police	100
Gendarmerie	109
Fire	199
Tourist Police	171
Roadside assistance	104

You will notice there is no number for the operator, to get a call for you.

Time

Greek Standard Time is two hours ahead of Greenwich Mean Time (1200 in London is 1400 in Athens), and Greek Summer Time from April to October is still two hours ahead of British Summer Time. (Remember that the USA is between four hours and nine hours behind Greenwich Mean Time, depending on the particular Time Zone and local Summer Time; 1200 in New York is 1800 or 1900 hours in Athens.)

Greece adopted the Gregorian calendar only in 1923, and the Orthodox Church still follows the Julian calendar. (For example, in 1979 Easter Day was April 15 in the West, but April 22 in Greece.)

Tipping

Normally on a modest scale in Greece; over-tipping is not admired. Ten per cent of a bill is the maximum for large restaurants, but leave a few drachmai on the table for the assistant-waiter. Greeks often give no tip to taxidrivers; 2–300 dr for hotel staff in an A grade hotel; 50 dr per couple in a *taverna* if you feel pleased. There is more small-scale tipping than in the UK. For example: usherette in a cinema or theatre, 5 dr; boy whom you *ask* to show you the way, 5 dr (unwanted guides – nothing); parking attendant, 5 dr; guide round a site in a party, 10 dr; tour guide, 50 –100 dr at the end of a tour. In general, no tips to NTOG employees. (These are only indications and may become unrealistic with price rises.)

If a stranger does you a real service, like pulling your car out of a ditch, or taking you some distance to a classical site or to accommodation, the likelihood is that it is done from kindness and pride in showing hospitality. Payment is then not appropriate, and the offer of payment puts your helper in difficulty, because refusal may offend you. For such occasions, keep a bottle of wine or *ouzo* and have a drink to friendship.

Toilets

Public toilets are scarce in towns; cafés and hotels usually don't mind your using their facilities if you look respectable. There are toilets at railway stations and bus stations but they are often far from immaculate. Toilets at NTOG sites vary from hygienic to palatial. The sign for 'Gents' is ΑΝΔΡΩΝ, for 'Ladies' is ΓΥΝΑΙΚΩΝ. Keep tissues in your pocket.

USEFUL ADDRESSES

(Tel. nos in brackets)

The **National Tourist Organization of Greece** is the first and best source of all further information. It acts as a publicity office, and its leaflets on individual regions provide a reasonable map, tell you what there is to see, and list all the hotels down to C grade. It is an information bureau, equipped to answer questions on travel, activities and what you will find. (Obviously, involved questions which entail detailed research are best put in writing, rather than on the telephone.) It has considerable control over the standards of provision for tourists within Greece, and runs various ski-centres and beaches. What it cannot do is substitute for a commercial operator in making bookings.

The organization is abbreviated in this book to NTOG; in North America it is GNTO, and in Greece it is EOT (Ελλυνικος Οργανιστνος Τουριστνου).

Addresses of the NTOG overseas are: **Australia and New Zealand** Greek National Tourist Organization, 51-57 Pitt St., Sydney, N.S.W. 2000 (241-1663/ 4). **Canada** Greek National Tourist Organization, 2 Place Ville Marie, Suite 67, Esso Plaza, Montreal, Quebec H3B 2C9 (87-115-35). **South Africa** Greek National Tourist Organization, 108 Fox Street, Home Trust Building, Johannesburg (8342-551). **UK and Ireland** National Tourist Organization of Greece, 195-7 Regent St., London W1R 8DR (734-5997, 3 lines). **USA** a) Greek National Tourist Organization, 645 Fifth Ave, Olympic Tower, New York, N.Y. 10022 (212-421-5777), b) GNTO, 627 West Sixth Street, Los Angeles, California 90017 (213-626-6696), c) GNTO, 168 North Michigan Ave, National Bank of Greece Building, Chicago, Illinois 60601 (312-641-6600, 782-1084).

In Athens, the head office of the NTOG is at 2 Amerikis Street (3223-111), with an information office at 2 Karageorgi Servias Street (Sintagma), and other bureaux at 4 Stadiou and at East Airport. Other NTOG offices in Greece at: Corfu, Crete (Hania and Iraklio), Kavala, Kos, Larissa, Patra, Rodos, Thessaloniki, Volos, Igoumenitsa and the four road entry points.

Consulates

Australia 15 Messoghion St., Athens (3604-611). **Canada** 4 Ioan, Genadiou St., Athens (7395-11-19). **Ireland** 7 Vass. Konstandinou Ave, Athens (7327 712). **New Zealand** 29 Vass. Sofias Ave, Athens (7275-14/5). **South Africa** 69 Vass. Sofias Ave, Athens (7498-06/9). **USA** 91 Vass. Sofias Ave, Athens (712951).

United Kingdom 1 Ploutarchou St., Athens 139 (736211-19; 16 Papalexandrou St., Iraklio (081-224012); 45 Thessalonikis St., Kavala (051-223704); 2 Zambeli St., Corfu (0661-30055, 37995); 2 Votsi St., Patra (061-277329); 23 25th March St., Rodos (0241-27247, 27306); Ag. Theodorou St., Vathi,

Samos (0273-27314); 11 Vass. Konstandinou Ave, Thessaloniki (031-278006, 278169).

Travel

Olympic Airways 647 Fifth Ave, New York 10022; 141 New Bond St., London W.1; 96 Syngrou Ave, Athens (Terminal). **TWA** 8 Xenofontos St., Athens. **British Airways** 10 Othonos St., Athens. **OSE** (railways, Europabus, railway buses) 1-3 Karolou St., Athens (5222-491). **KTEL** (Κοινον Ταυειον Ειαπραξεων Λεωρορειων) *ie* pools of operators of buses for long-distance buses, and ΗΛΠΑΠ for Athens and suburban buses; timetables from NTOG at 2 Kar. Servias Street. **ELPA** Automobile and Touring Club of Greece, Athens Tower, 2-4 Messogion, Athens (7791-615). Also Corfu, Igoumenitsa. **Motor Insurance Bureau** 10 Xenofontos St., Athens (3236-733). **Ceres Hydrofoil Joint Service** 8 Thermistokleous St., Freattys, Pireas (4528-994). **Pireas Port Authority** (4511-311) – for timetables try the NTOG.

Car repairs – 24-hr service in Athens: Tourmikiotis, 22 Maizonos St., Vathis Sq., (5220-258) and Frangos, 21 Minoos St., Kinosargous (9017-962).

Sports

Hellenic Skiing and Alpine Club, 7 Karageorgi Servias, Athens. **Hellenic Touring Club**, 12 Politechnou, Athens. **Hellenic Rowing Federation**, 34 Voukourestiou, Athens (3612-109). **Hellenic Federation of Excursion Clubs**, 4 Draganitsiou, Athens. **Hellenic Sailing Federation**, 15A Xenofontos, Athens (3236-818). **Hellenic Athletic Swimming Federation** (EKOF), 2 Nikodimou St., Athens (3227-318). **Water Skiing Federation**, 32 Stournara St., Athens (5231-875). **National Airclub of Greece**, 27A Akadimias, Athens (3617-242). **Hellenic Riding Club**, 19 Paradissiou Maroussi, Athens (6826-128). **Northern Greece Riding Club**, Mikro Emvolo, Thessaloniki. **Athens Tennis Club**, 2 Leotoros Vassilissis Olgas, Athens (9232-872). **Yacht Brokers** There are 28 yacht brokers in Athens and Pireas, including Alpha Yachting Co., B&R Yachting, Bouboulis E.N., Captain Louys and George Masselos, Hellas Yachting, Kavos Yachting, Marine Corner – addresses from NTOG; many more in *Greek Travel Pages*.

Miscellaneous

Lost property in Athens: general (4531-716), in buses or taxis (5230-111).

Aliens Bureau, 9 Halokokondilli St., Athens (3628-301), or for work and residence permits (3622-601). **Chamber of Hotels**, 6 Aristidou, Athens (3235-501). **American Express**, 15-17 Venizelou St., Athens. **General Post Office** (open Sunday morning, philatelic service), 100 Eolou St., Athens. **Greek Animal Welfare Society**, Athens (6435-391). **National Organization of Greek Handicrafts**, 9 Mitropoleos St., Athens. **Vaccinations:** Health Centre at Ambelokipi, corner Alexandras and Vass. Sofias, Athens (6427-846).

THE LANGUAGE

Modern Greek is described as *demotic*, the language of the *demos* (people). It is not difficult to learn if you make an effort, but it is more difficult for English-speakers than, say, French or German. Without effort you won't pick up much Greek during a few weeks' stay. This is a pity, because one of the real pleasures of travel is talking to people.

You can get by without Greek. On all the main tourist tracks English, of a sort, is spoken by waiters and guides, and in shops, hotels and travel offices. Place-names are given in Greek and Latin characters, and much public information is put up in English as well as Greek. Off the beaten track, English is rare although banks and government offices nearly always have someone who speaks English, schoolteachers speak English, and in quite remote spots somebody will proudly appear who has unfortunately forgotten most of the English he learned working in the States many years ago. In northern Greece the men now go to Germany, rather than the USA, to work, but don't rush in to speaking German – memories of the war are long. There is a weather forecast in English on the radio at 0635 and 0730, and five minutes of news on the television at about 1815.

A phrase book such as *Collins Greek Phrase Book* will usually get you by if you're stuck. Try pointing to a phrase rather than saying it.

Almost as useful as a phrase book is pencil-and-paper. This is particularly helpful for numbers and times, and it is surprising how much you can get across with pictures. You won't find a phrase book that says, 'My car is stuck in the sand and we need a tow to reach hard ground. The children have got lost looking for help.' A quick sketch produces a traffic jam of tractors, laden with children.

Greek is spoken in nearly the same way in all the towns, with little regional variation. There are local accents in the mountains and on some of the islands, which can be exaggerated to prevent outsiders from understanding.

Greek conversation is more frank than English, and more inquisitive. If you get into conversation, let your face move, don't be afraid to gesture, and don't be afraid to ask. Do watch people's reaction carefully – Greeks can be very sensitive, but not show it to foreigners.

If you can read the Greek alphabet sufficiently to know how a word sounds, many words that you see will be familiar. Unfortunately, spoken Greek is more difficult to get the hang of – it is spoken very fast, one word is run into the next, and many of the consonants are halfway between their nearest English consonants.

The Greek Alphabet

Half the Greek alphabet is the same as the Latin alphabet used for writing English, and it takes only a few minutes to learn the capital letters of the other half sufficiently to be able to understand road signs. The small letters are rather more confusing and seem designed to give you eyestrain, but half-an-hour's practice is enough to leave you wondering why it seemed difficult.

The table opposite shows the alphabet in the correct order, with the pronunciation and the transliteration (the Latin equivalent for each letter). Note that the transliteration does not tell you exactly how the Greek letter is pronounced, it is just a simplified phonetic representation, used on maps and notices for presenting Greek names in a form you can recognize.

Many Greek place-names have a transliteration that looks ugly, and seems intended to confuse people used to traditional spellings. For example ΔΕΛΦΟΙ appears as DELFI, ΚΟΡΙΝΘΟΣ appears as KORIN-THOS, and ΧΑΛΚΕΔΟΝ appears as HALKEDON. These are probably more familiar as Delphi, Corinth and Chalcedon, which are taken from the spellings used by the ancient Romans to represent the Greek name (as it was pronounced 2000 years ago) in Latin characters (as these were used 2000 years ago). However, the transliteration comes nearer to representing the modern Greek pronunciation, and is the same for all European languages; it is the system used on NTOG maps and leaflets and in this book, with certain exceptions.

GREEK ALPHABET

Name	Capital	Small	Sound	Transliteration
alfa	A	α	*l*ark	A
vita	B	β	*v*im	V
ghama	Γ	γ	(*see notes*)	G
thelta	Δ	δ	*th*en	D
epsilon	E	ε	*e*gg	E
zita	Z	ζ	*z*ip	Z
ita	H	η	m*ee*t	I
thita	Θ	θ	*th*in	TH
iota	I	ι	m*ee*t	I
kappa	K	κ	*k*iss	K
lamtha	Λ	λ	*l*ook	L
mi	M	μ	*m*ad	M
ni	N	ν	*n*ot	N
ksi	Ξ	ξ	fo*x*	X
omikron	O	o	n*o*t	O
pi	Π	π	*p*ig	P
ro	P	ρ	*r*at	R
sighma	Σ	σ	*s*un	S
	(*before v, m, n*)		*z*ip	
taf	T	τ	*t*op	T
ipsilon	Y	υ	m*ee*t	I
fi	Φ	φ	*f*ish	F
hi	X	χ	(*see notes*)	H
psi	Ψ	ψ	co*ps*e	PS
omegha	Ω	ω	n*o*t	O

Notes

1 Γ(γ) pronounced (i) before an 'e' or 'i' sound like *y*ellow; (ii) before any other sound it is like a 'y' or 'w' pushed to the back of the throat – get a Greek to show you. Some people can reproduce the sound by making an 'r' or a 'k' sound deep in the throat.

2 X(χ), pronounced (i) before 'a', 'o', 'oo' sounds as in Scottish lo*ch*; (ii) before 'i' or 'e' sounds as in *h*ue or *h*ear.

3 OY(ου), pronounced as in m*oo*n.

4 EI(ει), OI(οι), YI(υι), pronounced as in m*ee*t.

5 AI(αι) pronounced as in m*e*n.

6 A small sighma is σ except at the end of a word where it is *s*.

7 The transliteration of Δ as D is just a convenience; DH is sometimes used.

In words of two or more syllables, one syllable is much more strongly stressed than the other. Sometimes the stressed syllable is marked with an acute accent in print, but this is only for the convenience of foreigners and is not part of Greek spelling.

Other accents are used in writing educated Greek, but they serve no purpose for speech and their use is simply a leftover from classical or 'purified' Greek. Most Greeks get them wrong and simply put a dot. Such an accent does not necessarily mean that a syllable is stressed. In place of a question mark (?) Greeks use a semicolon (;).

The 'Language Question'

Ancient Greek was the spoken language of 2500 years ago, and the language in which the great classics were written. During the period 200 BC to AD 1200 the grammar was simplified, the complicated vowel system and pronunciation of the consonants changed drastically, and many words were replaced by the words of the invaders. Modern Greek is as different from classical Greek as modern English is from Chaucer's.

When Greek national pride revived at the end of the 18th century, writers felt that the common speech of the time was not good enough for the land of past glories, and purified the language by bringing back archaic forms and replacing foreign words with 'pure' Greek words. Any word used by Homer was of course 100% pure. This artificial literary construction was adopted as the official language of the kingdom when

Greece became independent; it was called *Katharevousa*, meaning purified. All laws, scientific books, even newspapers, were written in Katharevousa. Over the years, popular (*Demotic*) Greek was used more and more for writing; in 1900 there were riots and killings when a translation of the New Testament appeared in Demotic – this was seen as a betrayal of the great past and the holy book. Under the Colonels (1967–74), Katharevousa was imposed as the only language allowed in secondary schools, so textbooks had to be rewritten and children had to learn in a 'foreign' language.

The question of whether to use Demotic or Katharevousa was settled in 1978 when Demotic was made the official language.

Useful Words and Phrases

Phrases to use

oríste	οριστε	may I have your attention; listen; excuse me
kali méra	καλι μερα	good morning
kali spéra	καλι σπερα	good afternoon or evening
parakalo	παρακαλω	please
efharistó	ευχαριστω	thank you
né	ηαι	yes
óhi	οχι	no
ya sas	γεια σας	cheers
signómi	συγνωμη	I'm sorry
poli kale	πολυ καλε	very good

Signs you will read

ΑΝΟΙΚΤΟΝ	Open	ΞΕΝΟΔΟΧΕΙΟΝ	Hotel
ΑΠΑΓΟΡΕΥΕΤΑΙ	Forbidden	ΜΟΥΣΕΙΟ	Museum
ΑΣΑΝΣΕΡ	Lift (elevator)	ΣΟΥΠΕΡΜΑΡΚΕΤ	Supermarket
ΕΙΣΟΔΟΣ	Entrance	ΣΤΑΘΜΟΣ	Station
ΕΝΟΙΚΙΑΖΕΤΑΙ	For hire (let or rent)	ΣΥΡΑΤΕ	Pull
ΕΞΟΔΟΣ	Exit	ΣΤΑΣΙΣ	Stop
ΙΣΟΓΕΙΟΝ	Ground Floor	ΥΠΕΡΑΓΟΡΑ	Hypermarket
ΚΕΝΤΡΟΝ	Centre	ΥΠΟΓΕΙΟΝ	Basement
ΚΛΕΙΣΤΟΝ	Closed	ΩΘΗΣΑΤΕ	Push
ΛΕΩΦΟΡΕΙΟ	Bus	ΚΙΝΔΥΝΟΣ	Danger

Shop signs

ΑΡΤΟΠΟΙΕΙΟΝ	baker's	ΟΠΟΡΟΠΩΛΕΙΟΝ	fresh vegetables
ΒΙΒΛΙΟΠΩΛΕΙΟΝ	bookshop	ΜΠΑΚΑΛΗΣ	grocer
ΧΑΣΑΠΗΣ	butcher	ΥΔΡΑΥΛΙΚΑ	hardware
ΦΑΡΜΑΚΕΙΟΝ	chemist	ΥΠΟΔΜΑΤΟΠΟΙΕΟΝ	shoe-shop
ΓΑΛΑΚΤΟΠΟΛΕΙΟΝ	dairy	ΧΑΡΤΗΠΩΛΕΙΟΝ	stationer
ΨΑΡΑS	fish-man	ΡΑΦΤΙΣ	tailor
ΦΡΕΣΚΑ ΨΑΡΙΑ	fresh-fish		

Words on maps

Agios	Αγιος (Αγια)	Saint
Akra	Ακρωτηρι	Cape
Áno	Ανο	Upper
Archea	Αρχαιο	Ancient
Káto	Κατο	Lower
Kólpos	Κολπος	Gulf
Límni	Λιμνις	Lake
Naós	Ναος	Temple
Néa	Νεα	New
Odos	Οδος	Street
Óros	Ορος	Mountain
Pálea	Παλ	Old
Potámi	Ποταμι	River
Spília	Σπιλια	Cave
Hóra	Χωρα	Country or village

TEMPLES

DORIC

IONIC

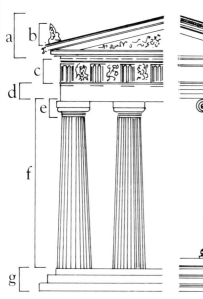

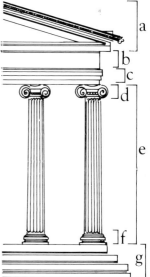

a decorated pediment
b acroterion
c frieze has upright triglyphs
separating the metopes
which usually carry carvings
d plain or ornamental architrave
e unornamented capital
f column, strongly tapered
– like a tree trunk
g no base, column stands directly
on the foundation

a pediment
b frieze
c architrave
d capital with volutes,
ornamented
e column,
slim very slightly tapered
f base
g foundation
(stylobate, euthynteria,
stereobate)

The land and its people

NORTHERN GREECE

Northern Greece consists of the provinces of Makedonia and Thraki, which were joined to the Greek kingdom only in this century and still have their own Minister for Northern Greece. This is the richest, busiest part of Greece, and the most 'un-Greek'.

The western part of Makedonia is mountainous (part of the Pindos range) and in places feels heavy and Balkan like neighbouring Yugoslavia, whose southern province is also called Makedonia. Elsewhere these mountains are more like those of southern Scotland, at their loveliest in autumn when the beeches turn golden. Between the mountains and the sea are rich agricultural lowlands, becoming richer still with irrigation schemes. The largest town, Thessaloniki – capital of the north, is a major centre of industry and modern cultural activity. Most other towns of this region are, to put it kindly, of no great interest. However, if you wander off the main road you will come to fascinating little villages.

North and east of Thessaloniki is a mixture of rather harsh mountain and rich plain devoted to tobacco, including the rather lovely old town of Kavala and some neglected but attractive seaside resorts. The Halkidiki Peninsula is a summer playground, apart from the beautiful land of Mt Athos which is a reservation for monks, forbidden to all women.

In classical times the Macedonians, speaking a barely intelligible Greek dialect, were regarded almost as barbarians until their king, Philip of Macedon, united the Greeks. His son, Alexander the Great, went on to lead the combined Greeks and Macedonians in spreading Hellenic culture all over the eastern Mediterranean. The Macedonian royal tombs and the remains of their palaces can be seen today at Pela and Vergina. The gold and silver mines of eastern Makedonia which financed Philip's conquests have been worked out, but today there are other riches – bauxite, copper, chrome and zinc, and, more interestingly, indications of uranium (near Drama and Seres) and oil (around the island of Thassos).

Under the Byzantine emperors Makedonia became more important, economically and culturally, than Greece proper, and Makedonia is still the richest Greek province; when the rest of Greece went republican in 1974, Makedonia remained staunchly royalist. Thessaloniki became the second city of the Empire next to Constantinople; today, it is the second city of Greece.

The Via Egnatia was the great highway connecting Imperial Rome with Constantinople, and today there are proposals to rebuild it to connect Igoumenitsa on the west coast with Thessaloniki and link up with the planned Trans-European Motorway.

The ancient Thracians were barbarians – wild, black-robed horsemen. Under the Ottoman Empire Thraki had a large Turkish population and even after the exchange of population in 1922, a minority of Thracians remained Moslem. (The official division is not between Greek- and Turkish-speaking people, but between those of Christian and Moslem religion.) Thraki is working hard to become Greek in spirit, just as Greece is preparing to merge its identity into Europe.

In winter, Northern Greece has snow in the mountains, rain or mist in the plains, and is no place to visit except perhaps for the skiing on Mt Vermio. In summer it is hot, but not with such a scorching heat as further south.

The food in restaurants reflects this northern character; there is more emphasis on meat, and less lavish use of olive oil, while mountain specialities such as wild boar and trout appear occasionally. The fresh fruit is perfection, and around the coasts there is more fish to be had.

Alexandroupoli E20

ΑΛΕΞΑΝΔΡΟΥΠΟΛΙΣ, ΑΛΕΞ/ΠΟΛΙΣ
Evros (pop. 23,000) The chief town and port of Thraki – airport, rail and sea connections. Alexandroupoli is only

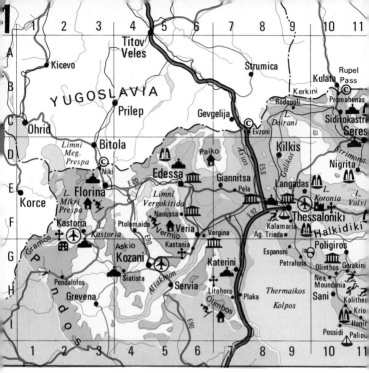

45km/28mi from the Turkish frontier on the River Evros, and from there it is 260km/162mi to Istanbul. The main boulevard, running parallel to the sea, is lively in the evening and the seafront itself is a broad, friendly promenade. This is a good base (hotels and restaurants) from which to explore Thraki.

A visit to the **Makri** cave (12km/7mi west of Alex/poli) is a good sightseeing expedition. The rubble of **Trajanopolis** (15km/9mi east) marks where Xerxes stood his army of two million men and counted them. *Thes/niki 341km/212mi.*

Drama (ΔΡΑΜΑ) C13

Drama (pop. 30,000) A rich town, centre of the tobacco growing 'Golden Plain'; much of it is newly built on a grid pattern. The shops suggest prosperity; the coffee places are very definitely cafés rather than *kaffeneinons*. *Alex/poli 214km/133mi, Thes/niki 165/103.*

Edessa (ΕΔΕΣΣΑ) E5

Pela (pop. 15,000) Beautifully situated above a steep bluff, Edessa appears to be well cared for – rare in Greece. Cascading streams run through the town meeting at the cliff edge in spectacular falls (24m/80ft). Carpets are manufactured here but don't expect to find them in the shops. There is a mosque and balconied Turkish houses to visit. Edessa is a favourite destination for a day's outing with people from Thessaloniki.

Pela, ancient capital of Makedonia (5th–2nd century BC), is halfway between Edessa and Thessaloniki, and has a fully excavated archaeological site alongside the main road. Here are the remains (a few columns) of the palace where Alexander the Great was born, and also the more interesting foundations of a great house of the Hellenistic period with mosaic floors – the much copied *Lion Hunt* and *Dionysos on a Panther*. The mosaics may however be covered with polythene to protect them.

If you stop for the antiquities, visit the two small towns of **Pela** and **Nea Pela** on the hill above the archaeological site. They are an interesting example of

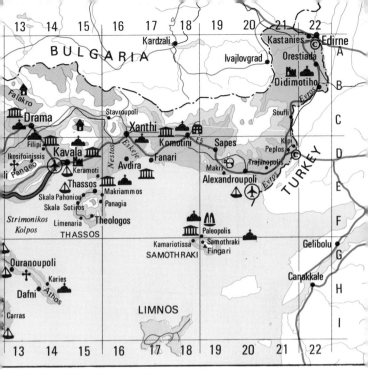

Greek 'suburban' development – a square grid of houses put up for refugees from Asia Minor. *Kastoria 118km/73mi, Thes/niki 89/55.*

Florina (ΦΛΩΡΙΝΑ)   E3

Florina (pop. 12,000) A gloomy mountain town, with derelict Turkish houses by the river; busy marketplace. The beech forests between Florina and Kastoria are good for picnics.

West of Florina are the **Prespa** lakes – the Great Prespa, shared between Yugoslavia, Albania and Greece can be visited only with a military permit (obtainable only if there is real cause), but the Little Prespa (L. Mikri Prespa) attracts many visitors. They come to see the bird sanctuary which is already established and attracting more and more wildfowl every year. *Kastoria 68km/42mi, Thes/niki 160/99.*

Kastoria (ΚΑΣΤΟΡΙΑ)   F3

Kastoria (pop. 10,000) A mountain town, on the neck of a peninsula which divides Lake Kastoria nearly in two from the west side. Kastoria makes the most of its lakeside setting. It is a V-shaped town climbing sharply up two sides of a mountain, overlooking the lake. There are cafés and eating-places on the water's edge and a rowdy quayside market. Kastorian furriers specialize in making *Megaic* blankets and fashions from fur off cuts; there is an exhibition of furs in March.

The 18th-century houses of the *archontika* – town worthies grown rich on trade – have trees between them in cobbled streets and alleys. There are also abandoned tower-like houses rising above the shore of the lake, and many Byzantine churches for the enthusiast.

Kastoria is an attractive centre for visiting the Prespa lake (see *Florina* above) but the road from Kastoria is unmetalled for over 30km/19mi. It is navigable but potholed and littered with fallen rock – at present there is no prospect of improvement. *Ioanina 219km/136mi, Thes/niki 207/129.*

Kavala (ΚΑΒΑΛΑ)   D14

Kavala (pop. 47,000) This is a major port exporting tobacco, beautifully situ-

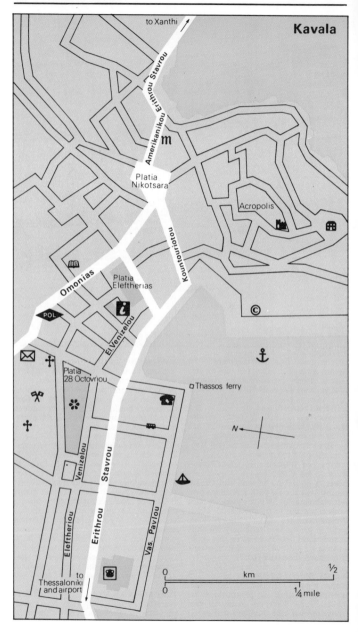

Kavala

to Xanthi

Amerikanikou Erithrou Stavrou

Platia
Nikotsara

Acropolis

Omonias

Platia
Eleftherias

Kountouriotou

POL

Platia
28 Octovriou

El.Venizelou

Thassos ferry

N

Venizelou

Erithrou
Stavrou

Vas. Pavlou

Eleftheriou

to
Thessaloniki
and airport

0   km
0   ¼ mile

½

ated at the head of a bay. Above the bustling quay rise red tiled roofs – the oriental maze of 'Old Kavala', climbing the eastern promontory. Here you'll find the almshouse of Mohammed Ali, founder of the Egyptian dynasty that ended with Farouk.

The nearby monastery of **Ikosifoinissis** is situated in plane woods (2-hr climb) – modern frescos, library, *etc.* There are several good beaches a bus ride out of town, a campsite by the sea 5km/3mi to the west, and 30km/19mi to the west is Mt Pangeo, with the worked-out gold mine of Alexander the Great, now a good area for shooting small game. Ferry to the island of Thassos every two hours (1½ hrs crossing). Good archaeological museum.

Filipi is an archaeological site 19km/12mi north west of Kavala. The ancient town of Philippi was named for Philip II of Macedon, and reached its height of prosperity in Roman times because of its strategic position on the Via Egnatia. This was the Philippi mentioned in *Julius Caesar*, where republican Rome died in the battle between Mark Antony/Octavian and Brutus/Cassius in 42BC. Here St Paul first preached the gospel in Europe and was imprisoned, but he visited the town again and later wrote his Epistle to the Philippians. Kavala was the new port for Philippi, called Neapolis in the Epistle.

The main road still passes through the middle of the site; it is mostly ruins, with standing columns and the cell of St Paul. You will need the detailed explanation found in the guide-book – obtainable in the museum. The Hellenistic theatre has been restored, and is used in summer during the Philippi and Thassos Festival – August. *Drama 36km/23mi, Thes/niki 163/101.*

Kilkis (ΚΙΛΚΙΣ) D9

Kilkis (pop. 11,000) Capital of the nome – an unremarkable town. Lake Doirani is about 52km/32mi north – good for fishing. (A military permit is required to approach the frontier.) **Rodopoli** is the centre of the Alpine area in the Kerkini mountains to the north. *Thes/niki 50km/31mi.*

Komotini (ΚΟΜΟΤΗΝΗ) C18

Rodhopi (pop. 31,000) A thriving market town. About half the inhabitants are Turkish and there are many **Bulgarian Pomaks**. Most archaeological finds from Thraki are in the museum here. The main places of interest are the Mosque of Yemi Djani and the local copper working shops.

Fanari has a good beach (30km/19mi away). *Thes/niki 276km/172mi.*

Kozani (ΚΟΖΑΝΗ) G4

Kozani (pop. 22,000) A wet night in Kozani is an experience to treasure. Mud, washed in from the side roads and out of the potholes, fills the main square, and the traffic slithers merrily about to an accompaniment of police whistles. But the crowds still parade cheerfully in side roads, closed to traffic, and there are enough restaurants to feed the population at one sitting. A very agreeable town; a few winding back streets, with no features of note but without the typical air of neglect. An important centre of communication, with buses to most places in Makedonia and to Ipiros. *Ioanina 222km/138mi, Thes/niki 135/84.*

Festivals: January 6 performances of folklore called *Bourbousaria*; at the end of Carnival – bonfires, songs in the local dialect, and traditional dancing.

Naoussa (ΝΑΟΥΣΑ) F6

Imathia (pop. 17,000) A long, narrow town on a mountainside, overlooking a vast plain where apple, cherry and peach trees blossom in May; in winter it is a centre for the skiing on Mt Vermio but is, nevertheless, remarkably cheerless. At Carnival time it comes to life. The dry red wine of Naoussa is one of the few Greek wines that really needs to age. *Thes/niki 93km/58mi.*

Festivals: May 27 cherry festival at Kolindio at Pieria.

Seres (ΣΕΡΡΑΙ) D11

Seres (pop. 40,000) In AD 1010, the Byzantine emperor Basil II defeated the Bulgarians, took 10,000 prisoners, blinded •them and sent them home, leaving one man in a hundred with one eye to lead the rest home. The Bulgarians did not occupy Seres again until 1913, when they took the town from the Turks in the First Balkan War. The Greeks ejected the Bulgarians in the Second Balkan War but, as they retreated, the Bulgarians burnt the town. Overlooked by the ruined Frankish-Byzantine castle, the town has been almost entirely rebuilt but rather boringly; there is a pleasant main square, bordered by poplars and willows, which has an abandoned mosque. It has an air of prosperity rather than enjoyment, being the centre of the rich Strymon plain (tobacco).

North of Seres (38km/24mi), **Sidirokastro** has a striking position in the foothills of the mountains between

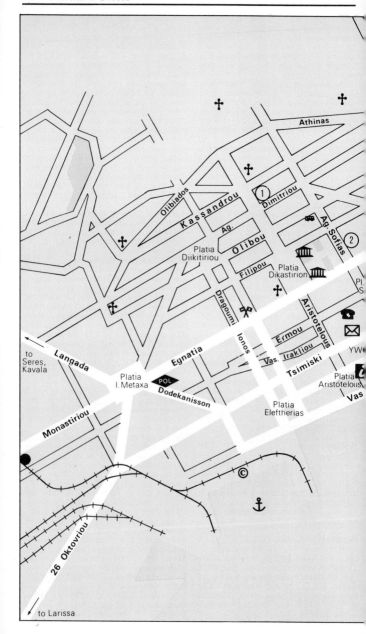

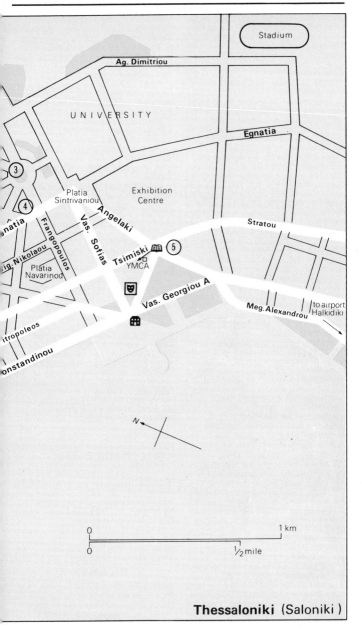

Thessaloniki (Saloniki)

Greece and Bulgaria, overlooked by the stone built 'Iron Castle'. The road from Sidirokastro leads to the grim Rupel Pass and on to Bulgaria. *Thes/niki 95km/ 59mi.*

Thessaloniki   F9
(ΘΕΣΣΑΛΟΝΙΚΗ, ΘΕΣ/ΝΙΚΗ)

Thessaloniki (pop. 750,000) Thessaloniki (abbreviated in speech to Saloniki) was called after Alexander the Great's half sister, Thessalonikeia, in about 316 BC. St Paul preached here in AD 49–50 and founded a church; in his Epistles to the Thessalonians he reminds them, 'If a man will not work, he shall not eat.'

Though the approach to Thessaloniki from the west is through miles of industrial dereliction, this second largest city in Greece and university town, has more of the style of a capital than Athens itself. The broad streets (often colonnaded) running down to the waterfront, the grand buildings, the squares, the futuristic international Exhibition Centre and the ghostly shells of mansions once loved by wealthy traders, make Saloniki a city unique in Greece for town planning and architectural richness. Its Byzantine monuments are surpassed only by those in Istanbul and although it suffers regularly from earthquakes, the damage is repaired. It has the only symphony orchestra in Greece.

In the centre, almost next door to the smart squares, with stores and boutiques, is the huge covered market for fresh produce (Vassil. Irakliou Street). The esplanade along the waterfront is a full kilometre of cafés and restaurants.

Saloniki has an airport, buses going everywhere and cars for rent so that it has become an excellent base for expeditions into Halkidiki, to Olympus, to the spa town of Edessa, and to the archaeological sites of Pela, Vergina and Lefkadia.

There is still scope for historical exploration in the city despite extensive rebuilding since 1950.

Off the Egnatia Odos, in Odos Ag. Sofias, is the **Panayia Akheiropoietos** (2) one of the earliest Christian buildings still in use, dedicated to the Virgin about AD 431.

The **Arch of Galerius** (4) was a triumphal monument to the Emperor's victories over the Persians in AD 297. It stands off the Egnatia Odos and was once part of a larger design containing a palace (the foundations have been recently uncovered west of Odos Frangopoulos), a hippodrome and a mausoleum. The Rotunda at **Agios**

Georgios (3) (the oldest monument in Thessaloniki) was probably built as this mausoleum. The building has been a mosque and is now a church. When repairs are completed it will be open from 0900–1300 and 1500–1700 (Sundays 1000–1400 free).

Agios Dimitrios (1) is reputedly the largest church in Greece. It was almost destroyed by fire in 1917 but has been reconstructed.

The **Archaeological Museum** (in the YMCA Square – 5) specializes in architectural and sculptural marbles, but also contains a great deal of gold and metalwork including the caskets from Vergina. Exhibits are marked in English.

In September there is a great international trade fair of local and foreign products, and the Greek Light Song Festival in the **Exhibition Centre**. *Athens 508km/316mi, Larissa 153/95.*

Veria (ΒΕΡΟΙΑ)   F6

Imathia (pop. 30,000) This is the centre of a small linen industry based on local flax. It is the nearest town to the skiing centre on Mt Vermio. There are plentiful eating places for visitors to **Vergina** (12km/7mi away), one of the most important archaeological sites of Makedonia.

At Vergina the Royal Tomb has a front like an Ionic temple, and the massive marble doors are still lying on the ground. A carved throne inside symbolizes the unknown king of the Hellenistic period. Excavations of the site of the Royal Palace beyond the tomb show that it was huge – it is clearly marked. Most fascinating of all are the excavations now going on by the modern village of Vergina; here in 1977 were found gold caskets (now in Thessaloniki museum) containing bones which the excavator believes are the remains of Philip of Macedon. *Thes/niki 75km/47mi.*

Xanthi (ΞΑΝΘΗ)   C16

Xanthi (pop. 25,000) A Turkish town with slim minarets, it straddles the valley of the River Eskeje and is the centre of a tobacco growing area.

Avdira (30km/19mi south) is a partly excavated Hellenic city. The coast is rocky and desolate. *Komotini 57km/ 35mi, Thes/niki 219/136.*

THE HALKIDIKI

(area 3281 sq km/1267 sq mi, pop. 75,000) At the height of the summer the classical sites of Greece are flattened by armies of tourists; the overflow who prefer lazing in the sun fill up the islands, so that their character, which is the main attraction, is being gradually changed. Yet there are plenty of undemanding holidaymakers – especially those with young children – who do not seek culture, are not really interested in 'going native' and ask only for the simple seaside pleasures of good food, good swimming and family entertainment for their precious two or three weeks away. For them, there is the Halkidiki.

The Halkidiki is a peninsula of eastern Makedonia, with a gently mountainous interior and a long coastline of beaches, rocky headlands and fishing villages, which are being groomed as a string of holiday centres. Almost the entire coastline has been taken over by the Greek Government and tourist hotels, campsites and whole tourist towns are springing up. However, the Halkidiki is big enough to absorb this development – for years to come it should not be too overcrowded. It has an affinity in many ways with parts of Southern France, and as Greek visitors far outnumber foreigners its atmosphere is relaxed and happy.

The most popular area is probably the western promontory of Kassandra which projects for 50km/31mi into the Aegean Sea. **Kalithea**, **Kriopigi** and **Haniotis** are three lively centres where a number of hotels have appeared, but there are many other little places where you can eat, sleep, play and be entertained. On the central promontory, Sithonia, the once quiet village of **Neas Marmaras** is next to a mammoth complex – **Porto Carras** – still being built. The north west corner of the peninsula, nearer to Thessaloniki, is popular with campers, *eg* at **Ag. Triada** and **Epanoni**. **Nea Moundania** and **Ouranoupoli** are little towns that are retaining a life of their own despite the influx of foreigners. In between the built-up centres are campsites and all along the coast are coves and beaches.

The holiday centres provide all the water sports and beach activities the family man could wish for; nightlife is pretty well confined to the hotels. If you want shopping, or slightly more sophisticated entertainment, Thessaloniki is at most 140km/87mi away (from Ouranoupoli). The 'capital' of Halkidiki, **Poligiros**, is a sleepy, dusty little village with a few agreeable restaurants and considerable charm – it is no 'hot spot'!

A Neolithic cave at **Petralona** and a pile of stones marking the site of the ancient city of **Olinthos** are the only sites of interest for the antiquarian.

The eastern promontory is the 'Holy Mountain', **Mount Athos**. This is a self governing 'monks' republic', with a frontier just south of Ouranoupoli which the casual visitor may not cross. There are about 20 occupied monasteries and about 1500 monks. Some of the monks are old men who have retired here from the world, while others are actively serving, or seeking, God.

The mountain landscape is one of the most beautiful in Greece and the monasteries are storehouses of Byzantine art. Adult male visitors are allowed to enter, if they are seriously interested; it is not a place for the idly curious. Women are totally prohibited. A permit to enter may be obtained from the Ministry of Northern Greece in Thessaloniki, or the Ministry of Foreign Affairs in Athens. In principle a request for a permit must be supported by a recommendation from the visitor's embassy or consulate, so this is not a sudden impulse outing. Entry is through the port of Dafni.

A monastery, Mt Athos

THE NORTHERN ISLANDS

The two islands close to the northern mainland are similar in structure and history but they have a very different appearance. In antiquity, both were centres of Greek culture while the adjacent mainland was barbaric, and both were covered by forest. Today Samothraki has lost most of its trees, while Thassos is still covered by pine and chestnut; Samothraki has one sandy beach, while the coast of Thassos is a chain of beaches. These factors have affected   tourist   development   –

Samothraki is barely visited and has only about 50 hotel beds, while Thassos has over 50 hotels (2300 beds in 1980). Which one is now a centre of Greek culture is a matter of opinion.

Samothraki (ΣΑΜΟΘΡΑΚΗ) G19

(area 176 sq km/68 sq mi, pop. 4000) Its name means 'the Samos of Thrace', for it was originally peopled by colonists from Samos. You arrive today at the little port of **Kamariotissa**, which has a jetty rather than a harbour. There is violin and *bouzouki* music on a Sunday night for the entertainment of the locals. A bus goes four times a day from the port to the main village, **Samothraki** (Hora) – basic shops and banks – which is guarded by the ruins of a Byzantine fort and overlooked by Mt Fingari, 1448m/4751ft. From the top of Fingari, Poseidon watched the Greek siege of Troy, but if you want to attempt the four-hour walk to the top, take a guide. There is snow at the summit except at the height of summer.

Paleopolis also is reached by taking a bus from the harbour. It follows the dirt road along the north coast, through wheat fields, to the thermal baths of Loutra. Paleopolis is the site of the Sanctuary of the Great Gods, a great attraction for archaeologists. Here was found the *Winged Victory* of Samothrace, which now adorns the grand entrance to the Louvre. The French sent a plaster copy back to Samothraki and it is now in the museum in Hora.

For all that there is not much to say about it, Samothraki is nearly as much a camper's paradise as its sister, Thassos. *Communications*: One ferry a day from Alex/poli (2½ hrs); one a week from Ag. Konstandinos (22 hrs) and from Kimi (18½ hrs).

Thassos (ΘΑΣΟΣ)   E15

(area 399 sq km/154 sq mi, pop. 17,000) Thassos is an island of gentle hills, green with pines and chestnuts, but with some dark gorges and switchbacks. The forest is alive with rushing streams; all round the coast are small sandy beaches and secluded coves. The evenings are pleasantly cool, even in August. In all, it is hardly surprising that Thassos is more popular than Samothraki.

Thassos (Limin or Limenas) is the capital, and the more important of the island's two ports. It says 'welcome' before you are off the ferry – decked out with the flags of all nations and, more importantly, with the signs, so absent elsewhere in Greece, with up-to-date information about transport and accommodation. The town manages to be gay, friendly and lively, with a busy nightlife but without the cosmopolitanism of Mikonos, for most of the visitors are Greek. The evening *volta*, through streets closed off to the traffic, is enthusiastic. There are many interesting classical remains in Limin. It is a pleasure to visit them rather than a duty. The Roman Agora manages to look lovely, though little more than broken stone. The Hellenistic theatre looking out to sea is used for dramatic performances during the annual Philippi and Thassos Festival.

The best beach for Limin is at Makriammos, but it is becoming rather an 'in' place; if you find this unappealing, there are plenty of other good beaches.

The road from Limin makes a circular tour of the island (about 3½ hrs in a bus). All the way round there are little villages, each a delight; they are all welcoming, though it cannot be long before the kind people of Thassos begin to wonder what benefits they get in return from the tourists. There is no reason to single out any one village above the rest, but the **Pahi** headland, west of Limin, is memorable for the spectacular views.

The west coast is less visited because it has less dramatic scenery. It includes the second port of Thassos, **Limenaria**, which remains essentially a fishing village but has *tavernas*, nightspots and accommodation.

There are four organized campsites on Thassos, but the whole island is (mosquitoes permitting) a camper's paradise – despite the notices at Limin, warning you that freelance camping is forbidden. Unfortunately, this could change.

The west coast has suffered from mining, mainly cadmium extraction which causes a red dust. Just offshore, oil has been discovered, and the first commercial recovery is expected in 1981. If the reserves are as big as some Greeks hope, Thassos will be the natural base for the oilmen, making it another Shetland.

Communications: Ferry frequent – up to one an hour – from Kavala (1½ hrs crossing). About ten ferries a day from Keramoti (40 mins), the nearest point if you are driving.

Festivals: August 6 at Skala Sotiros, August 15 at Panagia, August 27 at Limenaria, October 26 at Theologos, every summer weekend seems a festival in Limin.

WESTERN GREECE

This region consists of the mainland of north-west Greece which is the administrative province of Ipiros (mainly mountains), and the soft islands of the Ionian Sea. The mountains are the southern end of the Pindos range, backbone of the Balkan peninsula, and virtually cut off Ipiros from the east. Deep gorges and ravines make them a delight for viewing from a car, but they are hard going even for experienced walkers. In the valleys, you can find ancient tracks at the foot of gentle green slopes – a pastoral scene rather unexpected in Greece. The western seaboard offers sandy beaches and coves, little developed for holiday-makers. Of the islands, only Corfu has become well-known to tourists, and even there you will easily find deserted beaches; Zakinthos is now visited for its dreamy peace and Lefkada because it is easily accessible – almost joined to the mainland, but the others – Ithaki, Paxi and the largest of them all, Kefalonia – remain havens of peace, *ie* for most people there is nothing much to do. (Kithira is administratively one of the Ionian Islands, but it has been included in the Peloponnese (page 79) where it belongs in location and in feeling.)

In winter, the mountains of Western Greece are snow-covered (there is a ski centre at Metsovo) while the coast and the islands are very wet – hotels outside the towns tend to be closed. In summer the mountain valleys can be hot and oppressive, but at no great height the air cools and the sunshine is pleasant. The islands and seaboard are hot in summer, but it is a bearable heat. The best time to visit this area is probably May and early summer.

Ipiros was called 'Epirus' in ancient times meaning mainland, and to the classical Greeks it was not part of their shining island world but the start of the vast barbarian north, home of their ancestors. Still, the inhabitants were Greeks, even if backward, and they sometimes joined in the affairs of the southern world. Pyrrhus, King of Epirus (*c*318–272 BC) was one of the world's most brilliant generals.

The region was virtually independent during the time of the Byzantine Empire, and after Constantinople fell to the Latins was ruled by despots, nobles who aspired to the Imperial throne themselves. Under the Turks, Byzantine culture stayed very much alive in Ipiros, while the islands and much of the coast remained under Venetian control. Southern Ipiros was joined to Greece in 1881, and the north only in 1913. This history can be seen in the buildings – the churches are a mixture of Orthodox solidity and Romanesque striving; the old stone houses are the robust dwellings of a primitive but prosperous bourgeoisie.

The mountain remoteness of Ipiros has produced a clan life reminiscent of the old Scottish Highlands. Epirots have a reputation for meanness, but are among the friendliest and most hospitable of Greeks. The traditional men's costume (now vanished except for displays) was the *fustanella*, a long skirt from which came the kilt-like skirt of today's ceremonial guards. In between the periods of clan warfare the Epirots would unite against the foreign occupying forces of Turkey. Today they are great emigrants – to the United States or to Germany – but their heart remains at home.

Arta (ΑΡΤΑ) I7

Arta (pop.20,000) A bend in the River Arahthos half-surrounds this spacious town. The two main squares interconnect – one nearly always full of life (Platia Kilkis), the other quieter but with an occasional market (Platia Skoufas). The latter is dominated by the square church of the Parigoritissa which looks about to fall down but has stood for 700 years and now houses a museum of Christian antiquities. The many churches in Arta (indicating the town's past importance) are an interesting blend of Byzantine and Romanesque – see the tiled church of St Basil near the castle.

The city was depopulated by the

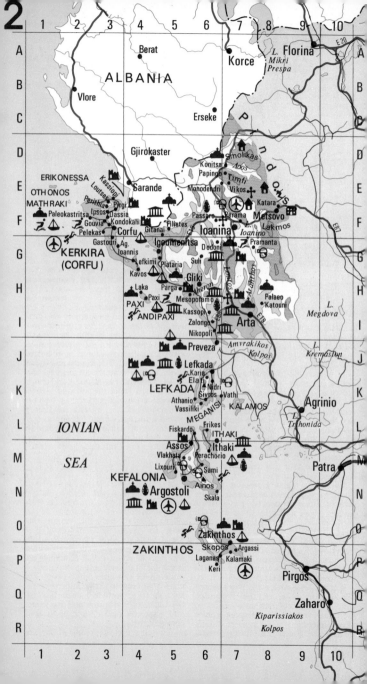

Romans when they tried to establish a town at Nikopoli (see *Preveza*, p. 53), but in the 13th century it became the capital of the Despotate of Epirus and the second city of mainland Greece. It fell to the Turks in 1449 but soon passed to the Venetians whose castle, on a low peak of rock overlooking the town, is now a hotel. A lopsided Turkish packhorse bridge spans the Arahthos south west of the town – best seen from the nearby modern bridge.

The town is surrounded by orange groves and distant precipitous mountains, except to the south where the land turns to marsh before reaching the Amvrakikos Kolpos (Ambracian Gulf) 10km/6mi away – good fishing. North, the road to Ioanina leads through the **Louros Gorge** 25km/16mi away, a deep valley shaded by plane trees. Darkness falls early as the high mountains cut short the evening sun. Following roughly the course of the Arahthos, then turning north east towards **Palaeo Katouni** (see the brilliantly coloured 'Red Church' – Byzantine), you come to a land of cliffs and firs and wild mountains. *Athens 360km/224mi, Ioanina 75/47.*

Dodoni (ΔΩΔΩΝΗ)   G6

Ioanina 19km/12mi south of Ioanina are the ruins of the most ancient oracle in Greece, Dodoni (8th century BC). In the reconstructed theatre, as at Epidavros, there is a summer festival of drama, (details from Pirrou Square in Ioanina). The eyes of the audience may be drawn away from the stage, across the little stream to the beautiful mountain opposite (Mt Tomaros, 1974m/6476ft) or to the surrounding, gentle, oak-covered hills.

Igoumenitsa   G6
(ΗΓΟΥΜΕΝΙΤΣΑ)
Thesprotia (pop. 4500) This little town exists for the ferry traffic; it is the nearest port of call in Greece for boats from Italy (a cheaper and considerably shorter crossing than going to Patra) and is also the terminus for traffic between Corfu and the mainland. It is unlikely that anybody would visit Igoumenitsa except in transit, but if you are stuck there for a day or so there are much worse places to be. There are two main streets; the harbour front lined with travel agencies and shipping offices, and the parallel shopping road with cafés and restaurants – staff are accustomed to the idea that ferry passengers may want to eat in a hurry.

There is a pleasant garden overlooking the water. Stay here for a quiet swim, or go to the better beach at **Plataria** 12km/7mi south. For an outing, there are the ruins of an ancient acropolis at **Gitanai**, 14km/9mi north east on the road to Filiates. *Athens 475km/295mi, Ioanina 100/62.*

Ioanina (ΙΩΑΝΝΙΝΑ)   F7

Ioanina (pop. 40,000) Tucked away in the mountains, far from the rest of Greece, Ioanina (Yanina) is a large, surprisingly unprovincial town. It sits on the western side of a large lake (11 kilometres long, 6 kilometres wide – 7mi/4mi), the old walled town projecting on a rocky ledge into the lake. Ioannines claim to speak the purest, clearest Greek. In early Turkish times Ioanina was the principal centre of learning in the ruins of Byzantine culture, and later under Ali Pasha it became the largest and busiest town in Greece.

The name of Ali Pasha, Lion of Ioanina, may be dimly recalled by students of European history. He was an Albanian adventurer, straight out of the Middle Ages, who took over Ioanina in the early 19th century and made himself ruler, nominally dependent on the Sultan, of much of modern Ipiros and Albania. He was an ally of the French and then the British in the Napoleonic Wars and was finally shot by order of the Sultan in 1822 in a monastery on the lake – his tomb stands in front of the former mosque in his fortress in the old town.

Ali Pasha's Mosque, Ioanina

At the foot of the old town is a half-derelict maze of back streets, where craftsmen still produce copperware and filigree silver of an Oriental style; the goods are sold in the decaying shops of Averof Street. At the top of Averof Street the belvedere in a small garden overlooking the lake is a centre of social life – it has a restaurant, a popular disco and the occasional cultural event. You might well expect the lakeside to be lined with shaded restaurants, but there are just a couple of dusty cafés by the landing stage. There is a boat once an hour to the island where you'll find six monasteries or churches among the flowers. There's also a restaurant, which occasionally serves frog's legs or eels from traps which you may see near the jetty. At the northern end of the lake the limestone caverns of **Perama** are well-lit, and from there the road leads across bleak marshland to the airport.

North west of the town (10km/6mi), off the road to Igoumenitsa, is the site of **Passaro** with the remains of a temple to Zeus Areios (paved courtyard). *Athens 435km/270mi, Kastoria 219/136, Trikala 145/90.*

Konitsa (ΚΟΝΙΤΣΑ)   D7

Ioanina (pop. 3000) The extreme north of Ipiros is a land of wild mountains, precipitous gorges, rushing torrents and austere, stone-built, often deserted villages. The only village of any size in the region is Konitsa – from the distance it looks attractive, a triangular clump of roof-tops in a narrowing valley, but close up it is rather seedy. The lovely Turkish humpback bridge is obscured now by a Bailey bridge.

The region between Konitsa and Ioanina is called the **Zagoria.** It will suit the real lover of rugged landscapes with a good head for heights and a stomach for hairpin bends. There are 20 or so mountain villages which are nearly deserted, but may revive with the aid of a government programme to restore and preserve 'traditional settlements'. There are two well-made roads into the region now from the Ioanina/Konitsa road – both dead-ends, but if you don't want to retrace your route back to the main road there are alternative dirt roads. Visit some of the villages: try **Monodendri** with 200 or so houses on its steep mule roads, and perhaps 100 inhabitants; go from there north east to the empty monastery of Ag. Paraskevi which you can go through (a white, painted hand points to the secret catch to let you in) to a 300m/1000ft drop over sheer cliffs into the **Vikos Gorge**; or **Papingo**, where the people claim to be descended from the original pre-

Greek inhabitants, offers a view of the northern opening of the Vikos Gorge.

To travel north of Konitsa, towards the Albanian frontier, you need a military permit. Enquire at the Tourist Police in Ioanina, but expect to be invited to go elsewhere. *Ioanina 68km/42mi, Kozani 156/97.*

Metsovo (ΜΕΤΣΟΒΟΝ)   F8

Ioanina (pop. 2800) A mountain village just before the Katara Pass (1707m/5600ft) on the only good road from west to east in the region, Metsovo is called by some the 'show village of Greece'. It still has the tall, stone houses and narrow, cobbled alleys from the days when the merchants of these mountains were the most prosperous in Turkish-held Greece. The Tositsa House is now a museum of handicrafts.

In winter, Vlach shepherds would retreat here from the bleak hills, speaking a language like modern Romanian. There are few Vlachs now and in their place come the skiers, for Metsovo is becoming a ski centre, with chair lifts and long ski runs. The local workshops use pine and fir from the surrounding forest to produce carpentry and woodcarvings which are on sale in the village. *Ioanina 60km/37mi, Trikala 90/56.*

Ipiros local costume, Metsovo

Parga (ΠΑΡΓΑ)   H5

Thesprotia (pop. 1700) With two bays, a jetty and a huddle of square white houses pushed up onto the rocks behind, this pretty seaside town has successfully absorbed the impact of tourism – its cafés on the waterfront still serve plenty of local custom. The golden beach to the north is reputedly the best in Greece and, with the greater demand, more facilities have been provided.

South of Parga, across 15km/9mi of bad road and marsh, is the Nekromanteion of Ephyra (sanctuary of Persephone, goddess of the dead) on a low hill above the village of **Mesopotamo.** 'Necromancy' means prophesy by consulting the dead (through an oracle) and in pre-classical Greece this was the entrance to Hell, where pilgrims were drugged and purified before consulting the oracle. It was a labyrinth of windowless corridors to encourage mystical transportation of the soul. Today only some ruined walls and an arched underground chamber remain. The nearby River Aheron passes through a gorge and it is here in mythology that the ferryman took the souls of the dead across to the Elysian Fields, provided some thoughtful relative had placed a coin under their tongue. Why this gorge should have been selected as the entrance to Hell is a mystery; today it seems a pleasant landscape, reached by a dirt track (motorable in fine weather) which starts from the south side of the bridge just before **Gliki.**

North east of Gliki are the most savage-looking mountains in Greece – not softened and moulded by erosion, but sheer rock faces and sharp peaks. This was the home of the Suliots, fiercest of all the Greek brigand-warriors; their village, **Suli,** is at the end of 18km/11mi of stony road that looks impossible even for a mule – until you see the bus going up. *Athens 450km/280mi, Igoumenitsa 45/28.*

Preveza (ΠΡΕΒΕΖΑ)   J6

Preveza (pop. 12,000) Standing at the very tip of a flat spit of land with the Ionian Sea on one side and the Gulf of Amvrakikos on the other, Preveza is lively, with a café-lined waterfront, a small garden, low buildings and shady streets. There is a ferry (twice an hour, taking ten minutes) across the narrow strait to **Aktio,** on a promontory similar to that of Preveza. There is little of Aktio now but the deserted ruin of a Venetian fortress, a deserted airport, and a memorial to the naval battle of Actium (31 BC) at which Octavian defeated Antony and Cleopatra.

To commemorate his victory, Octavian (Emperor Augustus) built a new city called Nikopoli, to which the people of all the surrounding towns were transferred. The extensive ruins of Nikopoli are scattered 10km/6mi north of Preveza; huge burnt-brick walls, and the level remains of a theatre, houses and basilica.

Beyond Nikopoli, the north-bound road to Parga forks. To the right is the ruin of **Kassopi,** which has not been built on since its destruction by the Romans and shows clearly the plan of a Hellenistic city; and the high cliffs of **Zalongo.** The curious carved figures which crown the cliffs represent the women of Suli (see *Parga* above) who danced one by one over the cliff to their death, to escape from Turkish-Albanian troops during the War of Independence. To the left, the new broad road to Parga, leads to a fine beach – and then turns into an unmetalled, bumpy mud track. *Arta 50km/31mi.*

THE IONIAN ISLANDS

The six Ionian Islands which lie along the west coast of Greece were a British protectorate between 1815–64; from north to south they are: Corfu, Paxi, Lefkada, Ithaki, Kefalonia, Zakinthos. Because of the higher rainfall throughout the year, these islands tend to be greener than other regions and their hedge-lined roads are unique. They are inclined to sudden changes of weather, and temperatures vary enormously from the scorching heat of summer to the cold of wet, overcast winters. Despite this the Ionian Islands, especially Corfu, attract thousands of visitors particularly in spring and autumn.

There is a seventh island, Kithira, which administratively is one of the Ionian Islands, but it is located south of the Peloponnese, is barren unlike the others, and so is not included here but in region six.

Corfu (KEPKYPA)   G3

(area 640 sq km/247 sq mi, pop. 91,000) Corfu (Kerkira) is different in many ways from the other islands and is exotically beautiful in the traditional sense – blue-green mountains, flower-filled valleys. After centuries of Venetian rule it came under the British between 1815–64 and the influence of both periods is still evident in the architecture and life style – cricket is played.

The island enjoys its popularity with holiday-makers and offers an enormous range of activities – wind-surfing, waterskiing and para-gliding, mountaineering, rambling and boating. Even so, like everywhere else in Greece, there is still space to breathe and miraculously empty beaches. Roads are excellent and there are mopeds, scooters or cars for rent.

The approach to **Corfu** town by boat is misleadingly unattractive – there is cheap food available in many *tavernas*

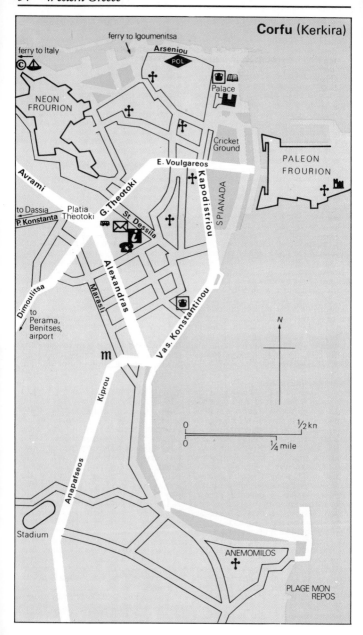

near the customs shed. The town itself is large, elegant French in some places, in others picturesque Italian with colonnades, cobwebby wrought iron and washing triumphant from alley to alley. It is dominated by the huge Venetian fort (Neon Frourion) – Edward Lear (1812–88), author of *The Book of Nonsense*, lived in a house nearby.

The Royal Palace, built as a treasury in 1819, is now a museum and in one wing houses the only Sino-Japanese collection in Greece. There are over 8000 items, *eg* porcelain and bronzes. Open 0830–1000; 1600–1800. Closed Saturday and Sunday afternoons.

Opposite the museum is the Spianada one of Europe's largest and most beautiful public squares. Here too is the island's rather worn cricket pitch, where British residents play against the natives.

The old fortress (Paleon Frourion) is the centre of Corfu's cultural activity. Corfu Ballet (Kerkyraikon Chorodroma) performs Greek dancing from early May until the end of September, 2030 – 2100. Price of admission includes Son-et-Lumière after the dancing, (in English on weekdays).

A short walk from the town (south) is the suburb of Anemomilos. There is a small pay beach overlooked by the royal palace of Mon Repos where the Duke of Edinburgh was born.

Most of the beach/hotel/restaurant complexes and most campsites are north of Corfu – **Kondokali, Gouvia, Dassia, Ipsos** and **Pirgi**. The waters are shallow and often hot.

The island's two youth hostels are at **Ag. Ioannis** (10km/6mi) and **Kondokali** (7km/4mi).

Founded by Pyrrhus of Epirus in about 300 BC, **Kassiopi** is a charming fishing village. It has a history of bloody battles but the fortress above the village is now full of flowers and sheep. In summer there is usually dancing in the *tavernas*.

Perithia, an abandoned village in the mountains (823m/2700ft), is a good goal for the end of a mountain walk (bus from Corfu town to Loutses).

The islands of **Othonoi, Erikoussa** and **Mathraki** are occasionally accessible by boat from Corfu. They are primitive, beautiful and mostly inhabited by women since the men fish or have gone to America.

The countryside of Corfu, springtime

Paleokastritsa is one of the major resorts. A stiff walk (8km/5mi) – or get a taxi – will take you to the forbidding 13th-century Angelokastro set above the town on the tumbling red rocks.

Pelekas has the island's only golf course, Ropas Meadow (Livaditau Ropa). **Gastouri** boasts the magnificently ugly Achillio built for Elizabeth of Austria in 1890. After her assassination the villa was bought by Wilhelm II who used to write letters home to Germany sitting at his desk astride a saddle! Today it is a casino and a few rooms have been made into a museum.
Communications: Daily flights from Athens. Bus from Athens to Igoumenitsa, via ferry (10 hrs). Frequent ferries from Igoumenitsa and Patra.
Festivals: Litany processions of St Spyridou's body through the streets of Corfu town – Palm Sunday, Saturday before Greek Easter, August 11 and 1st Sunday in November. July 8, at Lefkimi, local fair with folk dancing.
Specialities: sofrito, meat in a special sauce and *kumquat,* an orange liqueur.

Ithaki (ΙΘΑΚΗ)   M6
(area 113 sq km/44 sq mi, pop. 4000) Home of Odysseus, this is a rugged, barren island divided into two peninsulas by a narrow isthmus. In the valleys there is some effort to make use of scanty soil and on the hillsides there are vineyards, copses of myrtle, oleander and aromatic shrubs. Its men are mostly sailors and, like Odysseus (hero of Homer's *Odyssey),* tend to journey far.

Roads are unreliable and, though cars may be rented, a guide can be helpful as some of the inland villages are hard to reach.

Ithaki town (Vathi) is a horseshoe of white houses at the end of a deep inlet. It has been largely rebuilt since the earthquake of 1953. Walk south west from Ithaki (about 45 mins) to Marmarospilia Cave (192m/630ft) where Odysseus was said to have hidden his treasure. Bring a torch and wear stout shoes.
Communications: Ferry three times weekly from Patra. Bus daily from Athens via ferry (8 hrs).
Festivals: August 22–September 15 theatre festival at Ithaki. Early September wine festival at Perachorio.
Specialities: ravani, a sweet made of honey, sugar and rice, and *cherapa,* chicken and ginger beer.

Kefalonia (ΚΕΦΑΛΛΗΝΙΑ)   M6
(area 935 sq km/361 sq mi, pop. 31,000) This is the largest of the Io-

nian Islands and yet one of the least known. It is a rugged, grandiose island of sombre, pine-clad mountains and dramatically indented coastline. It was devastated by an earthquake in 1953 and many villages were destroyed. There is a tradition for adventure among the Kefaloniotes and a great many leave to seek their fortune in other parts of the world.

Most visitors arrive by car ferries from Patra and land at **Sami.** This pretty, modern port is the starting point for exploring the island. On the road between Sami and Argostoli, turn off for **Vlakhata** and you will come to a mysterious lake, running partially underground. Take a boat through the approach tunnel to a small clear lake and on to an inner cavern.

Argostoli (Sami 23km/15mi), the capital, has been completely rebuilt since the earthquake. There are some pleasant walks out of town eastwards around the shallow Koutavos Lagoon, cut off by a beautiful multi-arched bridge from the Gulf of Argostoli; or to the tip of the Lassis Peninsula where the sea pours perpetually into subterranean tunnels. There are pay beaches at Makri Yialos and Plati Yialos to the south. A 30 min. ferry-ride will take you to the second largest town **Lixouri,** situated on an isolated peninsula.

Assos, a delicious modern village, is one of the most spectacular places on the island – within sight of the mountains and the sea. Nearby (south) is the blinding white beach of Myrton.

Transport around the island is not easy. Roads vary in quality and buses are irregular – not always returning on the day of departure. Taxis will accept group bookings for economy.
Communications: Daily flights from Athens. Ferry three times daily from Patra (4 hrs), once daily to Ithaki (1 hr). Weekly ferry with Astakos, Kalamos, (from Mitikas), Meganisi, Vassiliki, Nidri, Frikes.
Festivals: April 23 Ag. Georgios, May 21 Ag. Constantinos, August 15 at Marcopoulon, August 16 and October 20 Ag. Gerassimos.
Specialities: tserepes, meat with spices.

Lefkada (ΛΕΥΚΑΣ)   K6
(area 325 sq km/125 sq mi, pop. 24,000) Although separated from the mainland by only 23m/75ft of shallow canal, Lefkada has the remote peace of an island. The crossing is by a chain-driven raft, and takes about 3 mins – at the height of the summer you can wait 30 mins before being taken over.

Lefkada, the ramshackle village which has grown around the harbour, has the faraway feel of Hollywood's Wild West, and behind, the island's heart – silent limestone mountains rising to Mt Elati (1082m/3550ft). Handmade lace from Lefkada is famous and the craft is still passed from mother to daughter. In August there is an international festival of art and literature and it is wise to book accommodation.

Nidri is a new but attractive seaside village opposite the wooded islets of Madouri, Sparti, Scorpio and Scorpios. You can sit here and listen to the serenading frogs.

All over the island are pretty villages each with its own personality. From **Sivros** there is a steep climb to the large Karouha Cave, Rodha and Sivota have good beaches, Vassiliki is shady. Roads are very dusty but are steadily being asphalted. There is a bus trip round the island (80km/50mi).

Communications: Bus three times daily from Athens to Patra, ferry to Lefkada town (7 hrs). Boat twice weekly from Nidri and Vassiliki to Ithaki, Kefalonia, Mitikas, Kalamos and Astakos. Daily to Meganisi.

Festivals: August 11-13 at Karia; the old folk wear national costume.

Paxi (ΠΑΞΟΙ)   H4

(area 18 sq km/7 sq mi, pop. 2250) The smallest of the islands (8km/5mi long), it is possible to tour Paxi by car in 30 mins. For those with a taste for lingering there is absolutely nothing 'to do', but that is the island's enchantment. Instead it offers acre after acre of silvery olive groves, producing the very best olive oil. The people are friendly and don't frown on careful campers.

Panayia, an islet off the east coast, is a pilgrimage centre and on August 15 (the feast of the Assumption) pilgrims return to Paxi and dance all night in the square at the village of **Paxi** (Gaios). The southern islet of **Mogonissi** is connected to Paxi by private caique. Run by the restaurant owner, it ferries visitors over to dinner in the evening. **Laka** has beautiful Russian bells in the Byzantine church – visitors may ring them on request.

One way to see the island is by boat and tours can be arranged to the Seven Sea Caves to see the seals of Ypapandi, and the impressive Mousmouli Cliffs on the west coast.

Just south of Paxi is the minute **Andipaxi** where only 50 families live. There are sandy beaches here unlike the rocky coast of Paxi. The island produces very

good red and white wine. There is no accommodation – bring a sleeping bag.

Communications: Ferry daily with Corfu (3 hrs), three times weekly with Patra (in summer).

Zakinthos (ΖΑΚΥΝΘΟΣ)   P6

(area 406 sq km/157 sq mi, pop. 30,000) Zakinthos, fragrant with spring and autumn flowers in the east, volcanic and mountainous in the west, is in no way braced for tourism. The airport is too small for international traffic and there is limited accommodation. Fortunately the people of Zakinthos are amazingly hospitable even by Greek standards. Offer an English cigarette or take their photograph and you will have found a friend!

Zakinthos town was almost completely rebuilt after the earthquake of 1953 and, though the arrogant spirit of the old colonnaded town has been re-created, there are many improvements making it a pleasant place to live in. There is a yacht-supply station and a youth hostel.

Summer transport is easy; there are buses to all parts of the island and bicycles to rent. **Kalamaki** and **Argassi** on the edge of currant country have sandy beaches.

Laganas, to the west of the airport, is the only real resort on the island. The beach has the finest sand, they say, in Greece and is backed by a curious rock formation. But as in many parts of Greece car-driving along the beach has spoilt it, and there is a better, less-known beach 30 mins cycle ride south.

On the southern peninsula there is hunting (August 25-March 15) for rabbit and fowl; **Keri** is the village centre. There are some strange pitch springs on the Bay of Keri; the pitch is used traditionally in caulking ships.

Mt Skopos (500m/1590ft) can be climbed in 2½ hrs from Zakinthos town. From the top there is a mystical view of sombre Mt Ainos in Kefalonia rising from the sea.

Communications: Daily flights from Athens. Six ferries daily from Kilini (1¼ hrs).

Festivals: Two weeks prior to Lent – carnival with masked singers and dancers. August 24 and December 17 for the feast of Ag. Dionysios – the streets are strewn with myrtle. Also in August, International Meeting of Mediaeval Theatre. Holy week at Easter is a riot!

Specialities: *mandolato*, a nougat with peanuts, fine currants and three good local wines, Verdea, Laganas and Byzantis.

THESSALY AND THE SPORADES

Thessaly is a vast agricultural plain shut in on all sides by mountains. On the east the mighty Olympus range (Oros Olimbos), home of the gods, divides Thessaly from Makedonia, and then the lesser mountains of Ossa and Pilio stand between the plain and the Aegean Sea. The giants, at war with the gods, tried to reach them on Olympus by piling Pilio on top of Ossa. They did not succeed, and today to 'pile Pilio on Ossa' means to add one superlative beauty to another – for Pilio, and to less extent Ossa, are renowned for their beauty. In the west, the Pindus range (Pindos Oros) is an extension of Western Greece, and includes the fantastic crags, surmounted by monasteries, of the Meteora region near Kalambaka.

The plain is Greece's richest agricultural region, producing most of the country's wheat, and in summer it is the most consistently hot region in Europe. The narrow coastal strip affords welcome relief – the afternoon breeze can feel almost cold but does not get past the mountains to the plain. Its beaches tend to be shingle, but you can't see this under the covering of Greek and Yugoslavian bodies.

The early Greeks settled in Thessaly

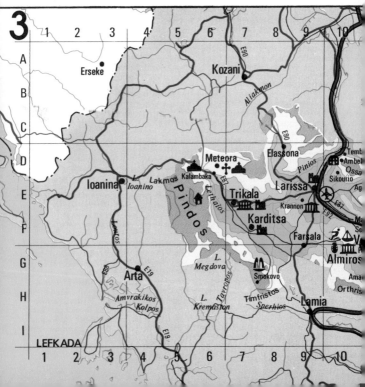

for many years before moving further south, and many of the pre-heroic myths are set here. The ark of Deucalion (a Greek version of Noah) rested in Thessaly; here too dwelt the centaurs, and Achilles among them. Jason and his Argonauts set sail from Pagasses, near modern Volos.

In classical times Thessaly took little part in the wars and culture of the Greek world – it was noted mainly for supplying horses. Even today, the agricultural life of the villages proceeds as if the 20th century had yet to arrive, though scooter-drawn carts have replaced horses and neon strip lighting the oil lamp.

In about AD 1150 the Thessalian plain was occupied by Slavs. It became the centre of a petty Bulgarian kingdom which fell to the Turks in 1389. The Greek kingdom recovered Thessaly in 1881, and all traces of the Slav and Turkish element have vanished, unless you fancy you can see it in the people themselves.

There are few archaeological remains. The objects of interest for the visitor are Mt Olympus, Tembi (the Vale of Tempe between Olympus and Ossa), the lush hills of Pilio and the Meteora region.

The Sporades (sporadic, *ie* scattered, islands) are a group of four largish and up to twenty small, uninhabited islands, which are outcrops of the submerged mountain range that rises on the mainland as Mt Pilio. They are rather similar in vegetation, hilliness, people and beaches to Pilio, but they have more appeal in that they are islands. There is isolated tourist development (especially on Skiathos, which has an airport), but on the whole these islands offer little to the sightseer but a great deal to the traveller with time. Most visitors are Greeks, seeking peaceful activity, not stimulus. Snorkelling is unsurpassed, for the seas are clean and clear and teeming with life. (Beware of jellyfish!)

There may be some confusion over the name of this group. During the Turkish occupation the 'Sporades' were all the islands scattered over the Aegean, apart from the Cyclades and those

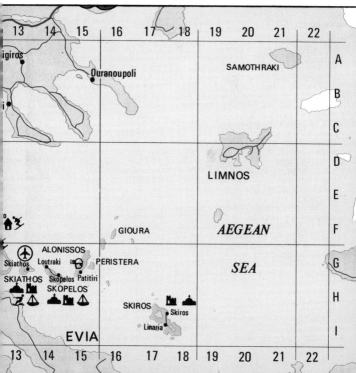

very close to the mainland. The islands adjacent to Pilio, now called simply 'Sporades', were the Northern Sporades, and you may still come across this name.

Many of the ferries to the Sporades are from Agios Konstandinos, which is on the main Athens-Volos road 166km/103mi from Athens (2½ hrs by bus).

Ambelakia (ΑΜΠΕΛΑΚΙΑ)   D10

Larissa (pop. 1000) A little village on the lower slopes of Mt Ossa, looking across the River Pinios to Mt Olympus. The village itself is interesting as the centre of an 18th-century workers' cooperative (spinning and dyeing based on natural pigments extracted from the vegetation of Ossa), and for the carefully restored, balconied houses of the leading citizens. The Schwarz House, a mixture of Islamic spaciousness and rococo decoration, has become a museum of folklore.

An interesting feature nearby is **Tembi** (the Vale of Tempe), through which the Pinios rushes to the sea. The valley, running at the foot of sheer cliffs, is beautiful, but rather easy to miss – it's a smaller version of some of the gorges of Ipiros. *Larissa 31km/19mi.*

Kalambaka   D6
(ΚΑΛΑΜΠΑΚΑ)

Trikala (pop. 5000) A pleasant little place in the Meteora foothills, it has a cathedral which is too large for what is really a big village. Good hotels, open all year, for Kalambaka is the base from which to visit the Meteora (9km/6mi, north).

The **Meteora** is a cluster of pillars of rock, rising perpendicularly from an eroded plain to a height of 200-300 metres (650-980ft) – giant, grey stalagmites reaching for the sky. The flat valleys between the pillars are a mass of green foliage, contrasting with the pinnacles which are bare, and crisscrossed by cracks.

The peaks initially offered refuge to religious hermits who by the 14th century were forming separate communities which built monasteries on top of many of the highest pillars. Today there are 13 monasteries, four of which are still inhabited by monks. The method of ascent used to be by basket, winched up on a rope; then came wooden stepladders, and finally, just before the monks began to leave, steps were cut in the rocks.

The inhabited monasteries can be visited in the mornings until 1200, and in the late afternoon; the Great Meteoron and usually the others are closed on Wednesday. There is a small restaurant at the monastery of Agios Stefanos. *Athens 394km/245mi, Trikala 21/13.*

Karditsa (ΚΑΡΔΙΤΣΑ)   F7

Karditsa (pop. 27,000) A trading town laid out in Turkish times on a rectilinear plan. From Karditsa there is a 26km/16mi excursion to the vast **Lake Megdova**, which provides hydroelectricity and irrigation for the plain. *Lamia 92km/57mi.*

Larissa (ΛΑΡΙΣΑ)   B9

Larissa (pop. 73,000) The capital of Thessaly, and the town which comes nearest to being a city in this region. It is a spacious, bustling but architecturally unnoteworthy town, whose most curious feature is the storks on the chimneypots and whose most famous resident was Hippocrates. In the centre of the town is a huge, lively square shaded with lime and orange trees. There is a covered market, a modern cathedral on the ancient acropolis overlooking the river, and a small museum in a former mosque.

From Larissa it is possible to visit the sparse remains of the former capital **Krannon** (24km/15mi south west). There are three chamber tombs in the Mycenaean style but dating from the 5th century BC.

Agia, 39km/24mi east of Larissa (bus twice a day), is a good starting point for the ascent of Mt Ossa – guides or mules may be hired here. *Athens 356km/221mi, Trikala 61/38.*

Olympus (ΟΛΥΜΠΟΣ)   C9

The Ancient Greeks made remote, mist-swathed Mt Olympus (Olimbos) the home of the gods. The highest peak in Greece (2913m/9570ft), the craggy, pine-forested ravines of the lower slopes and the faraway snow-covered summit, are as mystical as ever. Few people see Olympus at its best – by night – when the full moon silvers the streams and a handful of campers sit round their fires listening to the eerie braying of mules and – could it be – wolves howling?

A military road, carved from the mountainside, runs from the pleasant little town of **Litohoro,** past the monastery of Agios Dionysos, and ends half way to the top in a car park. Here the ramshackle Zeus Café serves bean soup and refreshments, and the last spring water is available. From here it is possible, if you are fit, to walk up the corkscrew track to Refuge 'A' at 2100m/

6890ft. (Food available.) The walk is hot, but often shaded and well signposted – possible even with children. Take drinks and snacks to keep you going. Allow 3 hrs.

From the refuge to the summit it is another 2 hrs, across scree and, even at the height of summer, snow patches. It is possible for a very fit walker to get from the car park to the summit and back in a day, but better to spend the night at the refuge. Stout footwear is needed, but not mountaineering boots. *Litohoro-Athens 430km/267mi, Thes/niki 92/57.*

Pilio (ΠΗΛΙΟΝ)   F12

The Pelion chain (highest point 1651m/ 5417ft) is the backbone of the narrow Magnesia peninsula and all of it is within sight of the sea. Scattered over the mountains are quaint, flower-scented villages where there is shade and cool. There are tall timber houses, long low churches, exuberant streams and seaside hamlets where the water is unbelievably clear. There is plenty of *taverna* life and accommodation but the entire region is unspoilt – so far. The climate is mild in winter, bearably hot in summer.

Perhaps the most memorable stopping places are: **Portaria**, a summer resort from which to start the climb up to Pliasidî (1548m/5080ft) one of the main peaks of Pilio. There is a ski lift at **Hania** (1158m/3800ft) reached by an incredible zigzagging road. *Volos 14km/ 9mi.*

Zagora The largest community on Pilio is reached by dropping down through a tremendous wooded valley to the ledge (500m/1640ft) where the four hamlets of Zagora look out over the Aegean. Further down this winding road (8km/5mi) are the beaches of Horefto. *Volos 47km/29mi.*

Makrinitsa, one of the most beautiful of the Pelion villages, preserved as a traditional settlement. The houses rise like towers one above the other from the hillside. *Volos 17km/11mi.*

Agria, where the fishermen celebrate in lively style every Saturday night. *Volos 7km/4mi.*

Trikeri The last little village of the Pilio, separated from the rest of the peninsula by miles of mountain. Reached only by sea, through the little harbour of Agia Kiriaki (occasional boat from Volos).

Trikala (ΤΡΙΚΑΛΑ)   E7

Trikala (pop. 34,000) An attractive riverside town with cafés bordering the banks of the trout-filled River Lethaios. Its population swells in winter when Vlach shepherds are driven down from the mountains by bad weather. There is a picturesque old quarter which is not too easy to find (near the Fort). It is a good base for reaching the Meteora. *Athens 328km/204mi.*

Volos (ΒΟΛΟΣ)   F11

Magnesia (pop. 51,000) The pretty, bustling but unremarkable chief port of Thessaly, exporting olive oil, sugar and soap; industrial outskirts. Ferry to Syria, greatly used by the big intercontinental road hauliers. Jason once set sail from Volos with the Argonauts to seek the Golden Fleece, and it is a good base from which to launch an exploration of the Pilio peninsula or the Sporades today.

The town of Volos had to be largely rebuilt after the earthquake in 1955, but the little hamlet of **Ano Volos** 792m/ 2600ft above was untouched. In the dense forests between the two once lived the centaurs – half beast, half man. In the village itself, in the Kondos House, are several remarkable frescos by the renowned primitive Theofilos; some of his other paintings are at nearby Anakassia.

The ruins of the four ancient cities preceding Volos are important and easily accessible. **Pagasses** and **Dimitrias** (3km/2mi south west) can be reached in 10 mins by car or bus, 30 mins on foot. Pagasses is, they say, where the Argo was built; now there is a beach and a *taverna*. **Dimini** and **Seyklo** (6km/4mi and 18km/11mi west, off the road to Larissa) have more meaning for the archaeologist than the layman but a preliminary visit to Volos museum is a help in explaining the sites. *Athens 316km/196, Thes/niki 130/81.*

THE SPORADES

Alonissos (ΑΛΟΝΝΗΣΟΣ)   G15

(area 62 sq km/24 sq mi, pop.1500) There are only 268 beds for visitors registered on Alonissos, so be prepared to sleep under the stars. There are a few rooms to let in private houses but not enough to disturb the peace of this island retreat. Most of the accommodation is provided by a single holiday beach club catering for the fun lovers – situated near the only real village, the port of **Patitiri**. The restaurants of Patitiri are good for fish and lobster and simple evening fun. There used to be a town called Chora or Alonissos, but it has been almost deserted since the earthquake of 1965.

There are only 10km/6mi of road; to see the rest of the 25km/16mi long island you have to walk or visit the beaches by boat. This is a hiker's paradise – shady tracks through vineyards, over wooded hills to deserted bays. Boats, usually rented by a group sharing expenses, take you to the remoter beaches or tiny off-shore islets inhabited only by sheep and their shepherds.

Communications: Ferry daily, early morning, from Volos (5 hrs) also Friday and Saturday afternoons. Three a week from Kimi (Evia), (3 hrs). Daily to Skiathos for the airport (3 hrs). Three a week from Ag. Konstandinos (5 hrs).

Skiathos (ΣΚΙΑΘΟΣ)   G13
(area 41 sq km/16 sq mi, pop. 4000)
Tiny Skiathos has 60 beaches and more than enough visitors to fill many of them in the height of summer, but there is a choice between those that are isolated and tranquil, and those that are picturesque and lively with people, *tavernas* and music. This is a good place for a beach-sampling holiday.

There are plenty of restaurants, a waterskiing school and *bouzouki* music at night, but you can easily escape into the hills – the island is flat enough for pleasant walking.

Communications: Flights from Athens daily. Boats run from Volos and Ag. Konstandinos (both 3 hrs) – tickets sell out early for these two.

Festivals: July 26 Ag. Paraskevi.

Skiros (ΣΚΥΡΟΣ)   I18
(area 205 sq km/79 sq mi, pop. 2500)
An island of folklore and tradition where the men still wear baggy blue breeches and the women long skirts and yellow headscarves. There is very little accommodation for visitors and sometimes in summer even bread can be short. You will learn when the boat leaves from a town crier in **Skiros** town. This is an island of contrast: the south is barren and Cycladic with white sugar-loaf houses; the north is forested. The people are friendly and proud to show off the ornately decorated interiors of their homes. There is one B grade and one E grade hotel.

Theseus, King of Athens, was murdered on Skiros, and the English poet Rupert Brooke (1887–1915) is buried here, near the bay of Tris Boukes on the southern coast.

Communications: Boat five times weekly from Volos (12 hrs) and daily from Kimi (2 hrs).

Skopelos (ΣΚΟΠΕΛΟΣ)   G14
(area 122 sq km/47 sq mi, pop. 4500)
A pine-scented island which has succeeded in keeping tourists at arm's length. Those who go to Skopelos must expect to take it as they find it, perhaps the most beautiful place in Greece. There are no souvenir shops, few synthetic entertainments and no tourist venues. The beaches are shallow and safe for children and, though there are few hotels (only 168 beds registered), some accommodation is available in private houses. There is no cheap or easy way of reaching Skopelos but the rewards are well worth the effort.

The economy of the island depends on plums and prunes, and in August it is possible to visit the prune oven near colourful **Skopelos** town.

Communications: Boat twice daily with Volos (4½ hrs); Skiathos and Alonissos in summer; three times weekly with Kimi (3½ hrs).

Festivals: February 25 Ag. Rigginos.

Skopelos town

NORTH-EAST AEGEAN ISLANDS

These islands are greener and on the whole more fertile than the Cyclades; they offer more in the way of sight-seeing, but are not nearly so visited by foreign holiday-makers. They are prosperous and quite heavily populated, and in summer are full of islanders who have returned from the mainland or abroad; a few thousand tourists can easily be absorbed in the native population. The old family ways and neighbourly traditions are preserved very strongly on these islands. The nearest to Turkey, they retain a vivid awareness of their Greek heritage and Greek character, and the liveliest memory of Turkish atrocities.

The North-East Aegean Islands figured prominently in the culture of ancient Greece: Limnos was dedicated to Hephaestus; on Samos the Temple of Hera was one of the wonders of the world; Hios has the best claim to being the birthplace of Homer; Lesvos was the home of Sappho.

Each island has a main town with fairly limited accommodation; the population is not concentrated in the towns but scattered over many small, lively villages.

Hios (ΧΙΟΣ)   K6
(area 858 sq km/331 sq mi, pop. 54,000) Hios (Chios), an island of abrupt contrasts – bare hills next to intensely fertile plains. Lemons, oranges and mandarins are grown in the north of the island, while the south is the only place in the world where the lentisk tree is cultivated, producing the mastic resin used to flavour chewing gum and an alcoholic drink. Most of the roads radiate from the main town, Hios – there is no circular tour of the island.

Hios town is home to many wealthy Greek ship-owning families, adding to its air of comfortable wellbeing. The old part of the town with its trellised windows, balconies and Byzantine baths is within the fortress walls. The harbour is overlooked by the ruins of the Genoese fort; down by the waterfront there is an old quarter with tiny, brightly painted houses, and nearby are modern quays backed by new shops. The archaeological museum, though small, is attractively laid out and drives home the long history of this place. Hios feels as though it has grown up, and not just

been planted fully grown. There are buses to the rest of the island from the square and municipal gardens, or cars may be rented.

Nea Moni (13km/8mi from Hios) is one of the best-known Byzantine monuments of Greece – an 11th-century monastery built by Emperor Constantine IX Monomachos. There are a few nuns here now. Open mornings until noon, and evenings from 1700 to 2000. Take the bus to **Karies**, and then there is a 6km/4mi walk through the pines if the bus does not continue.

Pirgi is a beautifully preserved, mediaeval fortress town, centre of the mastic country where almost all villages date from the 13th century. There are narrow streets with round-roofed houses decorated with *sgraffito* – curious blue and grey designs scratched into the stone, or scooped out of the cement rendering of the walls. Two other notable mediaeval villages near Pirgi are **Olimbos** and **Mesta**; some of the old houses of Mesta are being turned into traditional guest houses. The women in this area mostly wear the old island costume.

Psara is an islet off the north-west coast, reached by caique from Hios town two or three times a week. There is a little village, secluded beaches and a guesthouse. The islet of **Inousses** is a similar refuge.

Many of the beaches of Hios are stony, like the black pebbly beach of **Emborio**, and the east coast facing Turkey is rocky. However, there are good sandy beaches at **Marmaro** and **Ag. Markella**; **Karfas** has the best beach (though shadeless) near Hios town.

Communications: One hour by air from Athens – three flights daily. Ferries five times weekly from Pireas (14hrs) and Lesvos, weekly from Thes/niki and

Kavala; connections to many other islands of the eastern Aegean; daily boat to Cesme (Turkey) for an outing to Izmir (Smyrna).

Festivals: There are church festivals on saints' days at which all are welcome, but for homecoming islanders life is a round of visits and parties. Saints' days include: April 23 Ag. Georgios, July 18 Ag. Aemilianos outside Hios town, July 22 Ag. Markella at Volissos, August 15 at Pirgi, Nenita, Kambia and Ag. Georgios, August 23 at Nea Moni. Also in July-August the International Society of Homeric Studies holds the 'Homerics', a cultural and artistic event.

Ikaria (IKAPIA)   O6

(area 267 sq km/103 sq mi, pop. 9000) The god of wind is reputed to live in the mountains of Ikaria and the sea can be one of the roughest in Greece. It was here that Ikaros, flying from Crete with the wings his father Daedalus made for him, flew too near the sun so that the wax holding the feathers together melted and the boy plunged to his death.

Tourism of any scale only started here in 1977 and most visitors come for the hot springs, considered the most radioactive in Europe. The ten springs are claimed to help chronic rheumatism, arthritis and gout.

The southern shore presents steep cliffs or rocks, while the north shore has beaches. The interior is made up of peaceful green mountains with exceptionally dry air; the apricots are excellent. **Ag. Kirikos**, the little capital, has more trees than people (pop. 1000); there is a small beach, and buses to the villages. The hotels are at the two spa centres, **Therma** and **Therma Lefkadas**. The asphalt road from Ag. Kirikos ends at **Evdilos** (near lovely beaches) – from here an earth track continues to the west end of the island but most of this side of Ikaria is better suited to goats than to cars.

Manganitis, on the south side of the island, is built into a steep cliff. It has no road or electricity and can be reached only by track over the mountain from Evdilos or by daily caique from Ag. Kirikos. It can be one of the liveliest places on the island and, indeed, in all these villages of the southern shore they seem to enjoy life.

Communications: Ferry four times weekly to Samos and Pireas (15 hrs), less frequently to other islands of the eastern Aegean, to Thes/niki and to Kavala. *Festivals*: All through the summer, exiles return to the island for old-fashioned fêtes. One orders a *prothese* – a kilo of goat, a bottle of wine, a bowl of soup and a loaf of bread. Big festival on July 17 to celebrate the defeat of the Turks.

Lesvos (ΛΕΣΒΟΣ)   G7

(area 1632 sq km/630 sq mi, pop. 124,000) The third largest Greek island, silver with olive trees and scented with pine, once the home of the poetess Sappho. The villages are largely Byzantine in character and there is a long tradition of artistic activity with many musical and theatrical events during the year. Industries include tanning, textile-making and, most important, soap manufacture.

The main town, **Mitilini**, is the starting point for an exploration of the island. It is built like an amphitheatre above the sea and is guarded by the ancient Kastro which looks across to Turkey.

The women of Lesvos are not lesbian but in the 6th century BC, Sappho wrote beautiful erotic poetry about her women students – hence the island's rather dubious claim to fame! A white marble statue to the lady stands on the front at Mitilini. There is an exciting outdoor play area for children at the end of the town's shady park.

Buses to the beaches and *tavernas* of nearby **Neapoli**, **Achivala** and **Kalimari** leave from the square at the back of the harbour (you must reserve a seat), or you can rent a car, scooter or bicycle. South of Mitilini by the airport is one of the loveliest regions of the island; there are long, sandy beaches at **Kratigos** (tree-shaded) and at **Ag. Ermogenis.**

Molivos (Mithimna) on the north of the island is a pretty village with a long, sandy beach. There is a lively night scene for tourists and performances of the classics and modern drama. At **Petra**, just south of Molivos, there are paintings by Theofilos in the little museum, and more at **Varia**, 5km/3mi south of Mitilini.

The road west from Mitilini skirts the beautiful Gulf of Yera (Kolpos Yeras), with a partially submerged ancient port just past **Thermi Yera**. In many of the villages in this area, *eg* **Agiassos** on Mt Olympos (967m/3173ft), the people dress in local costume. **Thermi**, 11km/7mi from Mitilini, is a spa with a thermal spring and nearby archaeological site.

To the south west from Agiassos is the vast beach of **Vatera**, and to the north west the Gulf of Kalloni (Kolpos

The port, Mitilini, Lesvos

Kallonis) where there is fishing for sardines. Herds of wild horses graze around this land-locked sea.

On the far side of the island, north west of **Sigri**, there is a petrified forest (about 1,000,000 years old). The trees, preserved by volcanic ash and standing now to a height of 8m/25ft, are partially excavated. To get there entails a good hike, though there is a beach at Sigri for recovering. **Skala Eressou** (6km/4mi from Sigri) also has a good beach.
Communications: There are two airports with daily connections to Athens (1 hr). Daily ferry from Pireas (15 hrs); less frequent ferries to other eastern Aegean islands; daily boat to Ayvalik (Turkey).

Limnos (ΛΗΜΝΟΣ)   D3
(area 453 sq km/175 sq mi, pop. 23,000) Legendary home of the god of fire, Hephaestus (Vulcan) – lamed when he fell onto volcanic Limnos – this is the flattest of the North-East Aegean Islands. It offers a countryside of gentle hills, bare rock, peaceful meadows, deep bays and jagged headlands. The island is almost bisected by two deep sea inlets, the Gulf of Moudros (Ormos Mudru) on the south and the Bay of

Pournia (Kolpos Purnias) in the north – the isthmus connecting them is just 3km/2mi wide. Hot springs are the only trace of the volcanos of antiquity.

Parts of the island are very green with crops and pasture land, but towards the end of summer even they dry and turn yellow. The roads are steadily being asphalted. Game shooting available – partridge, rabbit, wild duck, woodcock.

Mirina is the main town, built on the ruins of an ancient city. It stands at the head of a pretty gulf, overlooked by an impressive Venetian castle. The streets are stone-paved and some of the houses, built by prosperous seamen, have glassed-in corridors. There are few hotels, but a luxury bungalow complex. You can tour the island by bus (infrequent) or rent a car.

Livadohori (10km/6mi east of Mirina) is an attractive village, just above **Nea Koutali** which is set in a pine forest overlooking Moudros Bay. At **Poliohni**, east of **Moudros**, are the island's most important archaeological remains. Four periods of settlement are one on top of the other; the earliest predating the Egyptian dynasties, the latest is Mycenaean. South of Poliohni is a desolate landscape known for its sand hills as the Limnos Sahara.

From **Plaka** in the north east you may rent a boat to glide over the submarine city of Kastello Plaka. But the most attractive part of the island that you can get to easily from Mirina is the south west; the vine-growing area centred around **Thanos** (good beaches here and at **Zimata** and **Plati**).

Communications: Daily flight to Athens (1 hr). Ferry two or three times weekly from Ag. Konstandinos (11 hrs) and from Kimi (Evia) (7 hrs); irregular connections to other east Aegean islands; weekly to Thes/niki and Kavala.

Festivals: September 7, there is folk-dancing, *eg* the *Kehayatikos* dance, centred on the monastery of Ag. Sozon. Saints' days include: April 23 Ag. Georgios at Kalliopi (horseracing), May 21 Ag. Konstandinos at Romano, August 6 Ag. Sotiris at Vlaka, August 15 at Kaminia and Tsimantria, October 26 at Ag. Dimitrios.

Samos (ΣΑΜΟΣ)   N9

(area 468 sq km/181 sq mi, pop. 32,000) Thickly wooded and mountainous, with many streams to keep it fertile, Samos produces a sweet red wine, the recipe for which is handed down from Bacchus himself. Shiny white rocks are scattered throughout the vineyards and olive groves, and all round the coast are golden sandy beaches, interspersed with low cliffs or rocky headlands.

Samos town, built on a hill overlooking the sea, spreads down to a lovely quayside bordered with elegant old-world houses. Morning excursion boat to Kusadasi (Turkey) for a visit to ancient Ephesus.

Vathi, a suburb of Samos town, is situated on a bay with wonderful views from the hillside to the coast of Asia Minor.

It is possible to get round the main sights of the island – ancient Samos, Ireo and Karlovassi – in a day. **Pithagorio** (ancient Samos) is named for Pythagoras, of triangle fame. The most renowned Samian after Bacchus, Pythagoras was born here in the 6th century BC. There are many relics of the days of the tyrant Polycrates (6th century BC), especially the Efpalinion Tunnel about a mile north of the town (1½km). This was one of the greatest engineering feats of antiquity, cut for over 900m/1000yd through the mountain to carry the water supply. A path runs halfway along the tunnel and can be reached by a climb down from the Tigani Temple – bring a torch.

Ireo (the Heraion or Sanctuary of Hera) lies on the coast by a long, shingly beach. There are extensive remains dating back to the Bronze Age.

Karlovassi on the rugged north coast is the second largest town of Samos. It is an ideal base for splendid walks on Mt Kerkis (1433m/4701ft), the highest mountain on the island. Karlovassi has its own peculiar aroma since it is the centre of the tanning industry. The road from Karlovassi to Samos town runs along a 40m/130ft cliff with spectacular views.

The hotels are scattered over these various places, but nightlife tends to be centred in Vathi/Samos.

Communications: Daily air connection with Athens (1 hr). Ferry daily from Pireas (16 hrs); daily to Ikaria, twice weekly to other islands of eastern Aegean; weekly to Kavala and Thes/niki.

Festivals: The big one is August 6, celebration of the Revolution. July 20, Profitis Elias in many villages. July 26 Ag. Paraskevi at Vathi, July 27 Ag. Panellemonas at Kokari (very popular), August 29 Ag. Ionnes at Pithagorio.

Pithagorio, Samos

CENTRAL GREECE

Central Greece is the bridge between the bright air of the Mediterranean and the more sombre, Balkan north; in spirit it is halfway between the two. Its eastern end is made up of two long, narrow strips of land. One of them, Evia (ancient Euboea), is an island now becoming a holiday playground with beautiful beaches and undiscovered villages. The other, mainly the nome of Voiotia (ancient Boeotia), has seen the passage of countless armies pressing south and offers historic sites such as Thermopiles (Battle of Thermopylae) and scenery which can be of unprecedented dullness, or, around Parnassos, unsurpassed beauty. In the centre, the nome of Evritania is mountainous, attracting the name 'little Switzerland'. Some of the villages, however, are desperately poor while others prosper. In the west is the nome of Aitolia-Akarnania, which was hardly part of Hellas in classical times – a land of marshy lagoons, lost beaches by the western sea, and lakes inland.

The administrative province of Central Greece (Sterea Ellas) includes Attica and Pireas, but in this book they are treated separately (see page 87).

The southern edge of Central Greece is the Gulf of Corinth (Korinthiakos

Kolpos) with many small coves and beaches, a couple of resort towns (Nafpaktos and Galaxidi) and a model workers' town at the aluminium smelter of Antikira. The eastern coast, between the mainland and Evia, has more resorts, flourishing because they are within easy reach of Athens. The western seaboard is almost unvisited – amenities for visitors are limited but do exist.

You may hear this region referred to as Roumeli. The Byzantine Empire was the surviving part of the realm founded by Augustus Caesar, and right up to its destruction in 1453 its official title was 'Roman Empire'. When the Peloponnese was taken by the Franks, the inhabitants of Central Greece proudly remembered that they were still 'Romans', and called this area Roumeli.

Agrinio (ΑΓΡΙΝΙΟΝ)   E6
Aitolia-Akarnania (pop. 31,000) Centre of the tobacco industry, the town was rebuilt after an earthquake in 1887 and has changed very little. Neither modern, nor decayed, its hotels and restaurants are mainly for local trade,

but serve tourists who want to experience the attractive surroundings.

The road south east gives a good view of Lake Trihonis (Trihonida), and leads to the monastery of **Mirtia** (built in 1491), and then to **Thermo** – a real country town, with the fallen columns of the Temple of Apollo nearby (¾km/ ½mi south).

The first road east of Agrinio, leading north towards Karpenissi, offers 'Alpine' driving once over the River Aheloos. Carry on across the head of Lake Kremaston, through little mountain villages, stopping occasionally to take coffee or admire the view.

Stratos (12km/7mi north west of Agrinio) is a large village of stone-built houses scattered over the ruins of ancient Stratos, whose massive stone blocks form the terrace walls. The square tower of the ancient town gate marks the entry to the old village which is now deserted, but for a few sheep and chickens. The inhabitants have moved down to the modern village of reinforced concrete along the main road. In the old part, only two or three roofs are

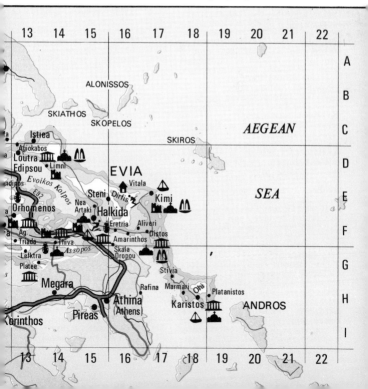

beginning to collapse; the other houses appear to be waiting for occupants who will never return. *Athens 227km/141mi, Karpenissi 107/66.*

Amfilohia (ΑΜΦΙΛΟΧΙΑ)   D6

Aitolia-Akarnania (pop. 5000) The remains of the ancient acropolis (some long walls with crumbling Byzantine additions) may attract the antiquary, but otherwise the town is just a waterfront at the head of the gulf, with whitewashed houses crawling up the hills; an agreeable stop.

The road to Lefkada passes a number of pine-shaded coves on the shallow Gulf of Amvrakikos where flat-bottomed boats with canvas tops are moored. *Agrinio 41km/25mi, Arta 47/29.*

Amfissa (ΑΜΦΙΣΣΑ)   E10

Fokis (pop. 6600) This sloping town is built round a spire-like rock topped by the ruin of a 13th-century Frankish castle. It lives on the olive trade. Amfissa olives are about three times the size of ordinary 'cocktail' olives, blue-black and fleshy. They come mainly from the plain between Amfissa and the Gulf of Corinth – the Plain of Hrison, formerly called the Sacred Plain. This was part of the holy region of Delfi where cultivation was not allowed in ancient times. Driving from Amfissa towards Itea you see an olive forest rather than an olive grove – some of the trees here are over 500-years-old.

North of Amfissa (168m/550ft) the road rises dramatically and dustily to the **Gravia Pass** (884m/2900ft), with the streams and waterfalls of **Eleona** before the pass, and of **Eptalofos** beyond. *Delfi 20km/12mi.*

Antirio (ΑΝΤΙΡΙΟΝ)   F8

Aitolia-Akarnania At the head of the Gulf of Corinth, Antirio is signposted from afar but there is nothing when you get there. It is just a landing stage for car ferries between the Peloponnese and north-west Greece. The crossing to Rio takes about 20 mins, and is at least every half hour. To take the ferry and then the toll road to Corinth (Korinthos) is the quickest way to Athens from western Greece.

The decayed but rather pretty mediaeval fortress which overlooks Antirio is called the Castle of Roumeli. *Athens 205km/127mi.*

Arahova (ΑΡΑΧΩΒΑ)   F11

Voiotia (pop. 3000) Some sights in Greece may be overrated, but the early morning view from high on Mt Parnas-sos can claim with some justification to be one of the marvels of the world. Arahova is probably the best base from which to visit Parnassos. It is a good four hours to the summit in summer (June or July), and since the signposting is uncertain it is advisable to allow longer unless you have a guide. In winter, Parnassos is Greece's best ski centre with ski-lifts, a road ploughed free of snow and an attempt at après ski – the installations are at **Fterolaka**, 23km/14mi north west from Arahova.

Arahova is also a base for a prolonged visit to the archaeological site of Delfi – it has the accommodation and the tourist shops, but fewer crowds than in Delfi village. Streams and fountains furnish the water for washing the wool used in local rug-making, and the main road winding through the village is lined with shops offering rugs, blankets and fleecy *floccatas*.

Ossios Loukas monastery (translated on timetables as Saint Luke) is 26km/16mi south of Arahova, one of the most celebrated Byzantine churches of Greece, noted both for architecture and for ornament – Dafni on a bigger scale.

The turning for Ossios Loukas is at Distomo. A few metres east of this turning is another, more obscure one to the north, signposted Davlia (ΔΑΥΛΕΙΑ) This junction, called **Tridos** in antiquity, is where young Oedipus, fleeing to Thebes (Thiva) to defeat the oracle he had just consulted at Delfi, met old Laius, King of Thebes. Oedipus killed him and became king himself, marrying Laius' widow. Stand at desolate Triodos, close your eyes to the asphalt road, and listen for the last shriek of Oedipus as he puts out his eyes on learning that he had killed his father and married his mother. *Athens 160km/99mi, Delfi 12/7.*

Bralos (ΜΠΡΑΛΟΣ)   E10

Fthiotis This little junction is the starting point for an enthusiast to seek the funeral pyre of Heracles. Heracles was killed by a poisoned robe, and to ease the pain in his dead body it was burned on the top of lonely Mt Iti. A shrine was built here later to mark the event, if not the actual spot; fragments of limestone blocks and carvings are all that remain on this bleak plateau, above forests of chestnut and fir. An illegible sign marks the site, which is about 8km/5mi from the hamlet of **Pavliani**, at the end of the road from Bralos. There is a mountain refuge on Mt Iti at Trapeza.

On the approach to Bralos from Lamia, the Pass of Fournataki offers some of Greece's best hairpin bends. *Lamia 35km/22mi.*

Delfi (ΔΕΛΦΟΙ) F11

Fokis This sacred place, set on the slopes of Mt Parnassos beneath the precipitous 'shining rocks' (the Phaedriades) which rise over 300m/1000ft above the road, was the centre of the world to the ancient Greeks – the most beautiful place they knew, and home of their most famous oracle. The site is half-encircled by a vast amphitheatre of mountains, and looks across the chasm of the Pleistos Gorge and across the dense olive groves of the Sacred Plain, to the shining sea of the Gulf of Corinth.

The oracle was a peasant woman of mature years who would purify herself in the Castalian stream, induce hallucinations by eating a laurel leaf, and then foretell the future for mighty and humble alike. Her incoherent mumblings were interpreted in verse by one of the priests of Apollo, and the 'Delphic prophesy' that resulted was usually double-edged – the forecast could be proven to be correct only after the event, and was so obscure as to be of no use to anybody needing to know the future.

Still, the fame of the oracle was so great that the whole area was sanctified, and adorned with temples and the treasuries of the Greek cities. The remains to be seen today are in two main parts. Below the road is the Sanctuary of Athena (Marmaria), approached by narrow tracks over the hills past some of the most gnarled olives you will ever see. The most photographed feature of this sanctuary is the Tholos; three standing columns capped by marble lintels, all that is left of a circle of 20 columns. The Tholos, which has become the symbol of Delfi as the Parthenon is the symbol of Athens, is best seen from the distance.

Above the road is the Pythian Sanctuary (Temenos of Apollo) approached by a wide, paved path. This was formerly covered in marble buildings, but earthquakes, landslides and robbery have destroyed most of them. Obvious points of interest are the Temple of Apollo (partly restored in 1939), the Athenian Treasury (re-erected in 1906) and the Theatre (one of the best-preserved in Greece, and a perfect echo of the bigger theatre presented by the surrounding mountains). Beyond the theatre is the Stadium, for the Pythian Games were held here, a sort of mini-Olympics in honour of Apollo.

To get the most out of a visit to Delfi you need a detailed guide-book, obtainable from the museum adjacent to the Pythian Sanctuary. The museum should not be missed as it contains a great deal of statuary from the site, *eg* the frieze from the Siphnian Treasury and the famous bronze charioteer.

Between the Pythian Sanctuary and the Sanctuary of Athena runs the stream which rises at the Castalian spring (in a cleft – through the Phaedriades); here all visitors to ancient Delfi purified themselves by washing their hair, while today's tourists must be content to drink its clear, warm water. You can spend six hours at Delfi – coach driver permitting – and still want to carry on exploring the site. In summer, the approach can be spoilt by heavy traffic and parking is difficult, but once off the narrow road and scrambling down to the famous white columns you will be glad you came.

South of the Sanctuary of Athena there is a delightful walk to the Cave of Sybaris. (Start at the dirt road just east

The Sacred Way, Delfi

DELFI
(PYTHIAN SANCTUARY)

of the site – allow 3 hrs.) Above the Pythian Sanctuary there is a more strenuous walk to the Korician Cave. (Start from Delfi village, otherwise just somewhere to spend your money on the way to the archaeological site.) *Antirio 111km/69mi, Athens 165/103, Livadia 47/29.*

Evia (EYBOIA)   **E16**
(area 3908 sq km/1509 sq mi, pop. 165,000) Evia (Euboea), the second largest island in Greece, runs parallel to

the mainland of Attica and Voiotia for 160km/100mi, and is separated from Voiotia at one point only by the narrow and treacherous Euripos Strait. The strong current of the strait changes direction eight times a day, and so perplexed Aristotle that he flung himself into the water in despair! The north/south current is indicated by a red ball and the south/west by a white ball. The bridge which links the island to the mainland is open only on the north/south tide.

Evia is a rural backwater. Although it has become a weekend retreat for Athenians, it has so far faced no great influx of tourists. The pleasantest way to explore the gentle countryside is by bicycle, since there are large areas of fertile plain rich in crops, and the roads, though rather poor, are passable.

Inland, running right down the spine of the island, is a range of chestnut- and pine-covered mountains, rising at Mt Dirfis (west of Kimi on the east coast) to 1745m/5725ft. There is a refuge hut at 1100m/3608ft which sleeps 36. (Details from the Hellenic Alpine Club in Halkida, Tel: 0221 25230.)

The east coast, with its sheer cliffs, is almost inaccessible – most of the island's beaches and resorts are on the more gentle west.

Aliveri (pop. 4000) Situated on a hillside, this old, red-roofed town is inhabited mainly by workers from a nearby lignite mine. It is the taxi-hire centre for visiting the ancient city of Distos.

Dirfis The ascent of the mountain is best begun from **Nea Artaki** on the east coast, to **Steni** (32km/20mi) below the summit. Mules and a guide may be hired in the village and the climb takes about 5 hrs. On the lower slopes the way runs through deciduous woodland, then there are pines until just beyond Metochi where the path deteriorates but the views improve!

Distos The well-preserved ruins of ancient Distos stand on an isolated hill overlooking a swampy lake. The walls of the city are 3m high and 2m thick (10ft/6ft) with 11 towers; inside on the terraces are the only known remains of 5th-century-BC houses.

Eretria (pop. 1760) has easy access to the mainland (ferry to Skala Oropou) and is being developed as a holiday resort. It was once one of the most important maritime states in Greece and has the best-preserved antiquities on the island. There is a Roman theatre, a Macedonian tomb with the marble funeral couches dramatically intact, and a gymnasium. The museum, closed on Mondays, opens every other morning.

Halkida (pop. 36,000) The capital of the island, Halkida (Chalkis) lies at the narrowest point of the Euripos Strait and has always therefore been strategically important. It is an industrial, noisy and rather unattractive town. There is an archaeological museum, a Turkish fortress called Karababa from which there is a wonderful view of the strait, and the church of Ag. Paraskevi.
Communications: Halkida is 88km/55mi from Athens, across the bridge. There are ferries between Rafina and Stira, Marmari and Karistos – one or two a day; every 30 mins between Skala Oropou and Eretria; and every two hours between Glifa and Agiokabos.
Festivals: May 21 Ag. Konstandinos at Vitala, Kimi, July 17 Ag. Marinas near Karistos, July 26 at Halkida, Myli and Rukia – long celebrations.

Itea (ITEA)   F10

Fokis (pop. 3400) Cruise ships heading for the Corinth Canal stop at Itea to pour their passengers into Delfi-destined coaches. Just outside the town is the small, commercial harbour, busy with mineral traffic. All this makes little Itea quite a lively place, with a palm-lined seafront with cafés and the occasional *taverna*.

Itea is accidentally a miniature resort, while its neighbour **Galaxidi** (15km/9mi south west around the bay) really tries to be one. It has picturesque old houses by the sea which are let out in summer, and an attractive yacht-filled harbour in a little inlet. *Athens 168km/104mi, Nafpaktos 85/53.*

Karpenissi   D8
(ΚΑΡΠΕΝΗΣΙΟΝ)

Evritania (pop. 4300) At the very head of the River Sperhios and overshadowed by Mt Timfristos (2315m/

Galaxidi

7595ft), this large village has not decided whether to be a mountain spa or an industrial centre. Some of the nearby villages are fairly prosperous from mining; others are so poor that aid has to be distributed by volunteers from Athens. Despite this, it is a very hospitable area.

South west of Karpenissi (30km/19mi) is the monastery of **Proussos**; there is an ikon of the Virgin Mary which is said to be the work of St Luke. The road is a succession of hairpin bends with gorges, cliffs, peaks and precipices which give the region its name, 'little Switzerland'. Along the way, the village of **Korishades** is preserved as a 'traditional settlement', and then there are the alpine villages of **Mikro Horio** and **Mega Horio** halfway to Proussos.

The better road north west from Karpenissi leads through still wilder mountains to Lake Kremaston, and then down to Agrinio – a good day's outing for the lover of scenery. *Lamia 75km/47mi.*

Lamia (ΛΑΜΙΑ)   C10

Fthiotis (pop. 37,000) Lamia, a provincial market town, lies in the rich valley of the River Sperhios, growing cotton and wheat. It is spread over hilly slopes which lead up to a 14th-century Spanish (Catalan) castle. A few of the streets are still stone-stepped, like an island village, and storks nest on the roofs. Lively and prosperous for an hour, but dull for a day's visit. *Athens 215km/134mi.*

Livadia (ΛΕΒΑΔΕΙΑ)   F12

Voiotia (pop. 15,000) Many of the lovely 'local' blankets which you can buy in other parts of Greece come from this busy little town. Textile-making is still a cottage industry, and water for washing the wool is supplied by the River Erkina.

The red-roofed town up on the hill is less interesting for the visitor than the river, spanned by an ancient Turkish bridge. The Erkina rises from springs at the foot of the hill and then flows over a series of weirs and waterfalls to drop away through the lower town. The broad waters create a cool, refreshing, tree-shaded area to sit and take a coffee, as the Turkish governors did before you.

Heronia (Chaeronia) is 12km/7mi north of Livadia, and is famous as the site of two decisive battles. In 338 BC Philip of Macedon defeated the Greeks here and brought to an end the world of classical Greece; the marble lion by the roadside marks the burial mound of the

254 warriors of the Theban Sacred Band who fell ĺn the battle against Philip – some of their armour is in the nearby museum. Two hundred and fifty years later, in 87 BC, Philip's Hellenistic world ended when Sulla's Roman army wiped out so many Greeks that the pass was blocked with their bodies. *Athens 118km/73mi.*

Messolongi   F6

(ΜΕΣΟΛΟΓΓΙΟΝ)
Aitolia-Akarnania (pop. 16,000) Known to lovers of English poetry as the scene of the death of Lord Byron, Messolongi is loved by Greeks as the last bastion of liberty during their War of Independence.

The town lies on a narrow spit of land between the sea and a marshy lagoon. On the outskirts the buildings are all single-storeyed and, unusually for Greece, well-spaced like country villas. Even in the centre they are low and shy, as though afraid of sinking into the marsh. They have good reason, for along the edge of the lagoon the old reed and daub huts are still inhabited but have sunk down so that their roofs sag like those of badly erected tents.

During the day a few flat-bottomed boats glide over the lagoon to the fish hatcheries which supply roe, a local delicacy. There are many marsh birds and at night the croaking of frogs can be heard for miles. In all, a rather eerie place, but romantic.

The most famous landmarks in the town are the Sortie Gate and the Heroes Garden and to savour these to the full you need to know something of recent Greek 'mythology'.

The Sultan's troops were engaged in suppressing Ali Pasha at Ioanina (page 51) when the War of Independence broke out in 1821, and at first the revolt was successful. But with Ali Pasha dead, Turkish forces were available for the reconquest of the unruly empire, while the Greeks quarrelled amongst themselves after the first flush of success. Before long Messolongi, which had been made the headquarters of a mixed bunch of brigands, intellectuals, peasants and soldiers, was the only place of any size left in Greek hands. Lord Byron (1788–1824) came here in 1824, bringing with him his title, gold collected by English lovers of Greece and promises of more support. Just what part he played in stiffening the defence is open to question, but he died of fever after a few months, and by his death mobilized British public opinion in support of the Greeks – the results appeared three years later at the Battle of Navarino. The defenders of Messolongi managed to work together, and set an example which the rest of Greece was to follow later. The siege intensified; the Sultan brought in Egyptian troops who pacified the Peloponnese and then joined the Turks in investing Messolongi. By April 1826 the position was hopeless, and the defenders decided to break out.

Those who made the sortie were cut to pieces by cavalry, warned by a traitor, and those who stayed behind blew up the whole town. Their desperate, heroic defence saved Greece – they had given time for forces to be organized against the Sultan both within and outside Greece, and showed their countrymen pride in their cause.

The entry to Messolongi today is through a reconstructed gate representing the famous Sortie Gate, and a memorial garden opposite honours the heroes who fell in the siege. *Athens 244km/152mi.*

Nafpaktos (ΝΑΥΠΑΚΤΟΣ) F8

Aitolia-Akarnania (pop. 9000) Like a Hollywood filmset, the tiny harbour of this seaside port is enclosed by castellated ramparts and guarded by white stone towers. The old village has a certain charm; the newer parts of this holiday resort for Greeks are squeezed against the sandy coast by mountains. The mountains themselves are deeply cut by gorges, covered here and there by fir and oak forests, and supply the streams which run through the town. There is a Venetian castle, caves at Anavriti and the best beaches are at Grimbovon and Psani. In July there is a Festival of Art and Literature.

Nafpaktos was the scene of the defeat of the Spartan fleet by the Athenians in 429 BC, and the more famous defeat of the Turks by the Venetians at the Battle of Lepanto in 1571. *Athens 215km/134mi.*

Thermopiles D10
(ΘΕΡΜΟΠΥΛΩΝ)

Fthiotis The story of a handful of Spartans holding the Pass of Thermopiles (Thermopylae) against the vast army of Persia (480 BC) is probably the best known of all the deeds of Ancient Greece, and the truest story. The pass lay between the steep side of Mt Kallidromo and the sea, barely wide enough for a chariot to pass, and the Persian army had to go through this pass from the north west to join the fleet.

For days on end the Greeks slaughtered the Persians as they tried a frontal attack on the pass, and then the traitor Efialdes led the Persian 'Immortal Guard' through a path over the mountain to take the Greeks in the rear. Most of the Greeks were sent back, but Leonidas, King of Sparta, kept 300 of his best men to delay the Persians – two million of them according to Herodotus. The Spartans did not win the battle but they won immortal fame.

It is difficult to envisage the battle scene today, for what was swamp has become dry land and on the land stands a restaurant and a car park. There is a marble memorial with a huge bronze figure of Leonidas; miniature copies of this figure are on sale in half the tourist shops of Greece.

The range of **Mt Kallidromo** is a favourite with walkers and one of the best ways into it is from the village of **Mendenitsa** (9km/5mi south east of Thermopiles) overlooked by the castle of Bodonitsa. If you prefer the sea, **Kamena Vourla** (20km/12mi along the coast east of Thermopiles) is a spa with mountains right behind it; **Agios Konstandinos** is more of a fishing village. *Athens 220km/137mi.*

Thiva (ΘHBAI) F14

Voiotia (pop. 16,000) In classical times Thiva (Thebes) was renowned as a heavy forbidding town, provincial in spirit, despite its size and importance. The town was destroyed by Alexander the Great in 336 BC, by Sulla in 86 BC, by the Goths in AD 248 and 396 and by various earthquakes, the latest in 1893. The present town stands high above the rubble but in spirit it has not changed – it is, frankly, dull.

The three great men that Thiva produced were the mythical Oedipus, Pindar the poet and Epaminondas, who led the first Greek army to defeat Sparta. Epaminondas' victory is commemorated by a monument at **Lefktra** 22km/14mi south west of Thiva. Pindar and Epaminondas are the names of the parallel main streets of Thiva, running to the top of the hill from the lemon-covered plain.

Ancient Thebes was known as the City of Seven Gates, but the gates have gone. The museum stands on the site of the North Gate, within the remains of a Frankish castle, and is worth a visit. The little chapel of Agios Lukas 500m/550yds from the museum is, allegedly, where St Luke lies buried (author of the third Gospel of the New Testament and the *Acts of the Apostles*). *Athens 72km/45mi, Livadia 47/29.*

THE PELOPONNESE

Twice in its long history the Peloponnese (Peloponnisos) has been all there was of Greece, but αιων παντα ρερει – time changes everything. Today this region is something of a backwater – a coastal strip in the west thrives on agriculture and the east is rich in antiquities; in between there are mountains.

The story of the area is told in two titles.

Peloponnisos means the island of Pelops, and indeed it is an island – the narrow isthmus which connected it to the mainland was cut by a canal in the 1890s, and now it is surrounded by water: the Gulf of Corinth (Korinthos) to the north, open Mediterranean to the south, and Ionian and Aegean seas to west and east. Pelops was the grandson of Zeus, and grandfather to Agamemnon who summoned the Greeks to the Trojan War.

The Morea was the mediaeval name for the Peloponnese, when it was taken by the Franks who betrayed the Byzantine Empire. Frankish rule was an almost welcome break of less than 100 years, in a long period of invasion and oppression, for the Morea became the setting for a court life of knightly courtesy.

All over the Peloponnese you can see Byzantine churches, Frankish castles and Turkish ruins. The remains of ancient Greece are concentrated in Argolis, with excursions to Vasses and Olympia. The three southern peninsulas offer a coastline of coves and bays with few amenities – there are more amenities in the smaller peninsula of Argolis. The western edge of the Peloponnese is a fertile and intensely cultivated strip with little roads that lead nowhere or, if you're lucky, back to your starting point. The towns are mostly dull, modern creations, providing a base for exploration of the sites of heroic, classical, and mediaeval Greece, and the sea, mountains, and villages of Greece today.

Andravida (ΑΝΔΡΑΒΙΔΑ)　F1

Ilia (pop. 3000) Formerly the capital of the Frankish principality of the Morea, this township straddling the road from Pirgos to Patra is now a market centre with an airport to the east, and to the west the pleasure grounds of the most westerly tip of the Peloponnese. **Kilini** (15km/9mi) offers a soft sandy beach, the carefully tended lawns of a modern miniature spa, and a view to the distant island of Zakinthos – ferry four times daily (1 hr). The Castle of **Hlemoutsi** (Castel Tornese) is the most impressive and best preserved Frankish castle of the Peloponnese; if you visit no other, visit this one. **Loutra Kilinis** (8km/5mi) offers hotels, another sandy beach with a campsite, and pinewoods. Further south at **Kourouta**, there is a huge campsite for the beach; freelance camping attractive but forbidden. *Korinthos 200km/124mi.*

Andritsena (ΑΝΔΡΙΤΣΑΙΝΑ)　H4

Ilia (pop. 1200) Straggling along the hillside, this lovely mountain village makes a perfect refreshment stop on the way to the temple at **Vasses** (see page 86) – restaurants in the shaded square (part of the road overlooking the edge of the mountain) and *tavernas* in the jumble of wooden houses in the back streets (pedestrians only). There is a river below, fountains, a church, a few poor shops, and a petrol pump. *Pirgos 63km/30mi, Tripoli 78/48.*

Areopoli (ΑΡΕΟΠΟΛΙΣ)　L6

Lakonia (pop. 800) A few cafés in the lively, narrow streets are enough to make this large village the centre for exploring the inner Mani and the Diros Caves.

The **Mani** is the middle of the three principal peninsulas of the Peloponnese, where the inhabitants of ancient Sparta took refuge from endless invasions. The Maniates still claim to be direct descendants of the Spartans, and to have preserved Spartan speech. Square, tower-like houses, each a miniature fortress but now mostly crumbling, show the recent defensive past, *eg* at **Vathia**. Shortage of water is acute in summer.

The spectacular caves of Diros (**Pirgos Dirou**, 12km/7½mi south of Areopoli) have a just claim to be the most beautiful caves in the world. There are two tours: get a numbered ticket for both as you go in, and prepare for a 2 to 4-hour wait until your number comes up. Good bathing while you wait, from a stony beach in a lovely bay (restaurant and café). Take jeans and a sweater for the caves.

Vlihada is really a subterranean river and boats are rowed between the translucent stalactites, through elbow-width chasms and head-bending tunnels. There are 2000m/6560ft of walkway. The natural colour of the rocks and the total silence are almost too intense. In the **Alepotrypa** cave, 200m/650ft east of Vlihada, visitors go on foot.

Between Areopoli and Sparti, **Githio** is a quiet harbour town with its cafés and shops sleeping round the bay. Ferries, which disturb the fish by the quay, leave regularly for Athens and occasionally for Crete. *Kalamata 82km/51mi, Sparti 72/45.*

Argos (ΑΡΓΟΣ)   G7
Argolis (pop. 20,000) A compact, thriving town; lively market place. This is a convenient base to eat or stay overnight when visiting **Mikines** (9km/6mi by bus or taxi).

Nearby are the remains of the Roman baths, the mediaeval castle on the site of a Mycenaean citadel (275m/900ft above the town), and the Hellenic theatre – all

worth a visit. Details from the museum in the central square.

After two hours of strenuous walking east from Argos, the Sanctuary of Apollo and Hera (Heraion) may appear a pile of ruins but it is situated, as a sanctuary should be, in peace and remoteness with an impressive view. *Athens 139km/86mi, Korinthos 46/29.*

Epidavros (ΕΠΙΔΑΥΡΟΣ)   G9
The car park at Epidavros gives the first hint that this is a 'sacred' place. It is a huge lawn, watered daily and brushed and combed twice a day, with rose beds to define the parking bays. Then the shaded walk to the theatre itself, up a broad path past giant trees, or through narrow tracks scented with the purple and yellow bushes, increases the mystery. A visit to the theatre in any town has its sense of occasion, but a play in this open-air theatre, one more in a programme that began over 2000 years ago, seems more like a religious experience. In fact, theatre and religious services went together in classical times, and for today's Greek visitors, Epidavros is a national shrine.

The theatre is a semicircular bowl cut into the hillside, with stone seats for 14–16,000 spectators to look down on the 'orchestra' – for ancient Greeks, where the chorus danced, today used as the stage. The acoustics are perfect – during the day, when it is open and free to casual visitors, you can see couples, one talking softly in the orchestra, the other, hearing every word, in the 55th row over 30m/100ft up.

Performances are given here every

The theatre, Epidavros

evening from Monday to Saturday for a ten week season in summer – two weeks of a comedy, then two weeks of a tragedy. The language is a modern Greek translation of the ancient Greek text, and the style is declamation rather than acting as we know it. The way to get the best from a visit – unless of course you understand Greek – is to find out the programme from the NTOG, and read an English translation before you go. However, it is enough to buy a programme – this describes the action in sufficient detail for you to follow what is going on.

It helps to take a cushion, as the ancient Greeks did before you, and some warm clothing for it becomes chilly when the sun finally vanishes.

Tickets are to be had at a kiosk on the site: open mornings until 1300, afternoons from 1530. The better seats may well be sold out, but it is rare indeed if you cannot get one of the cheaper (high-level) seats on the day. (Tickets obtainable, in advance, in Athens.)

While waiting for the evening performance – or if you just go to see the sights – you can visit the museum, the excavations which include a hotel for ancient theatre-goers, the gymnasium and at the head of a ravine the stadium where races were run in classical times, or eat in one of the many restaurants on the road between the site and the village of **Ligourio** 4km/2½mi away. After the show, the police allow you to camp or sleep out on the lawns once the last of the cars and coaches has gone.

Nea (New) **Epidavros** is a small village 12km/7½mi from Ligourio, and **Palea** (Old) **Epidavros** is a smaller fishing village about the same distance away, where you can also spend a comfortable few hours – good swimming. *Athens 150km/93mi, Nafplio 29/18.*

Kalamata (ΚΑΛΑΜΑΤΑ)   J5
Messinia (pop. 40,000) A busy town, full of cars, shops and restaurants, with a life that owes nothing to tourists. The beach, 2km/1¼mi from the town, is long, hot, safe for children, and the centre of nightlife created entirely for tourists.

From the beach and harbour the long main street (Aristomenous) broadens into a grand, tree-lined square which is the hub of local life, and continues to the Frankish-built, Turkish-destroyed, citadel.

The road south from Kalamata, towards **Areopoli**, leads through the small resort of **Almiro** (villas to rent) and then climbs high above the sea. It offers spectacular views inland, access to a number of secluded coves reached only on foot, and a Frankish castle at **Kambos**, ruined by an earthquake in 1947 (20km/12mi). *Athens 285km/178mi, Tripoli 90/56.*

Kalavrita (ΚΑΛΑΒΡΥΤΑ)   E5
Achaia (pop. 2000) The centre for some of the most sensational mountain scenery in Greece. The town itself has been rebuilt after its destruction in 1943, when the Germans set it on fire and executed 1500 male inhabitants. The hands of the church clock are stopped at the time of the massacre, 2.34.

North of the town, towards the sea at **Diakofto**, the road runs through the menacing Vouraikos gorge, but rather than going by road, take the rack-and-pinion train through tunnels, over bridges, and across mountain ledges.

The road south, towards **Kato** (Lower) **Klitoria**, and the one west to Patra, climb through wild, pine-covered country, offering spectacular views. *Diakofto 36km/22mi, Patra 80/50.*

Kithira (ΚΥΘΗΡΑ)   N8
(area 285 sq km/110 sq mi, pop. 4000) Hilly, though hardly mountainous, this island is visited chiefly by returning emigrants and has scant tourist accommodation. The two most popular 'visits' are to **Avlemonas** where in 2000 BC the Minoans had a trading settlement, and the Monastery of Panayia **Mirtidion** with its blackened, gold ikons of the Virgin and Child.

Milopotamos is a village laced with waterways; there are peaceful mills and nightingales. This is the most likely place to find rooms for rent, and there is a small hotel at **Ag. Pelagia**.
Communications: Flight to Athens four times weekly (1½ hrs). Ferry twice weekly from Pireas (10 hrs); hydrofoil once weekly from Pireas (4¼ hrs).
Festivals: May 29–30 at Mitata.

Korinthos (ΚΟΡΙΝΘΟΣ)   F8
Korinthia (pop. 20,000) Modern, rectangular, flat town, with a pleasant harbour frontage on the gulf (Korinthiakos Kolpos). A good base for visiting Mikines (44km/30mi), and, of course, Ancient Corinth.

Paleo (Old) **Korinthos** is a village 8km/5mi south of the modern town, a single street of tourist shops with the entrance to the excavations of **Ancient Corinth**. (Open 0900–1700 in winter, 0800–1800 in summer, museum closed 1300–1430.)

Ancient Corinth was the vice centre of classical Greece, with ¼ million people; it was totally destroyed in 146 BC by the Romans. The ruins you see now – apart from the sixth-century BC Temple of Apollo – are of the Roman city built 100 years later, and include the market place where St Paul was accused by the Jews, the theatre, the Fountain of Peirene, and the Lechaeon Road leading north to Lechaeon (**Leheo**), the ancient port, 4km/2½mi from modern Korinthos.

The Acrokorinthos is the citadel of Ancient Corinth, with the remains of Byzantine, Frankish, Venetian and Turkish fortifications. The climb to the top, nearly 600m/1900ft, is worth it for the view.

The Corinth Canal   Korinthos became a major port because it was at the head of the Gulf of Corinth – a short cut between the western seas and Athens even though ships had to be dragged across the narrow isthmus. The first earth for a canal was dug with a golden spade by the Emperor Nero; the last in 1893. The canal is 6km/3½mi long, 9m/30ft wide and takes ships up to 8m/26ft deep; the road passes 70m/230ft above the canal, and a current of 3km/2mi per hour flows through it west to east, from the Gulf of Corinth (Korinthiakos Kolpos) to the Saronic Gulf (Saronikos Kolpos). *Athens 83km/52mi, Patra 134/83.*

Methoni (ΜΕΘΩΝΗ)   K3

Messinia (pop. 1200) A mediaeval pirate city, this quiet townlet on the west side of the Messinian peninsula offers a huge sandy beach, a hotel, a couple of *tavernas*, camping and the nostalgic remnants of an imposing Venetian fortress by the rocky sea, with a Turkish fortified islet beyond.

Methoni's sister town **Koroni** (30km/18½mi) on the east side of the peninsula, offers another sandy beach, another Venetian fortress (less imposing but containing a convent), and good fishing. Elegant mansions crowd its narrow streets.

The roads north from Methoni to Pilos, and from Koroni to Kalamata, skirt the sea and you can scramble down to coves for a bathe. *Kalamata 62km/39mi, Pilos 11/7.*

Mikines (ΜΥΚΗΝΑΙ)   G7

Argolis The forbidding limestone ruin of Mikines (Mycenae) spreads out over the mountainside above the plain of Argos. This was the chief city of the first Greek civilization, 1000 years before classical Greece. Here were the royal palace, the citadel, and the tombs of the Mycenaean world which went to war with Troy. You can spend days here if you're seriously interested in antiquities, and hours even as a curious tourist. Be ready for a fair amount of strenuous scrambling to explore the site fully.

Gates open 0800–1800 in summer, 0900–1600 in winter. The large car park can be quite inadequate in summer, and it is safer to park near the village and walk up to the site if you want to ensure a speedy getaway. Mikines village (3km/1½mi from the archaeological site) offers limited accommodation but a good choice of eating-places.

The guide-book of the site, available at the entrance kiosk, is quite detailed. The citadel is surrounded by Cyclopean walls (*ie* built of large, dry, undressed blocks of stone), which in places are still 5m/15ft high. It is entered through the famous Lion Gate, so called from the bas-relief lions carved above the entrance. To the rights you go up the ramp from the Lion Gate are first the remains of the granary, and then the circle of graves and the remains of houses, which you look down on from the ramp. Straight up the ramp you come to the ruined palace, where you can easily identify the Great Hall, with the traces of its fireplace and the footings of four columns, and the red stucco bath where Prince Agamemnon was murdered. To identify the rest needs expert help or a detailed guide. Beyond the palace, small boys will love the sally port and the postern gate which now leads to a small collection of the huge jars used by Mycenaeans for storage; for 'bigger boys' there is the secret cistern, reached down 100 wet steps with no handrail – take a torch.

Outside the citadel are nine tholos tombs – beehive shaped, brick lined burial chambers. Best of them all is the Tomb of Agamemnon (13m/43ft high, 15m/48ft diameter) also called the Treasury of Atreus, which is cut into the hillside beyond the modern fence. The Tomb of Clytemnestra is nearer the citadel; the others are much less spectacular. These tombs are the burial chambers of great chiefs, almost certainly earlier than Agamemnon, who built them in their own lifetimes as the Pharaohs built the Pyramids. In 1874 Schliemann, who had already discovered and excavated ancient Troy, began digging at Mikines, and almost the first object he found was the gold death

Cyclopean walls, Mikines

mask, which is now the centre piece of the collection in the Archaeological Museum in Athens.

The Mycenaeans The question which this bleak site imposes on any visitor is: Did the Mycenaean Greeks really go from here to the war with Troy – was there really a Trojan War?

Roving bands of Bronze Age brigands, speaking Greek, came to this area about 2000 BC, and by 1500 BC they had become rulers of the Peloponnese and surrounding islands. Their best-known city was Mikines, but other Mycenaeans of the period took over the royal palace of the Minoans at Knossos in Crete. Mikines traded with Egypt, the Baltic and Asia.

Almost all that is known of this period is told in Homer's long poem the *Iliad*. According to Homer, Agamemnon was the Prince of Mikines and paramount prince of all the Greeks – Αναξανδρων Αγαμεμνων (Agamemnon, the Prince of Men). His younger brother Menelaus was Prince of Sparta, and it was Helen his wife who was abducted by Paris, son of Priam King of Troy. To avenge this insult, Agamemnon summoned all the Greeks to send ships and men to war with Troy. To appease the gods, Agamemnon had to sacrifice his daughter Iphigenia before the fleet could sail. For ten years the Greeks besieged Troy, until the famous Trojan Horse got them in, and they destroyed the city. On his return to Mikines, Agamemnon's wife Clytemnestra killed him for sacrificing Iphigenia; the subsequent revenge of his son Orestes provided material for generations of playwrights.

This is not historical truth as we

understand it – these events probably took place around 1250 BC, and the *Iliad* was written as much as 500 years later. Also, scholars believe that Homer was not just one poet, but several men at different times – there are at least eight places in Greece which claim to be his birthplace. However, the legends are based on some fact, and the home of this fact is here at Mikines.

Mikines declined after the Dorian invasions at the end of the 12th century BC, but remained an independent city for another thousand years. Then the site became deserted, and covered in rubble eroded from the surrounding crags; when Pausanias wrote the first guide-book to Greece in the 2nd century AD he could not find the tombs, but the local legends of the site of the Treasury of Atreus were sufficiently accurate for Schliemann to find it 1500 years later. *Argos 13km/8mi.*

Mistras (ΜΥΣΤΡΑΣ)   **J6**

Lakonia (pop. 20 nuns) The rich blue and terra cotta rooftops of the abandoned mediaeval ghost town of Mistras cling like the gardens of Babylon to the terraced hills 150m/500ft above the rich plain – a compromise between beauty and defence.

The entrance can be reached by car from the modern hamlet of Mistras (car park too small) or by bus from Sparti 6km/4mi away. Then there is the dusty climb up the cobbled alleys and steps through the ruins. It is strenuous but not impossible, even in the heat – after all people once lived here. Take a little sustenance with you – the only source of refreshment is a fountain in the museum courtyard. But why did the people of Mistras first build up here, where every step seems like an endurance test in the summer sun?

It was founded in the 13th century by the Franks as a citadel, but fairly soon passed to the Byzantine Greeks. The city became a flourishing capital of the Palaeologi (the last imperial dynasty), being out of easy reach of marauding invaders. After an interlude of Turkish occupation from 1460, it passed to Venice just before 1700, and reached a new peak of prosperity based on silk production (pop. 42,000) before the return of the Turks. When the Turks were expelled, Sparti was re-built in the plain and Mistras became deserted.

At the very top of the hill is the Kastro (Villehardouin Castle), the original Frankish fortress, with a fabulous view across the blue haze of the cypress-spiked Laconian plain. Below the Kastro the Upper Town is centred on the Palace of the Despots (Anaktora) – with its vast arched hall, now open to the sky, its chimney places, and its fig-shaded courtyard. The beautiful ornate Pantanassa Church now inhabited by a few nuns, is at this level. (Women are requested to wear skirts, long trousers for men.) On the lower level the Peribleptos Monastery visited on the way in, and the Cathedral (St Demetrius) on the way out, are the principal monuments, but everywhere else are the ruins of houses, small palaces, and churches. *Athens 260km/417mi, Sparti 7/4.*

Monemvassia   L8
(ΜΟΝΕΜΒΑΣΙΑ)
Lakonia (pop. varies, say 500) A great cliff face rises like the Rock of Gibraltar from the sea with the ruins of a castle at its peak, and below, on the seaward side, a melancholy Byzantine-Venetian city. Almost deserted now, the mansions overhang the narrow streets,

propped up by crumbling walls; and yet Monemvassia still feels like a miniature city. The inhabited houses have white-washed steps, and here and there in the paved alleys a few tables outside indicate an eating-house.

The sea-lashed walls surrounding the city (still nearly complete) have a donkey gate, too narrow for cars. The castle above (entrance through a tunnel) and the glorious Byzantine church on the edge of the cliff draw the artists at sunset.

Ferry from Pireas (8 hrs), also a daily hydrofoil (3½ hrs). Ferry twice a week from Githio in summer (3 hrs). *Athens 340km/210mi, Sparti 95/59.*

Nafplio (ΝΑΥΠΛΙΟΝ)   G8
Argolis (pop. 10,000) A leisurely, prosperous town, Nafplio (Nauplia) is a popular resort. The harbour front is one centre for eating; higher class hotels on the approach to the citadel (Akronafplia). This was the first capital of the infant Kingdom of Greece.

The Palamidi Fortress above the town (230m/700ft; over 1000 steps to the summit) is named after Palamedes who invented much of the Greek alphabet. It was in fact built by the Venetians and the Lion of St Mark can be seen on many of the gates.

Outside Nafplio, the village of **Tolo** (10km/6mi south) has many good beaches (sand and shingle), campsites and holiday activities. For antiquarians, there is the nearby site of ancient Asine, (Assini).

The site of **Tirins** is 4km/2½mi north of Nafplio – a Mycenaean palace-fortress surrounded by the Cyclopean walls recorded by Homer. They still stand to about half their original height of 20m/65ft, made of huge stone blocks, weighing up to 15 tons each. North west of the main courtyard are two secret passages leading to spring-fed cisterns. As at Mikines, take a torch. *Athens 147km/91mi.*

Olympia (ΟΛΥΜΠΙΑ)   G3
Ilia The first Olympic Games were run in 776 BC in honour of Zeus whose home was on distant Mt Olympus, and continued to be held every four years until AD 393. The games were the occasion of a holy truce between the endlessly warring Greek States, and the single year the truce was broken the Olympics Committee (then called the Olympian Senate) excluded the offending Spartans from the games; thereafter the truce was observed until AD 69 when Nero organized his own games, with

Mistras

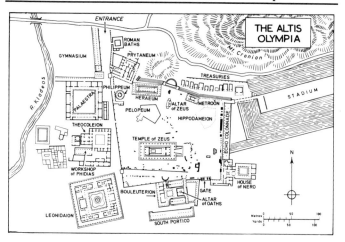

THE ALTIS
OLYMPIA

ENTRANCE
ROMAN BATHS
GYMNASIUM
PRYTANEUM
Cronion
TREASURIES
PHILIPPEUM
HERAEUM
PELOPEUM
ALTAR of ZEUS
METRÖON
STADIUM
PALAESTRA
R. Kladeos
THEOCOLEION
HIPPODAMEION
ECHO COLONNADE
WORKSHOP OF PHIDIAS
TEMPLE of ZEUS
HOUSE OF NERO
BOULEUTERION
GATE
ALTAR of OATHS
LEONIDAION
SOUTH PORTICO
Metres 0 50 100
Yards 0 50 100

himself as winner.

The site of the games, in a triangle of land between the Rivers Alfios and Kladeos, became covered with temples and sanctuaries (most famous of which was the Temple of Zeus), and functional blocks. These were mostly destroyed in AD 426 on the order of the Christian emperor; what was overlooked then was subsequently knocked down by earthquakes and covered by floods. Many winners erected illegal statues to themselves towards the end of the period of the games – mercifully this forest of statues has been destroyed too.

The site was uncovered from 1875 onwards, and now the ruins of many of the ancient buildings can be seen in a setting of shaded tranquillity. Best preserved is the Temple of Hera (Heraeum); the columns of the Palaestra (wrestling school) remind you that Doric columns were not reserved for temples; the arched entrance to the Stadium is still complete, and in the Stadium itself the ancient starting and finishing lines are preserved. The abiding impression of the site is still its green richness and the sweet air.

In the two museums, there is a collection of pre-classical statues, pediments and metopes from the Temple of Zeus, original sculptures, and the statue of *Hermes* by the most famous sculptor of antiquity, Praxiteles. The collection of armour, including a Persian helmet and the helmet of the Athenian commander from the Battle of Marathon, makes the museums more interesting than many others for the non-classical tourist.

The village of Olympia is a line of plastic-and-gilt souvenir shops, with cafés still selling neon-lit plastic food at two in the morning. Rare as the greenery of ancient Olympia is in the rest of Greece, so, fortunately, is the brashness of the modern town.

The modern Olympic Games were started in 1896 by Baron de Coubertin, to recapture his vision of the Olympic ideal, and the first games were held in Greece.

Patra (ΠΑΤΡΑΙ) D3

Achaia (pop. 120,000) This is the second port of Greece, where the ferries from Italy and the Ionian Isles arrive, and also a rather elegant modern city – the grid pattern streets, not so burdened with traffic as most Greek cities, are relieved by colonnades and arcades (neo-classical style). Although not a holiday centre in itself, it has many visitors who just like the life, centred on Olgas Square with its bands and barrel organ. Tennis (at 64 Club); mountain climbing (details from Hellenic Alpine Club, address page 33); the biggest carnival in Greece in March; wine-tasting at the winery of Achaia Klauss; museum, interesting for its Mycenaean armour; and of course the port.

Many tourists, having driven across Yugoslavia and unwilling to face the long haul back, wait here in summer for a ferry to Italy. Scores of shipping agencies line the harbour front and each agency will assure you the others are fully booked for days or weeks ahead; but with patience and persistence you

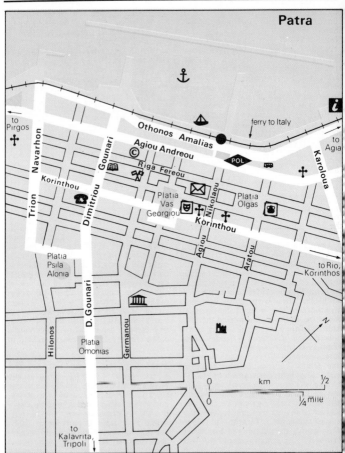

Patra

to Pirgos

Navarhon

Othonos Amalias

ferry to Italy

to Agia

Karoloua

Korinthou

Agiou Andreou

Gounari

Dimitriou

Trion

Riga Fereou

Platia
Vas
Georgiou

Nikolaou

Platia
Olgas

Korinthou

Agiou

Aratou

*to Rio,
Korinthos*

Platia
Psila
Alonia

D. Gounari

Hilonos

Germanou

Platia
Omonias

km   ½

¼ mile

*to
Kalavrita,
Tripoli*

will nearly always get a crossing within, at most, a couple of days.

Informal seaside camping just west of Patra, and further west at **Ities** and below **Mintilogli**; also to the east at an NTOG site and at **Rio**. From Rio, overlooked by the sombre Castle of the Morea, there is a car ferry across the Gulf of Corinth every 20–30 mins (hourly at night) to Antirio (for the drive to Corfu and northern Greece). *Athens 213km/132mi, Korinthos 134/83.*

Pilos (ΠΥΛΟΣ)   K3
Messinia (pop. 2500)   A small, elegant town of colonnaded houses and shops, its plane-tree shaded square facing the

bay, with cafés, sweetshops and eating-houses. The bay (5km/3mi long) is shut in on one side by the steep cliffs of the uninhabited island of Sfaktiria. It was the scene of the Battle of Navarino in 1827, during which the Turkish fleet was 'accidentally' destroyed by a combined British, French and Russian fleet, hastening the end of the War of Independence. A boat trip round the bay reveals the remains of ships on the bottom on a still day.

A superb small bay for swimming north of Navarino Bay is most easily reached by boat – you can risk scrambling down the cliff from the ruined castle on the headland above. From the bay you can reach Nestor's Cave; a 20m/60ft long cave, hung with animal-shaped stalactites – legend claims that Nestor kept his cows here.

Nestor's Palace is 15km/8mi north of Pilos, on the road to Filiatra. Built around 1300 BC, it is not in good condition but is better preserved and gives a more compact, more identifiable picture of a Mycenaean palace than the more extensive ruins of Mikines. The small museum – opening hours erratic – sells an excellent explanation of the ruins. Tablets written in Linear B script, similar to those found at Knossos in Crete, were discovered here as soon as excavation of the site began; see them in the museum at nearby **Hora**. *Athens 326km/203mi, Patra 222/138.*

Pirgos (ΠΥΡΓΟΣ)   G2

Ilia (pop. 22,000) A busy, currant-trading town; being on a hill, it avoids the flat rectangularity of many modern, Greek towns.

The nearby little resort of **Katakolo** (13km/8mi) has a broad flat beach bordered by simple Greek homes, unpretentious cafés with gardens on the sand, and a mole where cruise ships discharge passengers into coaches to be whisked off to Olympia. A short; shaded walk over the hill brings you to a smaller, better beach and the hamlet of **Ag. Andreas** (2km/1mi).

South of Pirgos, **Kaiafas** (28km/17mi) has a pine-covered bank of sand dunes between the road and the sea, concealing a long, sandy, steeply shelving beach. There is a cluster of dreary hotels and restaurants on an islet in the lagoon. From the sea, a dirt road leads to the hot springs of **Loutra Kaiafas** (hydrotherapy) past turtle-lurking waters (3km/2mi), and then to the village of **Zaharo**. *Athens 311km/193mi, Patra 95/59.*

Portoheli (ΠΟΡΤΟΧΕΛΙ)   H9

Argolis (pop. 1200) The holiday centre of the Argolis peninsula, with a few hotels, sandy beaches and a vast hinterland. Large scale development has been threatened for many years but Portoheli remains basically a fishing village, cut off from the rest of the Peloponnese by low mountains, orange groves and pines. From here you can easily reach Epidavros (62km/39mi) and other cultural centres, but essentially this is a place for an active holiday.

Kosta, 6km/4mi away, has frequent ferries and motorboats to the island of Spetse. For an outing, **Kranidi** (9km/5mi) is the main town of the Argolis for basic shopping, then on to the cave at **Kilada**, a real fishing village. Another outing from Portoheli is to **Ermioni**, a fishing village which is trying to establish itself as a wind-surfing centre. **Galatas** has constant ferries to the island of Poros, and there are sightseeing trips to the scattered ruins of **Trizina** (Troezen), home of Theseus.

The hydrofoil from Pireas connects this region to Athens: Portoheli six daily (2 hrs), Ermioni five daily (1¾ hrs, Zea).

Sparti (ΣΠΑΡΤΗ)   J6

Lakonia (pop. 12,000) Modern Sparti, which occupies about a quarter of the area of the ancient city of Sparta, is a square-planned town of broad streets and low buildings – built from nothing in 1834 on one bank of the River Evrotas (swimming pool). The main square (no traffic) has cafés along one side, a museum opposite and colonnaded shops between; a pleasant place to watch the evening *volta* or to take a drink before walking over the remains of ancient Sparta.

At the north end of the main street is the soccer stadium, from which a track leads to an olive grove containing scattered piles of stone – all that is left of Sparta; apart from the legend. (The more substantial remains of the theatre are Roman.) You can wander for hours in the thin shade of the trees, and remember that this is where the Spartans followed their strange ways for nearly 1000 years.

The Dorian invaders who destroyed the local Mycenaean civilization (see page 81) kept themselves separate from the original inhabitants, who were made *Helots* – halfway between slaves and a cowed peasantry. The Spartans' aim was to preserve not the purity of the race, but of the spirit. They had a vision of what a man should be, and tried to live accordingly.

Their system was formalized in about 800 BC in the laws of Lycurgus – his statue stands now in front of the cathedral in modern Sparti. However, following an expansion into neighbouring Messinia, the now vastly outnumbered Spartans evolved the brutal subjection of the Helots and totalitarian discipline of themselves which made them infamous and gave us the word 'Spartan'.

At birth the weaker boys were killed; at seven years of age those who lived were taken from their mothers to be trained. Life became a prolonged test of physical endurance and suffering; stealing was admired, but getting caught meant brutal punishment. At 20 they entered the police, who periodically beat up the Helots to keep them in their place, and at 30 they became 'Spartiates' – allowed to join the army proper. The troops were brave, tough, highly disciplined, and, if need be, merciless. They were invincible until refusal to adapt to modern ways led to defeat by new tactics.

The diet, even for Spartiates, was rigidly prescribed – one Greek visitor observed, 'Now I know why the Spartans do not fear death'. Spartan speech in early days was terse, biting and witty, but by the time of classical Greece it had degenerated to morose rudeness – called 'Laconic' by other Greeks.

The Spartan way of life was supposedly maintained by the rule of rapacious and corrupt kings, and was almost as austere and harsh, materially, for Spartiates as for Helots. That is the legend, but it is no doubt partly the propaganda of Sparta's enemy, Athens, and partly a fiction created by the Spartans themselves for state security. The way of life cannot have been so grim. Armed Helots, outnumbering Spartiates by seven to one, fought on the Spartan side in some of their worst battles. The Spartans themselves never sought to change it, despite prolonged contact with the rest of Greece which was richer and more joyful. The personal striving for a shared ideal gave each Spartan an identity. What they lacked was ideas; they had no need for doubt.

The Golden Age in Athens was only one half of the 'Glory that was Greece' – the other half was Sparta, from which we have as much to learn. Remember this as you walk past the memorial to Leonidas at the top of Stadium Street, and over the dusty path on the olive covered hillside. (For the descendants of Sparta in the Mani, see page 77.) *Athens 255km/158mi, Tripoli 60/37.*

Tripoli (ΤΡΙΠΟΛΙΣ)   H6

Arkadhia (pop. 22,000) A busy manufacturing town with narrow streets. Right in the centre of the Peloponnese, Tripoli is a good centre of communications. Three café-lined squares make this lively town agreeable to residents, and to visitors.

The plain surrounding Tripoli, although high above sea level, can be not only hot but heavily oppressive, with sudden, violent storms in summer. The road up to the plain from Argos and Nafplion is a spectacular series of hairpin bends with wide views over the gulf (Argolikos Kolpos); cars that have gone over the edge stay down below to encourage careful driving. *Athens 195km/121mi, Patra 171/106.*

Vasses (ΒΑΣΣΑΙ)   H4

Ilia One of the best-preserved and loveliest of the Greek temples, Vasses (Bassae or Vassai) has survived because it is so remote. The same remoteness, surrounded by empty limestone mountains cut by deep ravines, is its attraction – but why build a temple here? It was constructed around 450 BC by the local people in honour of Apollo Epikourios, the god who had saved them from a plague which devastated the neighbouring towns.

Many of the fallen columns of the temple have been re-erected and others are slowly being replaced, so the structure is likely to be covered by scaffolding for many years. You can nevertheless examine the detail and wander over the surrounding hills littered with temple stones; maybe you will be the one to stumble on a fragment with an inscription that will explain this bleak site further. More likely, you will trip over one of the baby tortoises that live amongst the scrub.

The easy way to Vasses is by the asphalt road from Andritsena (15km/9mi). The more rewarding, and more exciting, way is up the treacherous, precipitous track blasted out of the mountain, starting from Tholo on the main coast road between Kiparissia and Pirgos. A diversion from this road (two hours on foot) leads through the Nedas Gorge to a splendid waterfall. The whole area was at one time far more populous than today, and at any point you may find an unknown ruin.

Xilokastro   E7
(ΞΥΛΟΚΑΣΤΡΟΝ)

Korinthia (pop. 5000) A seaside resort on the Gulf of Corinth (Korinthiakos Kolpos). The sandy beach is backed by pines; there are subtropical gardens in the town; a good campsite to the east; and, above all, the mountains to the south. There is also a cement works.

An outing from Xilokastro to, say, Trikala is like going up into the cool Alps, where the tiny villages make you forget the scorching Mediterranean only 25km/16mi away. Mt Ziria is covered in snow until nearly midsummer.

A chain of resorts (smaller but similar) spreads west along the coast to Diakofto and on to Patra – Derveni is typical. Egio is a larger port. Wine festival at Zemeno in September. *Athens 294km/183mi.*

ATHENS
ATTICA AND THE ARGO-SARONIC ISLANDS

Greater Athens (Athina) is a concrete carpet sprawling from Pireas on the west coast of the Attic peninsula, over halfway to the Bay of Marathonas on the east coast, 40km/25mi away. Its flats and shacks are home to over 3½ million people and more arrive all the time. In 490 BC a warrior ran from Marathonas to the centre of ancient Athens to announce a great victory over the Persians; today when the traffic snarls up it feels as though it would still be quicker to run than take a taxi.

The official area of Greater Athens (Tmima Nomos Attiki and Tmima Nomos Pireas) is only 433 sq km/167 sq mi; the remainder of Attica – 2496 sq km/964 sq mi – is a playground and breathing space for crowded Athenians. In comparison, Greater London is 1606 sq km/620 sq mi, New York City is 829 sq km/320 sq mi and New York State is 20,295 sq km/7836 sq mi.

Despite its size and history, Athens feels like a provincial city; nevertheless there is a large colony of foreign residents who like life in the capital. Water from the tap is good to drink; the sewage system functions adequately; the streets are safe to walk in; advertising is restrained and, to our eyes, old-fashioned.

To enjoy Athens after seeing the standard sights, get one of the English-language guides from a kiosk around Sintagma Square – *The Athenian* or *Time in Athens*. These give details of shows, cultural and sporting activities, and restaurants. Athens is very strong in theatre (there are over 140 theatres, including experimental and avant-garde), poor in music, parochial in art, ambitious in dance.

Athens is not the place to take children to on holiday – there are few sights, parks, or entertainments to amuse them.

The Athenians' favourite pastime is talking – energy saving regulations may say that cafés close at two in the morning (early evening by traditional standards), but they don't say they can't re-open at four. When the chatter and the traffic fumes get too much, you can easily escape to the countryside of Attica or to one of the Saronic Islands for sport, entertainment, clean air, or even isolation.

Antiquities

The site which every tourist thinks of first is of course the Acropolis, the great rock crowned by the world's most photographed building, the Parthenon. But it is better not to rush to the Acropolis, approach it from the Agora, as Athenians of the Golden Age did before you.

The Agora (8) Agora in modern Greek means market, but in ancient Greek it meant 'gathering together'. The ancient Agora was a market where men came to buy and sell and do business, but it also housed the archives, council houses, dining hall, civic centre and gymnasium, and shopping arcades (stoas). They are all just rubble now, but at the entrance to the site (near Monastiraki Square, at the far end of Ifestou Street) there is a clear plan of the ancient site which will help you identify the remains and visualize what it was all like when it was the centre of Athens.

On a low hill overlooking the Agora is the **Temple of Hephaestus** (7), nearly as big as the Parthenon and to the same design, but much less impressive even though it is more complete. This is the best preserved of all Greek temples; only the outer roof is missing, and it gives you an idea what the interior of a temple was like before it was open to the skies. The metopes on the two long sides (four on each side) are decorated with carvings of Theseus in action, so the temple was thought to be dedicated to Theseus and is normally called the **Thissio** (Thesseion).

The colonnaded building at the end of the Agora, remote from the Thissio, is the **Stoa of Attalus** (9). The original Stoa was built in the 2nd century AD, a gift from Attalus King of Pergamum; the one you see now is a reconstruction

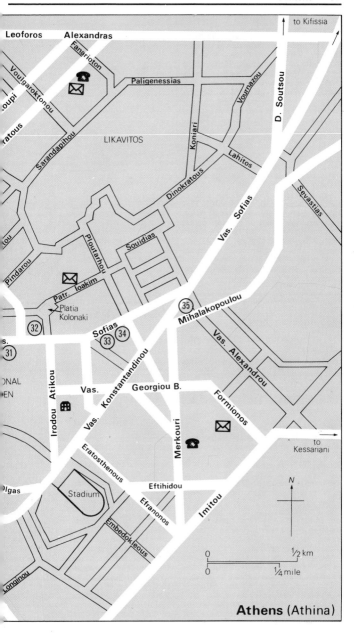

Athens (Athina)

(1956), a gift from private American donors. The new Stoa is a copy of the original, based on excavations, description and surviving remnants. From the distance it looks repetitive – a boring colonnade of 45 columns, Doric to the first floor, Ionic above. However, inside you can experience how Athens felt when all that fragmented stone was structured marble – cool, light and stimulating. The new Stoa makes a strong case for more reconstruction. Like the original, it is divided up into 21 'shops', but you can imagine what horrors would be on offer if it were leased to shopkeepers. Mercifully each 'shop' is part of a museum, displaying successive stages in the history of the Agora with findings from the site.

From the Agora, a path leads up to the west side of the Acropolis. This follows the ancient Panathenaic Way, the ceremonial road of classical times. This is a better approach to the Acropolis than by taxi to the car park. Don't time it so that you arrive at the Parthenon in the middle of a summer's day – there is no shade and the nearest refreshment is at the car park.

The Acropolis from the west

The Acropolis (19) The Acropolis (Akropoli) is a high outcrop of flat rock crowned by the **Parthenon (17)**, a landmark all over Athens and symbol of Greece. To look up at the Acropolis as you approach it from the Agora, or as you wander round the Plaka district on its lower slopes, creates the same sense of awe as looking up at a mountain-top. The Parthenon and the other three monuments on the rock need no description – you will inevitably want to go and see them – but it may help to know why they are there.

'Acro Polis' means 'High City', and on this rock grew the settlement that became the city of Athens. The flat top, nearly ten acres in area (four hectares), is about 120m/370ft above the surrounding plain; the walls rise almost vertically from the lower slopes, except

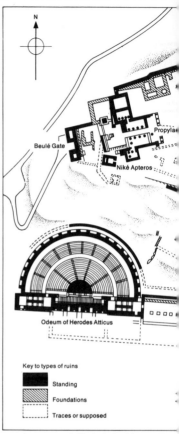

Propylaea

Beulé Gate

Niké Apteros

Odeum of Herodes Atticus

Key to types of ruins

Standing

Foundations

Traces or supposed

at the west end. Early in its history the rock had become a sacred site, adorned by temples, while the living city centred on the Agora below. In 480 BC, the city and all the temples on the Acropolis were destroyed by the Persians.

The retaining walls and buttresses which you see now were built soon after. Then under Pericles, the Athenians – with the riches and prestige that came from success in the Persian Wars, and yet with piety and almost disbelief that they had been saved – set about building other temples on the rock. The city itself was rebuilt quite simply, and their greatest efforts went into the first work undertaken on the Acropolis, the temple to their saviour, Athena Parthenon (Athena the Virgin).

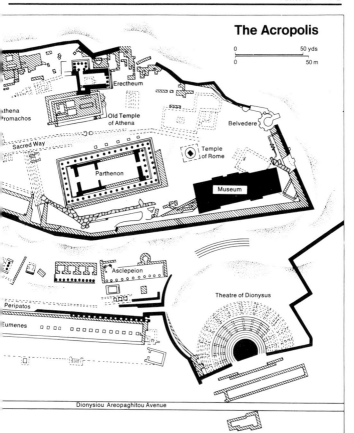

The Acropolis

0   50 yds
0   50 m

Erectheum

Athena Promachos

Old Temple of Athena

Belvedere

Sacred Way

Temple of Rome

Parthenon

Museum

Asclepeion

Theatre of Dionysus

Peripatos

Eumenes

Dionysiou Areopaghitou Avenue

The pattern of the Doric temple had become established, almost standardized, but this temple was to be the supreme example. The finest marble came from the new quarries of Mt Pentelis; it was gleaming white, its orange tint has come with the years. The architect Iktinos designed the building without using a straight line – it is all cunningly and exactly curved to create the optical illusion of straightness. It was richly decorated with sculptures, and was the first and only temple to have a sculpted frieze all the way round. The frieze was the work of Phidias, and represented the Panathenaic procession; the 192 male figures in the frieze are believed to represent the 192 Athenian soldiers killed at the Bat-

tle of Marathonas. When completed, the frieze and the sculpted pediments were brightly painted, but today what is left of the frieze is bare, corroded marble. Some of it was destroyed when a Turkish powder magazine in the Parthenon was blown up; some was commandeered by Lord Elgin, the 'Elgin Marbles' now in the British Museum; some is in the Louvre in Paris; and one panel (in good condition) is in the Acropolis Museum.

Erection of the Parthenon began in 447 BC, and it took 15 years to complete. It was a temple to house a huge statue of the goddess Athena (the sacrificial worship of Athena took place outside); it was a memorial to the dead of Marathonas; and it was a secure home for the treasure of the Delian League – the alliance of Greek states formed by Athens to keep away the Persians. The treasure was at first kept on the holy island of Dilos, but it was brought to Athens 'to protect it from pirates'. Some of the cost of building the Parthenon was met out of the Delian treasure, the rest came from the people of Athens. For whether the Parthenon was a temple, memorial or treasury, it was also an expression of Athenian pride and self-confidence – a monument to Periclean Athens.

Before visiting the Acropolis, study a picture of the rock as it was when the Parthenon and other buildings were just finished; there is such a picture in the lobby of many hotels in Athens. It is based on a model prepared by the American School of Archaeology, which can be seen in the Metropolitan Museum, New York. There is also a good model of the Acropolis as it is today in the British Museum, London. The statues, dividing walls, and Byzantine and Frankish additions, have all been cleared away, and today the three surviving buildings in addition to the Parthenon are the Propylaea (Gateways), a small temple to Athena of Victory, and the triple temple called the Erectheum; there is also a very absorbing museum tucked away discreetly at the east end of the Acropolis.

The approach to the Acropolis

The original approach to the **Propylaea** was up a ramp, but under the Romans this was replaced by grandiose marble steps. Today it is up some of the steps and then along a zigzag ramp (originally meant for sacrificial animals), leading you to the central and widest of the gateways. The Propylaea was the entrance hall to the Acropolis, intended to be as wide as the Parthenon is long (69m/228ft); work started as

soon as the Parthenon was finished, but was never completed because of the war with Sparta. The chamber to the north (left as you go in) housed a collection of paintings in classical times and then became the palace of Byzantine bishops and Frankish dukes; much of the damage of the years was repaired in 1909 –17. The outer columns of the Propylaea are Doric while the inner columns are Ionic, but though it looks like a temple this was a purely secular building – in its time the largest in Greece.

The temple to the right of the Propylaea, **Athena Nike** (Nike Apteros) was dedicated to the memory of the Athenian victories over the Persians. The goddess of Victory was normally represented as a winged figure, and a statue of Athena which stood here was wrongly believed to be a Victory deprived of her wings (to stop her from flying away). As a result, the temple is sometimes called the Wingless Victory. It is minute – only 18ft by 12ft (5½ × 4m) – but perfect, and some peoples' favourite temple. The original was knocked down by the Turks to make way for a gun battery, but the pieces were not lost and it was put together again in 1840. It was dismantled and rebuilt more correctly in 1936.

Caryatids, the Erectheum

The **Erectheum** was a confusing building for it housed three separate cults and its shape had to take account of objections to the possible desecration of the holy tomb which preceded it; in addition, it accommodated the sacred olive tree planted by Athena (not the one there now, which was planted in 1917) and the well of sea water struck by Poseidon. Only parts of it are standing today: the central temple contains the chamber of Athena Polias and the chamber of Poseidon/Erectheus; the North Portico which is an elegant porch of six Ionic columns; and the Caryatid Portico on the south side facing the Parthenon, a smaller colonnade which takes its name from the six carved figures of maidens (Caryatids) which support the roof in place of columns. The building was finished in the last days of the war with Sparta, just before total defeat, as a final act of piety. It has been reconstructed many times, and some of the columns are so eaten away by pollution that it needs further reconstruction. Get a detailed guide from the museum, and then with imagination you may see not scaffolding and iron braces, but the temple which for some artists is the finest in Greece.

The **Acropolis Museum (20)** (admission included in entrance fee to the Acropolis, but keep your ticket) contains sculptures found on the rock, mostly from the pre-Persian period. The Athens that built the Parthenon was intensely democratic, but 70 years earlier, under the Peisistratids, there was an elite in Athenian society, aristocrats – well-bred and well looked-after. It is mostly this earlier Athens which you see in the sculptures of the museum. The huge carvings from a temple pediment, representing the war between the gods and the giants, are from an earlier temple of Athena Parthenon built by Peisistratos and destroyed by the Persians. Exhibits are labelled in English but not very well; it is worth buying a guide-book at the entrance.

Herodes Atticus' theatre

Along the south slope of the Acropolis there are two ancient theatres connected by a stoa, or arcade. The **Theatre of Dionysus** (Theatron tou Dionyssou **21**), with seating, according to Plato, for 30,000, is where the plays of Sophocles and Euripides were first staged. The **Odeum of Herodes Atticus** (Theatron Irodou tou Attikou **18**) is a much smaller theatre, built in the second century AD, and now restored

and used for plays and concerts during the Athens Festival. The **Stoa of Eumenes** between the two – only a fragment now remains – was for walking and talking after performances in the theatres.

Other antiquities In the second century AD **Hadrian's Arch (28)** was erected to mark the boundary between the ancient city, the city of Theseus, and the new Roman extension, the city of Hadrian – and that is what the inscriptions on it say.

Temple of Olympian Zeus

The **Temple of Olympian Zeus** (Olympieion **29**), just beyond Hadrian's Arch, was finished by Hadrian having been started 700 years earlier under the Peisistratids; when finished it had 104 Corinthian columns, of which 15 are still standing. It was the most enormous Greek temple ever built, and when you see the great fat columns you may think it demonstrates megalomania rather than piety. Worth seeing before you go to the Acropolis – it will help you appreciate the proportions of the Parthenon.

The **Tower of the Winds** (**14**) was built as a meteorological station and public clock in the first century BC; it is an octagonal tower with each face decorated by a relief showing the wind prevailing from that direction – hence its popular name. Its official name is the Clock of Andronicus of Kyrrhos (Horologion tou Andronikos Kyrrhestes), after the astronomer who built it.

The **Roman Forum** (Romaiki Agora **15**) was begun in the days of Julius Caesar and finished under Hadrian; it was a marketplace, much smaller than the Greek Agora, and is represented now by a few standing columns.

The **Cemetery** (Kerameikos **4**) of ancient Athens is interesting now for the funeral monuments, vivid representations of family life.

'Diogenes Lantern' is the popular name for the **Monument of Lysikrates** (**22**), winner of a 'choregic' contest (singing and dancing); there must have been hundreds of such winners, who were allowed to erect a bronze tripod on a pedestal as a temporary sign of their triumph, and lucky Lysikrates, winner of a very small-scale contest, still has his memorial.

Museums

There are 15 museums in central Athens, and if you are going to make a tour of Greece, taking in antiquities and historic sites, you should take at least a quick look at the principal ones because this will give meaning and interest to what you later see on the ground. If you go back to the museums after a tour of Greece, you will notice and appreciate objects that you would have otherwise passed by. If you have a deep interest in archaeology, sculpture, art and history, you should go round each of the museums first to pick up the catalogues and study them before you visit the museum. Greece is not a world leader in the presentation and explanation of museum exhibits.

Benaki (Moussion tou Benaki **32**) This houses the private collection of a man of rich taste and richer pocket, and should be enjoyed as Mr Benaki enjoyed it – as you find it. Very good collections of objects illustrating the War of Independence, paintings, objects of fine workmanship (all periods) from the Middle East, and in the basement a display of popular costume and art through which you can try and imagine what it felt like to be Greek in the past.

Byzantine (Vyzantinon Moussion **33**)

Contains sculptures and ikons of the Byzantine period, sufficiently numerous and sufficiently well arranged to allow you to see their development over the centuries, but also to feel the unchanging tradition underneath. More interesting, perhaps, are the representations of a 5th-century Basilica, an 11th-century Greek-cross church, and a post-Byzantine church (mixture of oriental, Turkish and rococo).

Kanellopoulos (Kanellopoulos Moussion **16**) Another private, eclectic collection but on a much smaller scale than Benaki. Vases, ikons and stones from ancient buildings.

Kerameikos (Kerameikos Moussion **3**) A small museum at the ancient cemetery. It contains sculpture and, more interestingly, vases and pottery arranged in chronological order, showing the development of Greek pottery.

National Archaeological (Moussion ethnikon Archeologikon **12**) Nearly all the good finds from past excavations of ancient Greece (apart from Crete), covering the period from pre-history to the Byzantine era, are located here. The tendency now is to keep finds near the sites where they were discovered, and even to return some exhibits to their place of origin.

The centre of the museum is the Mycenaean Hall, and as soon as you enter the hall you see the golden mask. This is the mask that Schliemann found when he started digging at Mikines, after successfully excavating Troy. He proved his belief that Homer's account of the prehistoric war between Greeks and Trojans was based on fact.

Archaic sculpture is in Rooms 7–13; 'Archaic' means pre-classical – the figure of a youth is called a Kouron and of a maiden is called a Kore. Classical sculpture and grave ornaments are in Rooms 14–20; don't miss the bronze Poseidon in Room 15. Hellenistic works are in Rooms 28–30.

Vases and pottery are upstairs in the extension, the sequence of rooms (Roman numerals) being in roughly chronological order. The pottery in Room 4 has black figures, the earlier form of decoration, with the red-figure style in Room 6, representing near perfection in Greek pottery; some of the financial prosperity of Periclean Athens lay in the production of this pottery which was clearly superior to its competitors from Corinth.

National Gallery (Ethniki Pinakothiki **35**) This is a collection of paintings, and apart from four El Greco's they are mainly 19th-century.

Popular Art (Moussion Ellinikis Laikis Tehnis **27**) Handicrafts, pottery especially from Rodos, clerical robes, embroideries and costumes.

War (**34**) This was set up by the Colonels and is militaristic. It does, however, give a very good picture of Greek history up until the Second World War, as expressed through warfare. It is propaganda, but instructive, and children will love it.

Central Athens

Central Athens contains nearly all the antiquities and museums which are the first attraction for the visitor, and most of the shops and squares. This area, roughly a square mile (2½ sq km) between the Acropolis and Mt Likavitos, is small enough for you to get around on foot if you plan your expeditions with a map.

The chief **districts and squares** (*platia*) are described below.

The **Plaka** is all that is left of 19th-century Athens, spread over the north-east slopes of the Acropolis. At every turn you find a little alleyway, looking up at a different view of the Parthenon. This is the great area for *tavernas* and restaurants, with nightclubs and cinemas – nowhere pretentious or up-market. Despite the huge numbers of tourists, it remains Greek, and even on a summer's evening when you may have to hunt for a table, it attracts more Greeks than foreigners. Many tavernas have gardens, others are down steep flights of steps; when the Plaka is not too crowded, the tavernas where you still have to wait for a table are the best. When the dancing starts, it is spontaneous.

The Plaka is not just for evening eating; you can find a good, substantial breakfast here too – fried eggs and cake is a favourite. There is a fair number of cheap, 'student' hotels, and a few tourist shops. The layout is confusing, but the area is so small that by the time you have found your first destination you know your way around.

Monastiraki Square is by Monastirion Station on the electric line. The surrounding Monastiraki district is really an extension of the Plaka, but it is devoted more to shops than to entertainment. On Sunday mornings there is an open-air market in the square, the flea market, where you can take along any old junk you have and try to raise a few drax for your next meal. The narrow alley lined with open-fronted shops that runs from the south-west corner of the square (under the sign 'Flea Mar-

ket') is **Ifestou** (street). The shops here are open every day but are very crowded on Sunday mornings – the atmosphere is that of an eastern bazaar. The shops sell tools, cheap new clothes, second hand clothes, metal-work, tourist bait, footwear, tools and more tools, car parts, records and cassettes, pottery and plastic goods.

The Plaka and Monastiraki are lively and convivial, cheap and cheerful. **Kolonaki Square**, the centre of the Kolonaki district, is very 'smooth', similar to London's Mayfair. The square itself offers good cafés, and there are boutiques and rather select shops scattered throughout the residential district on the lower slopes of Mt Likavitos. **Marasli Square** is a less plush extension of Kolonaki.

Parliament Building, Sintagma Square

Sintagma Square is the centre of Athens, halfway between Likavitos and the Acropolis. Here are the more stately hotels, Parisian-style cafés, and the prestigious offices of airlines and international companies. On the east side of the square is the **Parliament Building** (Vouli **31**), the former royal palace, where there is still a ceremonial changing of the guard on Sunday mornings. *Sintagma* is Greek for constitution – the first king of modern Greece granted a constitution from the palace steps, and the square is sometimes called by the English name, Constitution Square.

Omonia Square is just 1km/½mi away from Sintagma, but is much more commercial – car rental firms, stores, travel agencies, restaurants. *Omonia* means harmony, but in this case it is usually translated as concord. **Kaningos Square** (Platia Kaningos **13**), a few steps away from Omonia (north east), is the terminus for a number of bus routes. Shops in the backstreets between Kaningos and Omonia tend to have cut-price goods.

Street names The word Street is

usually dropped; the Street of Hadrian is Odos Adrianou, but it is simply called Adrianou. However, the word for Avenue, Leoforos, is retained. Some of the better known streets of Athens are:

Panepistimiou is a one-way street from Sintagma to Omonia, with shops and insurance offices on the left and an imposing array of public buildings on the right – the **Roman Catholic Cathedral** (Aghios Dionysios **26**), and then the **Academy** (Akadimia **25**), the **University** (Panepistimion **24**) and the **National Library** (Ethniki Vivliothiki **23**). From the middle of Panepistimiou down to Omonia the street is lined with bus stops – make sure you wait at the right one. The official name of Panepistimiou is **El Venizelou**, but most people use the old name meaning university.

Stadiou, parallel to Panepistimiou, is one-way from Omonia to Sintagma. It is lined with shops and stores which are very smart at the Sintagma end, but decline rapidly towards the Omonia end.

Akadimias, formerly called Rouzvelt after the American president, is also parallel to Panepistimiou, and again full of bus stops. The side roads off Akadimias contain one-man tailoring businesses.

Athinas runs from Omonia to Monastiraki, and is a main shopping street, while the narrower and dingier **Eolou**, parallel to Athinas, has department stores. Between Eolou and Athinas, at the top end, there is a large fruit and vegetable market, and further down a covered meat and fish market

A market, central Athens

Leoforos Amalias leads from Sintagma past the **National Garden** and the **Zapio Garden** (Zappeion Exhibition Hall **30**) to Hadrian's Arch; it is a continual rush of traffic. Any turning off the side opposite the garden leads into the Plaka. **Leoforos Singrou**, which is the extension of Amalias after Hadrian's Arch, leads straight down to

the seafront at **Faliron**. Halfway along Singrou, near the Olympic Airways Office, the car rental firms congregate. The backstreets around here are full of car repair workshops. The **Planetarium** is at the southern end of Singrou.

Vassilissis Sofias is one of the most elegant streets of Athens; its north side is lined with the embassies and institutes of the fashionable Kolonaki and Marasli districts.

Patission starts as a shopping street at its junction with Omonia, containing Athens' largest department store, and then turns into small shops, flats and restaurants as you progress to the National Museum.

Athens as a whole is desperately short of **open spaces**, but in central Athens there are several hills and gardens where you can retreat for air and refreshment.

The **Acropolis** is, of course, the best known hill of Athens, but here you can feast only your eyes. The three hills adjacent to the Acropolis are green, in a Mediterranean way. First is the **Areopagus** (Areios Pagos – Hill of Mars **10**) where the supreme court of ancient Athens sat, and where St Paul preached. Higher than the Areopagus is the **Pnyka** (Hill of the Pnyx). Here is the site of the **Pnyx** (**6**) where the Athenian popular assembly met; performances of Son et Lumière are held at night on the terraced hillside. On slightly lower land to the north is the so-called Hill of the Nymphs with the **Observatory** (**5**). Highest of the three is the **Mouseion** (Hill of the Muses), officially called **Filopapou** (**11**) after a 2nd-century-AD benefactor whose monument stands on the hill to provide a viewing point for camera enthusiasts (Philopappos Monument); the wind here can be quite strong.

The highest hill is **Likavitos** which can be seen from all over the city, rising like a rock out of a sea of concrete. The municipality has managed to prevent the entire hill being used for housing, and there are many paths through its fir covered hillsides. There is an *ouzeri* halfway up. At the top (277m/910ft, nearly 122m/400ft higher than the Acropolis), there is a 19th-century chapel, next to which is a restaurant with fabulous views all over Athens. A cable car runs through a short tunnel to the top, from the end of Ploutarhou (street). (Operating until 0130 hours.)

The **National Garden** (Ethnikos Kipos) is a labyrinth of wooded paths with many shaded corners; ducks, swans and peacocks. **Areos Park** (Pe-

Mt Likavitos from the Parthenon

dion Areos) is popular for family strolls and often has a band.

Transport

Airport at Ellinikon, on the west coast about 10km/6mi from Sintagma. There are two terminals, **Ellinikon West** (Δυτικος Αεροσταθμος) for Olympic Airways internal and international flights, and **Ellinikon East** (Ανατολικος Αεροσταθμος) for other international flights. (There is a free shuttle service between the two.) Bus for the west terminal leaves from the Olympic Airways Office in Leoforos Syngrou (reached by bus 63/64 from Kaningos). Bus for the east terminal leaves from Leoforos Amalias, just off Sintagma. Duty-free shop at East terminal.

Passenger facilities at the airport are not extensive enough for the volume of summer traffic, especially when there are delays (usually caused by night flying restrictions at European destinations). There are plans to build a new airport at **Spata**, inevitably on the best agricultural land and causing rows.

Métro (Electric Train) This runs above ground from Pireas to central Athens: **Thissio** and **Monastiraki** (Monastirion Station), then underground via **Omonia** and **Viktorias** to **Attiki** Station. From there it goes above ground to **Kifissia**. The line is called the *Elektriko*. There are only two fare stages – cheap for a long journey, very cheap for a short journey. You must have a ticket to pass the barrier onto the platform.

Railway The railway station is just over 1km/½mi from Omonia as the crow flies, but there is no straight road to it. The best way to the station from Omonia is along the No. 1 trolleybus route, *ie* west along Ag. Konstandinou to Platia Karaiskaki and from there you can see the blank walls of the railway at the end of Deligiani (street). There are really two stations: **Stathmos Larissis** (Larissa **1**), larger one, for the mainline trains to Thessaly and Makedonia, and at its side **Stathmos Peloponnisos** (**2**) for trains to Korinthos and the Peloponnese. The railway buses destined for northern Greece and for the Peloponnese start out from the same stations as the trains.

Taxis A taxicab is labelled sometimes in Greek, ΤΑΞΙ, but usually in Latin characters, TAXI. (The stress is on the second syllable, taxí, not táxi which means class or classroom.) A taxi standing at a cab rank is obliged to take you; a passing taxi is not obliged to pick up a passenger. Fares are as displayed on the meter. A tip can be small change but, in any event, should not be over 10 percent.

Taxis are cheap, even by the standards of relatively poor Athenians, and used fairly freely. Past the city limits, the fare per kilometre doubles.

Buses There are 12 trolleybus routes in Athens (yellow buses) which serve only the city centre, and endless bus routes (blue buses) serving the outer suburbs. The green bus runs between Athens and Pireas every five minutes. Buses run until about 0100 hours; the green bus has a 24-hour service (hourly in the early morning). On most buses you enter at the rear and pay the conductor seated by the door; on others there is an honesty box, and everybody can see that you drop in some coins. The standard fare within the city is only 10 dr for a short journey, 15 dr for a long journey, but will soon go up. You can get on and off only at a bus stop. Bus stops are marked with the number of the service and the destination; there is no queuing at bus stops as in London, but less aggressive pushing than in New York.

You can get a list of bus services from the NTOG. Otherwise, ask at one of the turning points in the squares. Some turning points in the centre are: Platia Kaningos; Thissio Gardens; Mavromateon (street – south west corner of Areos Park); Platia Eleftherias; Leoforos Olgas (opposite the Temple of Olympian Zeus).

Buses to central Greece and southern Thessaly leave from the terminal at Tris Gefires (260 Liossion Street), reached by bus 63 or 34 from Leoforos Amalias, outside the National Garden. Buses for other provincial towns leave from the terminus at Kolokinthou (100 Kifissou Street) reached by town bus 62 from the corner of Vilara and Menandrou (streets), near Omonia.

On foot Sometimes the traffic gets choked up, but one-way streets keep it moving fast most of the time. When it is moving, you take your life in your hands if you attempt to cross except at a crossing. Many Athenians do. It is illegal for pedestrians to cross the road when the lights are against them.

Suburbs

Central Athens is visited for the antiquities and museums, maybe for the shops and flea market, and of course, for the life of the Plaka. Thereafter, most people will want to escape to one of the outer suburbs. Most of them have little to distinguish one from another, but there are some you may feel like seeing.

Faliron (Paleo, *ie* old, Faliron), at the bottom of Leoforos Syngrou (bus from Othonos, Sintagma Square), has a small beach, is the easiest to get to from the centre, and has a fair choice of undistinguished *tavernas* along the front. The racecourse is here. **Neo Faliron** last stop on the electric railway before Pireas, is by the sea but industrial.

Glifada is decidedly smart and fun-loving. Set in a small bay with a green headland, it is nearest to being the centre of the resorts of the Apollo Coast. There is a golf course, tennis courts, a sandy beach with cafés and restaurants, and a large number of *bouzouki* nightclubs; Glifada is fashionable, and not the place for a cheap night out. Bus 84 from Leoforas Olgas.

Kessariani, 5km/3mi east from the centre, is famed for its 11th-century monastery shaded by cypress and plane trees, making it an oasis of peace high in the foothills of Mt Imitos. Bus 39 from behind the university (**24**); a further 3km/1½mi on foot to the monastery.

Kifissia is a garden suburb on high ground north east of the centre, at the end of the electric railway. Roughly the equivalent of London's Hampstead, with a number of big hotels, and restaurants that have become reasonably cosmopolitan. It is well known as a desirable residential quarter, but many of the big houses in their own grounds have given way recently to the inevitable flats. The YMCA and YWCA are here. Bus from Platia Kaningos.

Kolonos, a very working class area on the 'wrong' side of the tracks, west of the railway stations. The home of Sophocles, who set his last play, *Oedipus at Colonus*, here. Blue-hazed *kaffeneinons* as in a country village, and raw wine on tap from the barrel.

Maroussi a fairly spacious area on the hills leading up to Kifissia, is a good centre for buying pottery. Paradissos Tennis Club is here.

Melissia, another version of Maroussi, further north; some friendly, unpretentious restaurants.

Patissia-Kipseli, a commercial district (north of Areos Park) with a lively market on Saturdays and Sundays. Very popular with Athenians as one of the better residential areas, with restaurants to match.

Perama (bus from Platia Eleftherias), the terminal for the Salamina ferry; there are many small shipyards.

Pireas the main port of Greece, formerly noted for its bawdy harbour front, but now very respectable, to suit the major shipping companies whose headquarters are here. The harbour – for inter-island ferries and international shipping – starts right outside the terminus of the Athens electric railway, which is next to the terminus of the Peloponnese railway. There is a noisy market – or, rather, bazaar – with every imaginable foodstuff; good restaurants and nightclubs, and *tavernas* overlooking the water; and a municipal theatre. The evening air in summer is mercifully cooler than in Athens. Zea and Tourkolimano (see below) are included in Pireas.

Psihiko is one of the smoother residential suburbs; the flats are creeping up, but there are still many comfortable (and expensive) houses in their own grounds. Very popular with foreigners and people working in the arts. Not an area to visit, but an area to stay in if you have friends here.

Singrou has a park which attracts residents who are prepared to pay for open space, and they in turn attract a reasonable standard of restaurants, tucked away in little back streets. (Don't confuse with Leoforos Singrou.)

Tourkolimano is the third harbour of Pireas, used for racing yachts. A very cheerful little bay, with bright canvas and bobbing masts, which you can watch from any of the waterside restaurants. Many fish restaurants and plenty of *bouzouki* (canned) and guitar (live) music. On Kastela Hill, overlooking the yacht basin, is the marble open air theatre where performances are held during the Athens Festival. Many offices for boat/yacht rental. Reached on foot from Neo Faliron Station on the electric railway, or by bus from Platia Klafthmonos. Tourkolimano means Turkish harbour; the Turks being out of favour, its new official name is **Mikrolimano**.

Tzitzifies, on the bay between Neo Faliron and Paleo Faliron, has a small yacht harbour and is usually very lively in the evening.

Voula by the sea is where the concrete of Athens begins to give way to the pines of Attica. There are two large beaches run by the NTOG (well equipped for beach sports) and villas are available for rent.

Vouliagmeni is the big beach for Athens, run by the NTOG; miles of golden sands with every possible facility for sea sports. There is a yacht harbour, boat club and two waterski schools in the eastern bay, and another boat club and waterski school in the western bay. There is a hotel complex, and a rather sulphurous spring which feeds a lake, now a bathing establishment reputed to be good for muscular aches. It is, as one brochure says, a 'vibrant summer resort'.

Zea is the second harbour of Pireas. It has a very pretty inner basin for small yachts, overlooked by the white houses on Zea Hill, and a long quay used by fishing boats, where you can still see fishermen mending their nets with their feet. At the end of the quay is the departure point for the hydrofoil service (Flying Dolphins) to the Saronic Islands. The naval museum is opposite the quay.

The Royal Yacht Club basin, Tourkolimano

ATTICA

The ancient land of Attica is the area now covered by the nomes of Attica and Pireas, surrounding Greater Athens. In prehistoric times the land was, reputedly, a rich grazing ground where 'men ate ox every day'; but over grazing had exhausted the soil even before Theseus was king, and throughout history it has been able to produce only vines and olives. At no great distance from Athens you can come to a landscape of rural peace that has changed little in 3000 years; most Athenians fleeing the city at weekends head for the coast, but the interior of the Attic peninsula is attractive in a dry way. One of the most memorable features of Attica is the light – the famous hard, clear light which is the essence of Greece.

No place in Attica is more than an hour by car from the city; you are well served by buses; you can plan your own tour.

On the whole, the west coast has been turned into a string of resorts (the Apollo Coast), while the east coast, with many bays and beaches, has been left to itself.

Places to Visit

Amfiaraio, with one of Greece's best preserved temples, in a wooded area on the way to Skala Oropou. (Bus from Mavromateon.)

The monastery, Dafni

Dafni The Monastery of Dafni has a notable 11th-century church inside fortified walls. There are some of the finest Byzantine mosaics in Greece – most impressive is the interior of the dome, with a painting of Christ surrounded by the prophets, against a background of pure gold. The monks left during the War of Independence, and in the grounds there is now a tourist pavilion and large campsite; in September and October the Attic Wine Festival is held here. (Bus from Platia Eleftherias.)

Elefsina (Eleusis) The ancient city was the home of a sacred cult of the classical era. Initiates underwent a revelation which they afterwards praised as an enriching personal experience, but the nature of the ceremony and revelation has remained a mystery. The site of the sanctuary of Demeter has been excavated and is open to visitors, but get a detailed guide from the museum to explain it. Modern Elefsina, spread along the old road from Athens to Korinthos, is a dusty industrial town. (Bus from Platia Eleftherias.)

Lagonissi is a summer resort on the west coast, with discos, nightclubs, restaurants and sports facilities. (Bus from Mavromateon.)

Lavrio is a port on the east coast, with sailings to certain islands in the Cyclades; shortest crossing to Kea (1¼ hrs). The wealth of classical Athens came from here, when the silver mines echoed with the groans of the slaves. Today Lavrio is a dusty village mining zinc and manganese. (Bus from Mavromateon.)

Marathonas (Marathon) is the name of a village, of the lake which supplies Athens' water, and a rather good beach. But, above all, it is the name of the battlefield where in 490 BC the Athenians first showed the Great King that free men fight harder than conscripts. A burial mound still covers the Athenian dead; there is a museum, ancient ruins (always open) and *tavernas*. Marathonas is, of course, 42km/26½mi from the Agora in Athens, setting the distance for the modern marathon race. (Bus from Platia Kaningos.)

Markopoulo is the chief village of the Messogeion Plain, the red-soiled centre of the Attic peninsula which produces the famous *retsina*. If you feel dry, you know how to quench your thirst here. (Bus from Mavromateon.)

Megara on the north shore of the Saronic Gulf (Saronikos Kolpos) was a major city of early Greece, but interesting today only for its fair held on Easter Tuesday. (Bus from Thissio Gardens.)

Nea Makri A popular, pine-backed bathing beach near Marathonas. (Bus from Mavromateon.)

Parnitha (Mt Parnes) is visited mainly for mountain climbing; there is an alpine refuge at Bafi. However, there is also a casino, restaurant and night-club at the Mt Parnes Hotel. (Bus from bottom of Alkiviadou (street); cable car up to the hotel.)

Peania is another wine-producing village of the Messogeion Plain. On the outskirts of the village is the Koutouki Cave, its stalagmites and stalactites displayed by artificial illumination. (Bus from Thissio Gardens.)

Penteli This village on Mt Penteli (Pentelikon) was the source of the marble used for the temples of the Acropolis. Iron in Pentelic marble weathers to produce the orange patina that is so noticeable on the Parthenon and Propylaea. The ancient quarries can be seen all around – they are supposed to be worked out, but Pentelic marble can still be dug out for special purposes. The area is used now as a summer campsite, with impressive views. (Bus from behind the National Archaeological Museum.)

Porto Rafti has one of the best sandy beaches on the east coast of Attica (NTOG beach), with one of the prettiest settings around a nearly circular, enclosed bay. (Bus from Mavromateon.)

Rafina is the port for some of the northern Cyclades (Andros 2½hrs) and for Evia (Karistos 1¾hrs). Good sea bathing. (Bus from Mavromateon.)

Ramnous is situated on a lovely, remote headland facing Evia. There is no development here, and it is almost the only place in Attica where you can feel really alone. There are the remains of two Doric temples – one to Themis, the other to Nemesis. (No public transport – it can be reached either by car (Athens 50km/31mi) or in about one hour's pleasant walk from Marathonas.)

Skala Oropou is a ferry port with sailings to Evia (the shortest crossing). A pleasing bay, with several *tavernas*; rather shallow. (Bus from Mavromateon.)

Sounio is a rocky cape at the end of the Attic peninsula – as you look south west across the sea, the next piece of land is Crete 250km/155mi away. The headland is crowned by the 5th-century Temple of Poseidon, of which 15 columns still stand – probably the most impressively sited of all Greek temples. At its best towards sunset, but most visited then. (Bus from Mavromateon.)

Varkiza is a resort on the Apollo Coast – golden NTOG beach, hotels, restaurants, *tavernas* – a miniature Vouliagmeni. (Bus from Mavromateon.)

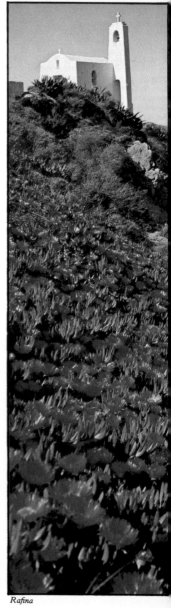

Rafina

Vravron is the site of a Temple of Artemis (5th-century BC); some of the Stoa has been re-erected. The Stoa was home to the little bears of Vravron (Brauron), the priestesses of Artemis. (Bus from Mavromateon.)

THE ARGO-SARONIC ISLANDS

The islands in the Saronic Gulf (Saronikos Kolpos) and those south of the Argolis peninsula are used by the Greeks as places to escape to from Athens, and some of them are used as holiday centres by package tour operators. On the whole, the further an island is from Athens, the more peaceful it is.

Egina (ΑΙΓΙΝΑ)   K4

(area 85 sq km/33 sq mi, pop. 12,000) Egina (Aegina) is very dry and depends for its water on wells or water ships. Despite this, it does not have too hot a summer climate. The west of the island concentrates on growing pistachio nuts, the north is pine covered, and the south offers bathing and walking. **Egina** town, which is also the port, has restaurants and *tavernas*, and a limited nightlife; it is noted for its beautiful sunsets. **Perdika** is an attractive fishing village, about 10km/6mi south of Egina

town. **Ag. Marina** is the seaside village of the island with a long sandy beach.

The Doric Temple of Aphaia (east of Egina, 11km/7mi) was built at the end of the sixth century BC. Of the original 32 columns, 15 are still standing (some re-erected in 1960), and it is thought to be one of the loveliest of the Greek temples. (Bus every 30 mins between Egina town and Ag. Marina passes the temple.)

Egina is close enough to Athens to be used by commuters, but you can easily get away from the crowds; bicycles (rented in Egina town) are useful for getting around the island.

Angistri is an islet west of Egina, with a few pine fringed beaches and some *tavernas*. There are two hotels, and a boat three times a day to Egina.

Idra (ΥΔΡΑ)   P4

(area 52 sq km/20 sq mi, pop. 2550) Idra (Hydra) is a mountainous, barren island, but its little town of **Idra**, where nearly the whole population lives, is very attractive. The town is lively, full of restaurants and shops – similar to Capri. Swimming is from the rocks; there are no beaches. There are no roads and no cars, for there is nowhere to go – Idra town is the attraction.

Idra town

Poros (ΠΟΡΟΣ)   N4

(area 21 sq km/8 sq mi, pop. 6450)
This is really two islands, connected by
a narrow strip of land. The larger island, green and lush – covered with
pines, is almost empty of people, and
offers many shingle beaches with a few
sandy beaches. The smaller island contains **Poros** town which provides hotels
and restaurants, a yacht station and a
waterskiing school, but is still peaceful.
It is very pretty, looking across to Galatas on the mainland which is almost its
mirror image. The nightlife of Poros is
simple and cheap.

(Don't confuse this island with Paros
in the Cyclades.)

Salamina (ΣΑΛΑΜΙΣ)   I4

(area 93 sq km/36 sq mi, pop. 23,100)
There are up to 70 ferries a day between
Salamina (Salamis) and Perama, which
is about 20 mins by bus from central
Athens, so the island is really an extension of the mainland. The north coast
faces the industrial shoreline of Elefsina
and is unattractive, but the south coast
(no bus) offers sandy beaches by pine
woods.

Spetses (ΣΠΕΤΣΑΙ)   Q1

(area 18 sq km/7 sq mi, pop. 3500) is a
wooded, hilly island, very popular with
families for holidays because there are
many beaches safe for children. There
are no cars, and most places outside
Spetses town are reached by water-taxi.
Spetses town offers an enormous choice

of *tavernas*, and is lively at night, but
you can easily walk out to seclusion.
There are two buses on the island. A
favourite outing is to **Ag. Anargiri** and
nearby **Ag. Paraskevi**, for beaches and
wind-surfing, with a visit to Bekiris'
Cave in the afternoon.

Communications: The ferry for the
Argo-Saronic Islands (apart from Salamina – see above) leaves from Pireas
harbour, a few minutes' walk from the
terminus of the electric railway from
Athens. The hydrofoil for Egina also
leaves from Pireas harbour, but for
Poros, Idra and Spetses it leaves from
Zea, a yacht harbour about 20 minutes'
walk from Pireas electric station. There
is a bus to Pireas from each of the
Athens airports. The hydrofoil is about
50 percent more expensive than the
ferry, but remember that people with
large trunks, goats and crates of chickens must use the ferry, not the hydrofoil. (Ferry/Hydrofoil – Egina 1¼hrs/
½hr; Idra 3hrs/1¼hrs; Poros 2½hrs/
1hr; Salamina ¼hr; Spetses 4½hrs/
2hrs.)

In Athens you can book a day's
round trip of Egina, Poros and Idra,
which allows time to look around each
island. (Booking agencies around Omonia Square.) For ferry information –
Pireas Port Authority (Tel: 4511–311).
Ferry bookings along the Pireas front or
at the electric station. For hydrofoil
information and bookings – Hydrofoil
Joint Service (Tel: 4528–994).

Poros town

THE CYCLADES

A white painted village high above the sea, reached only by donkey up a hundred stone steps from the little harbour where you fall ashore from a fishing smack; windmills, still, against the cloudless sky; and the timeless, peasant peace of a land with no riches for the 20th century to despoil. That is the picture conjured up by the words 'Greek island' and in the Cyclades it is nearest to the truth.

Some of the islands – Mikonos, Paros, Sifnos, Tinos, Ios – are prospering now from tourism, but even they have their corners where the old life continues. The remaining inhabited islands, and the small uninhabited ones, are each someone's ideal – fertile or barren, mountainous, hilly, terraced or flat; with cliffs or beaches, woods, living monastery or haunting ruin.

The Cyclades are the peaks of a submerged mountain range that is a southeast extension of the slope of Attica. The islands project from the sea bed (180m/600ft below) in a rough circle around the holy isle of Dilos (Delos) – hence the name, the Cyclades, the encircling isles.

These islands have been inhabited since 6000 BC, or maybe earlier; in prehistoric times they portrayed their fertility goddess in the sculpted figurines now loved by collectors for their simple purity. Cycladic culture grew at the same time as the Minoan culture in Crete, and then came the Hellenes. The islands kept out of the worst troubles of classical Greece, and even the Turkish oppression was fairly lightly felt. Pirates were the worst problem, which is why most towns grew up on the hills, not by the sea.

The windmills are there for the wind, and in July and August that wind – the Meltemi – can whip up very disagreeable seas, sufficient on occasion to interrupt the ferry; mercifully the Meltemi also keeps temperatures down. Shortage of water is acute on some of the islands, one of the causes of depopulation since the turn of the century.

The larger Cycladic islands can be reached by daily ferry from Pireas (about eight lines) or from Rafina, east of Athens (one regular line); the smaller islands are linked by ferry to their larger neighbours. Tours of the islands also run from Pireas. Small boats for a day's outing can be rented informally on many islands – enquire at a *taverna* – or, with better insurance but higher cost, from a broker at Siros, Mikonos or Pireas. For the not-so-poor, yachts can be rented at Pireas (many brokers, see page 26). Airports at Mikonos and Thira (Santorini) with connections to Athens. The island bus is replacing the donkey on all the larger islands, but the donkeys are still there for work as well as play.

Amorgos (ΑΜΟΡΓΟΣ)   G10

(area 134 sq km/52 sq mi, pop. 2000)
An unexploited island with over 160km/100mi of lonely beaches and towering cliffs. About an hour's hike above the port of **Katapola** is the ruined city of **Minoa** on Mt Profitis Ilias. In the south is the ancient city of **Arkessini** near the modern village of **Kastri**, where there are even more extensive ruins. At the eastern end of the island, the little village of **Egiali** (remains of Helleno-Roman baths) is a modest resort – best reached by caique from Katapola. Undoubtedly the best excursion of all is the ride by bus from Katapola across the mountains, through the capital **Amorgos**, up to the huge **Hozoviotissa** fortress/monastery – an eagle's nest set against the cliff. It contains precious manuscripts and ikons, one in particular of the Virgin.

There is a yacht supply station at Katapola but there is only one road serving the island, and transport to the many antiquities is somewhat limited. There are only simple hotels, and rooms to rent. Water is restricted to supplies from a few springs and wells so use it sparingly. A number of islets lie between Amorgos and Naxos – ideal for lovers of remoteness prepared to live and sleep rough – but they are very poor.

Communications: In summer, daily boat from Naxos; in winter, mail caique two

or three times weekly. Infrequent links during the summer with Ios and Thira (Santorini), Rodos, Kos, Kalimnos, Folegandros and Pireas (11½hrs).

Festivals: July 26 at Arkessini, August 15 – feast of Panaghia Exochoriani, November 21 at Hozoviotissa monastery.

The tradition of Amorgos festivals is that you bring a dish and eat free – the price the villagers pay for the struggle of their guests to get there; but we can't promise that this custom will survive easy mass travel.

Andros (ΑΝΔΡΟΣ)   A6

(area 380 sq km/140 sq mi, pop. 11,000) Andros is one of the largest and best wooded islands of the Cyclades, famed for sailors and shipowners who built large mansions here. It is popular with Greeks in July and August as a holiday island. The only antiquarian interest is the unexplored site of **Paleopoli**, the ancient capital, with the remains of the acropolis, temples, theatre and stadium.

There are some small hotels, good swimming beaches and plenty of locally popular eating places, but only at **Batsi** on the west coast is there any real tourist development; sandy beach, disco, villas and hotels. **Andros** town has a yacht supply station and there is a good bus service linking the island villages. The Sariza mineral water springs are close by, and south of the town is **Kamara** where there is excellent diving, though the beaches can be very windy.

From **Lathinou** village near **Aladino** there is a two-hour donkey ride to **Panahrando** monastery, walled like a fortress in the mountains and containing many saintly relics.

Communications: Daily ferry from Rafina (2½hrs), connected by same line to Tinos, Mikonos and Siros. Separated from Evia by the dangerous Doro Passage.

Festivals: Theoskepasti – 15 days before Easter. June 19, Analapsis.

Dilos (ΔΗΛΟΣ)   D7

(area 5 sq km/2 sq mi, almost uninhabited apart from archaeologists) Dilos (Delos) is reached by a regular caique service from Mikonos across 12 nautical miles of open sea. The crossing can be unpleasant and cold in rough seas, even in August. Dilos was the religious centre of the Aegean in 1000 years BC with a teeming population; later it had an oracle second only to that of Delfi.

The archaeological discoveries cover the entire island and even run under the sea. They are well worth an extended visit though they can be seen in four hours. The maritime and commercial city, docks, harbour and warehouses have all been unearthed, and the streets of the 3rd-century BC town are to be compared with those at Pompei. This is an island for the antiquarian to savour, with a vast array of temples, statues, theatres and other remains. The huge white marble lion statues are a symbol of the Cyclades – it is an island frozen in time.

There is a tourist pavilion clearly explaining the antiquities (restaurant and bar). Camping is allowed and there is one hotel.

Communications: Caique from Mikonos daily – too many tourists take the round trip and are back in Mikonos for lunch.

Ios (ΙΟΣ)   G7

(area 105 sq km/40 sq mi, pop 1270) A bare, hilly island believed to be the resting place of Homer; named after the Ionians who originally colonized it. It has many fine sandy beaches edged with *tavernas*, no metalled roads and an incredible 400 churches or chapels dotted amongst the hills and terraced pastures.

The loveliest beach is at **Manganari** but it is very popular with young, guitar-playing travellers with too little money to please the locals, and often noisy at night with its more affluent package tourists. There is a yacht supply station at the port of **Ormos** and **Ios** town (½mi inland) is a fine old Cycladic town with 12 remaining windmills.

Water is a great problem on Ios and so is sanitation! It is very hot and exposed.

Communications: Daily in summer with Thira (Santorini), Paros, Mikonos, Pireas. Less often with most of the other main Cyclades, and with Iraklio (Crete) once weekly. Out of season, connections are erratic and liable to change – enquire at Pireas.

Festivals: June 24 St Barbara church fête, August 28 – big festival at St Ioannes Kalamos.

Kea (KEA)   C3

(area 121 sq km/46 sq mi, pop. 1500) Only 40km/25mi from the coast of Attica, Kea (Tzia) is a rugged, rocky island with wooded valleys, many secluded inlets and beaches and few commercial attractions. There are one or two hotels at the southern end of the island; many of the restaurants have live music.

White painted **Korissia** is the main port, connected by bus to the minute capital, **Kea**, high above the sea. There is some agreeable archaeological pottering to be done amongst the ruins of **Poiessa**, ancient Karthea, or at the former Ag. Marina monastery (near **Pisses**) built around the finest Hellenic tower in Greece.

Communications: Daily ferry from Lavrio in winter, twice daily in summer (1¼ hrs). Ferry once a week from Kithnos and Pireas. Ferries should be checked for unannounced changes in date and place of departure.

Kimolos (ΚΙΜΩΛΟΣ)   G4

(barely 8km/5mi across, pop. 1000) Kimolos was once a notorious pirates' nest and is now a barren, white island with a variety of interesting rock formations. It has one small cobbled village, **Kimolos**, 2km/1mi from its little harbour, **Psathi**, and is best noted for the production of fuller's earth. Springs and lush growth at **Profitis Ilias**; many caves. Accommodation tends to be very limited – unless you prefer to sleep on the beach.

Communications: Ferry twice weekly with Pireas (6hrs), Serifos, Kithnos. Caique twice daily from Apolonia (Milos).

Festivals: July 20, July 27, August 4, August 27, November 21.

Specialities: Dark red Mavriti wine, apricots and honey.

Kithnos (ΚΥΘΝΟΣ)   D4

(area 86 sq km/33 sq mi, pop. 1500) Kithnos is a flat, barren place formerly infested with snakes and wild animals. The hot springs bubbling from the deep red rocks around **Loutra** are good for eczema, gout and sciatica. Pleasant walks will take you to see Byzantine ruins, wall paintings, ikons and the many caves.

There are some good beaches, a few small hotels and a new holiday village, but most visitors to Kithnos sleep under the stars. Lively traditional festivals in national costume take place in many villages.

Communications: Ferry six times weekly with Pireas (4 hrs); four weekly with Lavrio (3½ hrs); Serifos, Milos, Siros and Thira (Santorini) very occasionally.

Festivals: August 15 Panaghia Kakala.

Mikonos (ΜΥΚΟΝΟΣ)   C7

(area 60 sq km/23 sq mi, pop. 4000)
Mikonos, like St Tropez, is not for the
puritanical – anything goes and, usually, most of it does! This island is *not* for
a 'family' holiday.

Nearly all the population congregates
in the blinding white harbour town of
Mikonos; also the first place to attract
tourists, with its cubist, whitewashed
houses in typical Cycladic style. Its
maze of streets, constructed originally
to confuse pirates, is now top-heavy
with boutiques and tourist paraphern-
alia, but consequently is bursting with
cosmopolitan life and colour.

Prices are high – cheapest food is
found by the square. There are plenty
of discotheques, hotels (often full),
tourist complexes and rooms to let in
private houses. Remember that if you
have a quiet hotel away from the noise
of the town, you may have trouble
finding public transport in for evening
entertainment!

Mikonos town

This is the snap-happy tourist's
dream. Only one of the town's round-
thatched windmills still works but Pet-
ros II, the pink pelican mascot, swims
in the harbour and calls in at the *tavernas*; there are green pepper trees and
dozens of delightful churches built by
wealthy fishing families. There is an
airport and a yacht supply station in the
harbour where boats may be rented.
The youth hostel closes in September.

During July and August the island is
very crowded and the many beautiful
beaches are decorated with less beautiful nude sunbathers of both sexes.
Some beaches are accessible by car but
many lonely coves can be reached on
foot.

At **Alefkandra** a row of lovely old
houses is washed by the sea; there is a
drive across the island to **Ano Mera**
where there is a little monastery, should
you feel like a break from the sea. Taxis
or mini-motors may be rented in the
main square of Mikonos (fixed charges
displayed).

Communications: Flight from Athens at
least once a day. Ferry from Pireas
three times daily (5½–7½ hrs); three
times weekly ferries run from Mikonos
to Kalimnos, Kos and Rodos. There is
a day trip to Dilos.
Festivals: Life on Mikonos appears to
be one long festival.

Milos (ΜΗΛΟΣ)   G4

(area 160 sq km/62 sq mi, pop. 4500)
Milos was a centre of the Bronze Age
civilization that flourished in the Cyclades at the same time as the Minoan
culture in Crete, and was also important
during Mycenaean and classical times.
It is perhaps best known as the original
home of the *Venus de Milo*, discovered
in the 19th century and forcibly removed to the Louvre in Paris.

The island has an indented, whiteish
volcanic coastline and a huge natural
harbour which nearly divides it in two.
A series of rippling hills rises up behind
the harbour, much gashed by mining
activities through the centuries.

Although Milos is not so obviously
beautiful as some of the other islands, it
has a lot to offer. There are the dimly-lit
Roman catacombs at **Milos** (Plaka), the
old capital, reputed to be the best
preserved of all the early Christian
monuments in the world; the rainbow-
coloured, rock-fringed beaches near the
site of ancient **Zefiria**; and the remains
of the three successive prehistoric cities
near **Phylakope**.

There are still some isolated beaches
at Agios Dimitrios, Voudia Bay, Man-
drakia, and at Ahivalolimni (renowned
for seafood). To the north west by boat
from **Apolonia**, there are some curious
volcanic islands known as Glaronisia
(gull islands) where there are remarkable caves and crystalline rocks. On the
uninhabited island of **Andimilos** it is
possible to hunt wild goat.
Communications: Ferry weekly in summer with Ios and Thira (Santorini);
daily with Pireas (8½ hrs), Sifnos, Serifos. Less frequently with Kimolos and
Kithnos.
Festivals: May 7 and September 25 Ag.
Ioannes Theologos at Chalaka, June 20
and October 31, July 17 Ag. Marina,
July 19 Profitis Ilias on the mountain,
July 25 Ag. Paraskevi at Apolonia, July
26 Ag. Pantelemonos at the Chora,
August 5 Sotiris at Paraskopou, August
14 at the Chora, August 28 at Ioannes
Prodromou.

Naxos (ΝΑΞΟΣ)   E8

(area 448 sq km/173 sq mi, pop. 14,200)
The largest and most beautiful of the

Cyclades, beloved of Lord Byron, this is where the god of wine, Dionysus, lived and where Theseus abandoned Ariadne.

The mountain range which runs from north to south is divided by well watered valleys, luxuriant in groves of olive, orange, lemon and pomegranate. Mt Zeus (997m/3280ft) is the highest summit in the Cyclades.

The town of **Naxos** itself, founded largely by Venetian dukes in the Middle Ages, has been surprisingly sidestepped by visitors. Yet it has a personality all of its own with a labyrinth of steep, narrow lanes and alleys which have a rather mysterious Venetian atmosphere. The remains of the Mycenaean settlement are at **Grotta**, just north of the town; and the entrance of the Temple of Apollo can be seen on the nearby islet of **Palatia**, reached by a causeway. There is a yacht supply station in the harbour, and a youth hostel.

The island can cater for a wide range of interests: there is excellent folk art, dancing and good swimming beaches, but it is also delightful for mountain walking. Rented scooters or buses will take visitors to the many historic and classical sites at **Halki, Apiranthos** and **Filotio** (Cave of Zeus), and to Byzantine churches and mediaeval fortresses.

Communications: Ferries daily from Pireas (7 hrs). In summer, caique daily to Amorgos and frequent connections with Paros, Ios, Thira (Santorini), Siros, Tinos. Twice weekly with Rodos, Kos, Kalimnos. Tourist boat daily to Mikonos.

Festivals: On Naxos locals improvise verse – an ancient custom. There are many festivals, the most important being May 20 and July 17 at Koronos, July 1 at Sangri, July 14 at Naxos, August 15 at Filotio, August 23 at Tripodes, August 23 at Kinidaros, August 29 at Apolonas and Apiranthos.

Specialities: Naxian white wine, honey and a liqueur called *citron* distilled from lemons.

Paros *(ΠΑΡΟΣ)*   E7

(area 209 sq km/81 sq mi, pop. 7000)
The marble isle, the quarries of Paros once provided the translucent white stone for the Temple of Solomon. From the sea, the welcoming white buildings of **Paros** town (Parikia) straggle along the waterfront, broken by blue domes and windmills, set amongst olive groves and orchards.

The gentle daily routine of wandering sheep, goats, oxen and asses gives Paros the timeless, ageless sounds and smells

Paros town

of a land where it is always afternoon.

Paros has been inhabited since the 7th century BC and has fairly happily come to terms with its tourist visitors today. There are good hotels everywhere, shops, fishing opportunities and reasonable beaches which justify more than a day's visit. It is possible to see nuns weaving at the St Theodoron Convent (men not allowed), or monks painting ikons at the Monastery Longovarda (women not allowed) – turn right off the road to **Naoussa**, just out of Paros. You can visit the Petaloudhes sanctuary where in summer the trees and creepers are covered by clouds of reddish gold butterflies. There are many richly painted churches; visit the Byzantine church of Ekatontapyliani (Our Lady of 100 Gates) at Parikia – perhaps the most beautiful of the Orthodox churches. In Parikia it is possible to rent a car, bike or mule.

From Paros a caique ferries visitors to the tiny islet of **Andiparos** (pop. 540) where you may rent mules to visit the well-lit stalagtite caverns or simply swim on deserted beaches. There is a hotel on Andiparos and a few restaurants.

Communications: Ferries per week in summer: 12 with Naxos, 20 with Pireas

Sunset, Santorini

(6½ hrs), 4 with Crete and Mikonos, 11 with Ios, 7 with Siros, 3 with Leros, Kos, Kalimnos and Ródos, 9 with Thira, 2 with Amorgos and Anafi, 1 with Donoussa. Daily to Andiparos.

Festivals: 40 days after Easter at Riso Iwadi, April 23 at Angeria, May 21 at Parikia, June 24 Prodomos, July 1 at the monastery, August 15 at Parikia, August 23 at Naoussa, November 9 at Parikia.

Santorini (ΣANTOPINH)   I8

(area 76 sq km/29 sq mi, pop. 6400) Santorini (also known as Thira, Thera, Fira) is by far the most extraordinary

The track to Skala Thira

island in the Aegean. It is here that archaeologists believe they have found Metropolis, the capital of the lost continent of Atlantis. Recent excavations have uncovered the remains of a city of some 30,000 inhabitants, buried, as at Pompei (Italy), beneath lava.

Santorini was a huge volcano, which rose from the sea in prehistoric times. Its explosion in about 1450 BC not only destroyed the cities of Santorini but created a tidal wave which devastated Crete and the Minoan empire. Today, where the core of the volcano sank there is a huge lagoon surrounded by a weirdly coloured half-moon of precipitous cliffs. In the middle of this lagoon are a number of tiny active volcanic islands.

It is far from beautiful in the accepted sense, with its cliffs and the long black beaches on the east coast, but this is an island of continual surprises. There is the capital, **Thira**, perched on the edge of a striped cliff plunging 274m/900ft to the sea; there are the excavated, ash-preserved remains of ancient **Akrotiri** where shops, houses and palaces are explorable and where there are frescos finer than those of Herculaneum (near Pompei); and probably the most extraordinary trip of all is by boat to the steaming craters of **Nea Kaimene**. Buses on Santorini are irregular and mules are not necessarily less expensive than taking a taxi.

There are two ports. **Ia** (or Oia), 10km/6mi north of Thira, is where the domestic ferry calls. Larger ships, and sometimes the ferry, anchor offshore, below Thira at Skala Thira, and passengers are carried to the town by mule up a steep, zigzagging paved track. In Thira there are many white domed chapels, a museum, lots of souvenir shops and a small carpet-weaving workshop hanging on the edge of a precipice (near the cathedral).

In season (September) visitors may tread the grapes – and taste the wine! The island is not short of *tavernas* and there are some reasonable hotels and a youth hostel. **Monolithos**, with the closest beach to Thira, is used for camping.

Ancient Thira is about 20km/12mi from the modern town (above **Kamari**). It was the Dorian settlement and has the remains of their acropolis, together with the excavations of a number of Hellenistic houses.

Communications: Airport. Frequent ferries to Iraklio (Crete) Naxos, Ios, Mikonos and Pireas (12 hrs).

Festivals: July 19–20 Profitis Ilias, August 15 Mesa Goria, September 1 at Thira (Ag. Artenian), October 26 Karterado.

Serifos (ΣΕΡΙΦΟΣ)   E4

(area 65 sq km/25 sq mi, pop. 1100) The island where Perseus used Medusa's head to turn King Polydeuces to stone. Like Kithnos it is rocky and barren, dominated by towering cliffs and mountains which are divided by two fertile valleys. The cliffs are softened in summer by the profusion of indigenous pinks.

Boats land at **Livadi** and visitors climb or ride by bus, up the precipitous, terraced rock past well-tended vegetable gardens to the capital, **Serifos** (Hora), 1½km/1mi above. The white village is overlooked by a row of circling windmills. This is not an island for easy swimming as beaches are remote and mostly accessible only on foot – worth the effort if you can make it. There is a fine beach at Psili Ammos. You will find dancing and much enthusiastic lute and violin music in the villages if you chance on a wedding or a religious festival. Accommodation is limited to a few small hotels and rooms in private houses.

Communications: Ferry daily with Pireas (5 hrs), Kithnos, Milos, Sifnos. Twice weekly with Ios and Thira (Santorini).

Festivals: Fava beans are the speciality of Serifos festivals. July 27 at Livadi, August 7–17 different village each day, August 15 Panayia and September 7 at Livadi.

Sifnos (ΣΙΦΝΟΣ)   F5

(area 89 sq km/34 sq mi, pop. 2400) As rich in architecture, churches, craftsmanship and local colour as it once was in gold and silver. Sifnos (once Meropia) is a beautiful, mountainous island where mules and white-stoned monasteries offer the traveller transport and shelter. The finest olive oil in the Cyclades is made here and the standard of food is better than on most of the islands. There are some new tourist hotels offering good accommodation.

Ships arrive between high cliffs in the bay of **Kamares**. The visitors are taken ashore by motorboat and then go by bus up steep cliffs to the capital, **Apolonia** (20 mins away). Here, flat-roofed white houses rise in an amphitheatre on three terraced hills.

There are nearly 40 classical towers dotted around the island, lovely walks and good bathing. Kamares with its shaded waterfront has reasonable hotel accommodation and some excellent pottery workshops. The tourist centre is

Platis Gialos with its fine beach, and the village of Artemonas is renowned for nightlife and *tavernas.*
Communications: Ferry daily with Pireas (5½ hrs), Serifos, Milos, five weekly with Paros, two weekly with Ios, Thira (Santorini). Frequent to Kithnos.
Festivals: July 20 near Kamares, August 29 in Vathi, September 1 near Kamares.

Sikinos and Folegandros   G6

(ΣΙΚΙΝΟΣ and ΦΟΛΕΓΑΝΔΡΟΣ)
(Sikinos, area 40 sq km/15 sq mi, pop. 330. Folegandros, area 36 sq km/14 sq mi, is the smallest of the inhabited Cyclades; pop. 695.) These are probably the least visited of the Cyclades but, like Amorgos, have some of the finest cliff scenery in Greece. Sikinos is fertile with figs, olives and vines but Folegandros is rocky and barren. Neither has much tourist standard accommodation, though it is possible to find a homely bed for the night. There are caves on Folegandros, game birds on Sikinos.
Communications: Folegandros, ferry four times weekly from Pireas (12 hrs). Weekly with Rodos, Kos, Kalimnos, Astipalea and Amorgos. Caique to Sikinos. Sikinos, ferry three times weekly from Pireas (10½ hrs).
Festivals: August 15, and at Easter when ikons are paraded and boat trips made round the island.

Siros (ΣΥΡΟΣ)   D6

(area 86 sq km/33 sq mi, pop. 18,648). The administrative capital of the Cyclades, and substantial shipbuilding centre. Siros is a pleasant, scenically unspectacular island whose main town **Ermoupoli** has many 19th-century buildings and a life of its own. It is the home of Greek Roman Catholicism. The port is usually busy with cargo ships and the harbour is lined with animated cafés, *tavernas* and shops, fish markets and caiques. This is a good place to see Greece minding its own business, and to watch the modern Greek world go by.
Possidonia and **Finikas** are both excellent holiday centres and **Ano Siros**, high on a hill crowned by the Roman Catholic Cathedral, is a mediaeval delight with arched, narrow alleys and high walls. North of Ano Siros is the hill of Vrontado, the Orthodox quarter.
Communications: Ferry daily with Pireas (4½ hrs), two weekly with Ikaria and Samos, frequently to Paros, Tinos, Mikonos, Ios, Naxos, Thira (Santorini). Daily boat for Rafina via Andros

and Tinos (5 hrs).
Festivals: Last Sunday in May, finding the ikon at Ag. Dimitriou. September 24 Orthodox and Catholic celebration at Faneromeni, October 26 Ag. Dimitriou, December 6 in Ermoupoli.
Specialities: *Ioukoumi*, the Greek version of Turkish delight.

Tinos (ΤΗΝΟΣ)   C7

(area 195 sq km/75 sq mi, pop. 8300). Holy Tinos, whose northerly tip almost touches Andros, has many amenities for tourists. It even has a luxury beach hotel north of the capital, **Tinos**, and plenty of evening life. It is a place of pilgrimage – the Lourdes of the Aegean – rich in religious attractions. The white marble Panagia Evangelistria Church houses a miraculous ikon with great healing powers; it can hardly be seen for gold, diamonds and pearls!
The island is carefully cultivated and throughout its mountainous heart is dotted with white villages. Everywhere are towered dovecotes. There are lovely walks and a good bus service to remote coves such as Xera and Porto. There is a yacht supply station in the port at Tinos.
Communications: Ferry daily from Pireas (5½ hrs) and Rafina (4½ hrs) via Andros; daily to Mikonos, Siros, twice weekly to Leros, Patmos, Kalimnos, Rodos, Kos, Ikaria, Samos; more often with Naxos, Paros.
Festivals: January 19 at Ktikades, March 25 at Kardiani, August 15 at Panagia Evangelistria, August 29 at Komi, October 20 at Falatados, October 26 at Tinos, and December 21 at Tripotamus.

Minor Cycladic Islands

Donoussa Typical Cycladic. (**E9**)
Iraklia An archaeologists' paradise. Ruins, graves and statues – largely unexcavated. (**F8**)
Koufonissi A fishing shelter with a few inhabitants. (**F9**)
Shinoussa Minute; two small fishing settlements. (**F8**)
These islands, close together, can be reached by ferry from Pireas or Naxos. Three ferries per week to Donoussa, Koufonissi and Shinoussa.
Anafi A few inhabitants – reputed to wear local costume. Typical Cycladic. Reached by occasional ferry from Thira (Santorini). Sunken inland city at Katellimatsa. (**I9**)
Astipalea Belongs administratively to the Dodecanese, though it is nearer to the Cyclades both in spirit and in distance. See page 113.

THE DODECANESE

Off the south-west coast of Asia Minor lie the Dodecanese, meaning the '12 islands' (there are actually 14 of them). They have been occupied in turn by Minoans, Achaeans, Dorians, Egyptians, Romans, Byzantines, Crusaders and Turks. In 1912 the Italians took 'temporary' possession of the islands which were united to the Greek kingdom only in 1947. Since then the Dodecanese, with their lovely weather, have become increasingly popular as all-year-round holiday centres. Only Rodos and Kos have become well known to tourists but each of the islands has a fascinating personality of its own.

Astipalea (ΑΣΤΥΠΑΛΑΙΑ)   I2
(area 96 sq km/36 sq mi, pop.1200) The westernmost island of the Dodecanese, Astipalea is the most Cycladic in character. It has one fertile valley and a rocky indented coastline, with an abundance of fish in the many sheltered bays. Inland the hills rise to 482m/1581ft. Elaborate national costume is worn in many of the villages.
   Astipalea, the capital, is a growing port in the shadow of a Venetian castle. There are two beaches just outside the town – one unofficially 'nude'. There is a bus to the villages of **Analipsi** and **Vathi**.
Communications: Ferry twice weekly Pireas (13 hrs), Amorgos, Kos, Rodos, Kalimnos.
Festivals: August 15 Panayia Portaitissa.

Halki (ΧΑΛΚΗ)   K7
(area 29 sq km/11 sq mi, pop. 360) The people of Halki are 'shy of strangers', for the island is not visited much by tourists. The interior is bare and marshy, and there are no springs and few wells. Apart from **Halki** town there is only one other village which is almost abandoned (**Horio**). Formerly a copper-mining centre, the island's only occupation today is fishing. If you like solitude – this is your island!
Communications: Ferry twice weekly with Rodos, Ag. Nikolaos and Sitia (Crete), Karpathos, once weekly with Pireas (30 hrs).
Festivals: August 29 St John.

Kalimnos (ΚΑΛΥΜΝΟΣ)   G4
(area 109 sq km/42 sq mi, pop. 13,000)

Kalimnos is the only Greek island where the people still practise the art of sponge diving. The fleet leaves a week after Easter for four months, and its departure and its return are occasions for great festivity. The last night before the fleet leaves is known as *Ipnos tis Agapis*, the Sleep of Love. There is a school for sponge divers in Pothia, the main town.
   Kalimnos is a peaceful island with high cliffs and barren mountains, rising to 700m/2300ft. There are sandy coves everywhere and unforgettable sunsets.
   Inland roads are variable, but taxis can be hired (no buses) for exploring the tangerine and lemon groves of the south, or the eerie castle at **Horio** 2km/1½mi above Pothia. South of Pothia is the ruined Castle of the Knights. The northern peninsula of **Arginonda** is ideal for rugged, lonely hikes. **Kalimnos** town (Pothia) is very lively in autumn and winter when the sponge divers are home; less so in summer. It is an attractive town, built like an amphitheatre overlooking the bay. Many shops sell sponges. Try the two hour sea trip to the Cave of Zeus (stalactites and stalagmites) on the south-west coast.
Communications: Ferry twice weekly with Leros, three times weekly Kos and Patmos, four times weekly Rodos, eight times weekly Pireas (14-19 hrs). Weekly to Mikonos, and some of the lesser Dodecanese.
Festivals: The week after Easter – The Iprogros, July 27 Ag. Panteleimon.

Karpathos (ΚΑΡΠΑΘΟΣ)   N5
(area 285 sq km/110 sq mi, pop. 5000) The people of lonely Karpathos play their own special music, fast and furious, on the three-stringed lyre and goatskin bagpipes (*tsabouma*). Their

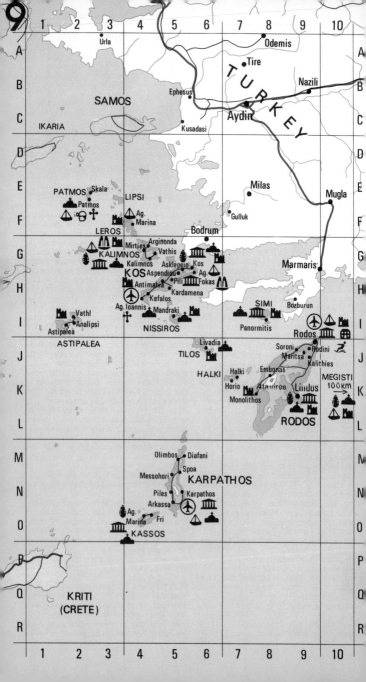

dances are extremely hard to learn.

The chief port and capital is **Karpathos** (Pigadia) in the fertile south, green with gardens and citrus trees. The centre of the island is reached by mule track to windy **Spoa**, below Mt Kalilimni (1215m/3986ft).

The isolated north is most easily accessible by boat from Pigadia to **Diafani**. From here a new road runs up to the astonishing village of Olimbos – 300 years behind the rest of the island. Traditional costume is worn as everyday, working dress and the unintelligible dialect has many Doric words.

Communications: Flight twice weekly from Rodos. Ferry twice weekly from Rodos, Halki, Kassos, Sitia and Ag. Nikolaos (Crete), Thira (Santorini), three times weekly Pireas (26 hrs).

Festivals: March 25 Evangelismos at Pigadia, July 19-20 Ag. Panteleimonis, August 15 at Olimbos, August 29 in the Church-in-the-Cave (Ag. Ioannes Vorgunda) near Olimbos, September 8 Tis Panayias at Messohori.

Kassos (ΚΑΣΟΣ)   O4
(area 65 sq km/25 sq mi, pop. 1350) This southernmost island is the most remote and difficult to land on. The coast is rocky, with caves and tiny beaches, and if the sea is rough ships won't enter the little port of **Fri**. Passengers then have to go ashore in a caique, taking about an hour. The mountains are formidable, the climate superb. There are two hotels.

Communications: Ferry twice weekly with Rodos, Halki, Karpathos (Pigadia and Diafani), Sitia and Ag. Nikolaos (Crete), Thira (Santorini), four weekly with Pireas (23 hrs).

Festivals: April 23 Ag. Georgios, July 7 at Fri, August 14 at Ag. Marina.

Kos (ΚΩΣ)   H5
(area 282 sq km/109 sq mi, pop. 17,000) A 'floating garden' surrounded by long, sandy beaches, Kos is an extremely popular holiday island – the poor man's Rodos. It is very crowded in summer although there is usually somewhere to escape to. Kos has always been a wealthy island, trading both in precious goods and in ideas. Hippocrates was born here in 460 BC – his medical school was known as the best in Greece, and laid the foundations of modern medicine.

The buildings of **Kos** town are eclipsed by its exotic profusion of trees, flowers and orchards. The best known export is perhaps Cos lettuce. There is a museum containing some fine statues including one of Hippocrates himself which was found with other statues after the 1933 earthquake. (Open 0900 to 1300, 1600 to 1800, closed Sunday.) Kos harbour has a yacht supply station, and there are two shingle beaches one shaded with tamarisk. If Kos itself is full, you may try the overspill village **Kefalos** at the other end of the island for accommodation.

Hire bikes to see the Asklepeio, one of the most sacred shrines of Asclepius, a god of healing (4km/2½mi west of Kos). There is a modern healing centre at Ag. Fokas on the south coast.

Although there is a mountain range – rising to Mt Oromedon (847m/2780ft) – running through the south of the island, for the most part, bikes or scooters are the best way of seeing the sights. There is the Byzantine church of the Virgin Mary near **Pili**, supposedly containing the bones of the 12 apostles; the château at **Antimahia**, built by the Knights of St John; and the apparently endless beaches of **Kardamena** where chickens and donkeys sunbathe on the sand.

Communications: Daily flights from Athens (50 mins). Ferry daily with Rodos, four times weekly Patmos, Leros, three times weekly with Nissiros, Samos, Mikonos, twice weekly Thessaloniki, Ikaria and several of the Dodecanese, eight times weekly Pireas (15 hrs). Irregular excursions to nearby Bodrum (Turkey), ancient Halicarnassus.

Festivals: March 25 Evangelismos at Aspendiu, April 23 Ag. Georgios at Pili, July 29 Agavastori at Antimahia, August 15 Panayias at Kardamena, August 29 Ag. Ioannes Kefalos, November 21 Isodia Tis Panayias, December 6 at Mikoleas (suburb of Kos).

Megisti (ΜΕΓΙΣΤΙ)
(area 9 sq km/3½ sq mi, pop. 270) The smallest of the Dodecanese, retirement home of wealthy émigrés, Megisti (Kastelorizo) is hilly with a precipitous coast and few beaches. Yet there is a lively folk tradition and interesting remains. The Parasta (blue grotto, like the Blue Grotto of Capri) is 30 mins by sea from the little town of **Megisti**.

Communications: Ferry twice weekly from Rodos.

Festivals: March 21, local fair.

Patmos (ΠΑΤΜΟΣ)   E2
(area 40 sq km/15 sq mi, pop. 2500) This is where St John the Divine wrote the Book of Revelation, having been banished from Ephesus. It is an irregu-

lar island of volcanic masses and little vegetation; its water is supplied by one of the largest desalination plants in the world at **Skala**.

Patmos town is scattered round the foot of a hill crowned by the monastery of Ag. Ioannes Theologos (St John) one of the richest of the Greek Orthodox churches. Inside there are beautiful frescos, gold and marble, and one of the most important monastic treasuries in Greece, including a superb library of the scriptures. Easter is an impressive time to see the monastery. Remember – no shorts, and skirts for women.

The monastery apart, Patmos is rather like a Cycladic island – peaceful, whitewashed houses, rather brown and bare, with many good beaches and *tavernas*.

Communications: Ferry daily with Samos, four times weekly Kalimnos, Leros, Kos, Rodos, six times weekly Pireas (10 hrs), twice weekly certain other Aegean islands, weekly Naxos, Kavala, Thessaloniki.

Rodos (ΡΟΔΟΣ)   K8

(area 1400 sq km/540 sq mi, pop. 66,000) Rodos (Rhodes) is the largest of the Dodecanese, the 'rose island', the 'butterfly island', the 'island of eternal summer'. It is richer in flora and fauna than any of the other islands in this group. The mountain-tops are covered in aromatic plants – lavender, sage, marjoram and styrax; and deer, foxes, hares and badgers, live in the wild, watched by vultures. There is even a species of large lizard – the Rhodes dragon – which grows up to 14 inches long (36cm).

This is by far the most popular of the Dodecanese, but with good reason. There are plenty of attractions – a casi-no, a golf course, a wine festival from July to early September, a festival of drama in the ancient theatre, it is a duty-free port, and there are many ancient and mediaeval sites to visit. It has a cosmopolitan main town (Rodos), a quaint second town (Lindos), and in between there are quiet villages where you can still hope to escape from other tourists.

In ancient times, around 290 BC, the harbour entrance of **Rodos** town was supposedly spanned by the mighty Colossus – a bronze statue of Helios the sun god (27m/90ft) – one of the seven wonders of the world.

The old town lies within a great wall (12m/40ft thick), built on Byzantine foundations in the 15th century. There is a three mile tour of the wall (5km) on Saturdays and Mondays starting at 1600, during which you overlook the exotic domes and the sunny squares and fountains. Start at the Amboise Gate. Inside the inner wall is the Palace of the Grand Masters, a fortress built by the Knights of St John. (Open all-year-round, 0730 to 1930, Sunday 1000 to 1800, closed Tuesdays.) There is a Son et Lumière show here (in English) between April 1 and October 31, tickets at the gate. Rodos museum (2), housed in the 15th-century Knights' Hospital, contains some remarkable statues – open 0730 to 1930, Sunday 1000 to 1800.

The only practising mosque in Greece is here, the Mosque of Suleiman. If you find it open, remove your shoes before entering. This is the heart of the old city, a maze of wooden balconies, crumbling arches and overhead houses. There are real Turkish baths nearby (1). Go there to relax or just admire the vaulted reception room

Mandraki harbour, Rodos

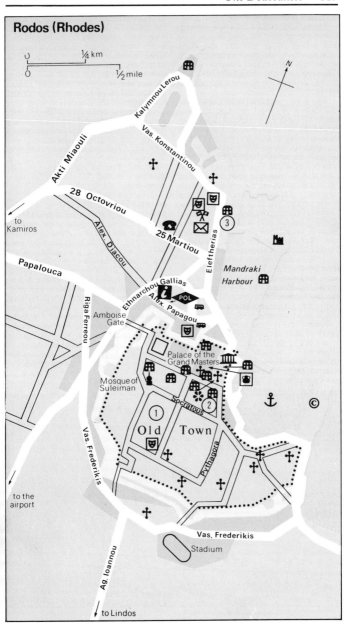

Rodos (Rhodes)

¼ km
½ mile

N

Kalymnou Lerou

Vas. Konstantinou

Akti Miaouli

28 Octovriou

to Kamiros

Alex. Diacou

25 Martiou

Eleftherias

③

Mandraki Harbour

Papalouca

Riga Ferreou

Ethnarchou Gallias

Alex. Papagou

Amboise Gate

Palace of the Grand Masters

Mosque of Suleiman

Socratous

②

①

Old Town

Vas. Frederikis

Pythagora

to the airport

Ag. Ioannou

to Lindos

Vas. Frederikis

Stadium

©

with its white marble floor.

The new part of Rodos town, extending north of the old city, boasts over 100 hotels. It is laid out along the waterfront of Mandraki harbour which is dominated by the massive square Campanile of the cathedral (**3**). There are many taxis or buses to all parts of the island, and guided tours.

The road from the main town along the east coast, runs through a fertile plain of orange groves and a Saharan landscape of date palms, with white cuboid houses and beaches off side-tracks along the way. It leads eventually to the village of **Lindos** (55km/35mi) which lies at the foot of a rocky headland and is classed, in its entirety, as an ancient monument. New building is not allowed and accommodation is in village houses only. Traffic is barred from the cobbled streets. Donkeys may be hired for the ascent of the Acropolis, past lines of local elders sewing day in, day out. The Acropolis, with its mediaeval castle and earlier remains, is open 0730 to 1930, and 1000 to 2000 on Sunday. The beach is long, sandy, and dotted with *tavernas*, as is the whole of the south-east coast. The desolate area at the southern tip of the island, Prassonisi Cape, has no accommodation except in the Skiadi monastery.

Round the rugged west coast is the castle of **Monolithos**, high on a precipitous rock (240m/775ft) – reached by a single path – and with superb views out to sea. Travelling north again (about 48km/30mi), you come to the tobacco growing village of **Embonas**, base camp

for the climb up Mt Ataviros, the highest peak on Rodos at 1214m/3986ft. The climb takes two hours up and two hours back – a hot shadeless walk in summer, but with a view of the whole island as compensation.

Communications: Rodos is well served by air and sea, with non-stop flights from London and ferries from all the main ports of the Aegean, *eg* ferry nine times weekly with Pireas (20-28 hrs). Daily flights from Athens (1 hr). Daily flights to Kos and Karpathos (50 mins). Check with your travel agent.

Festivals: Donkey races on July 29-30 at Soroni, August Dance Festivals at Kalithies, Maritsa and Embonas, folk dancing at Rodini, November 7 carnival at Apokries.

Minor Dodecanese

The following islands are accessible but seldom visited by tourists and perhaps only by connoisseurs. **Leros** is wooded and fertile (**F4**), **Nissiros** has a dormant volcano and sulphur springs (**I5**), **Tilos** has beautiful beaches (**J6**), **Simi** has a monastery (**I8**). They all offer the pleasures of beautiful islands untouched by the tide of tourism and quite unsophisticated. Tour operators have discovered Simi and Leros, but ... Read between the lines – beaches only accessible by boat sound romantic, but the novelty can soon wear off.

Communications: reasonable, but it is best to enquire. Ferry six times weekly Pireas to Leros (12 hrs), twice weekly to Simi (24 hrs), once a week Nissiros (22 hrs) and Tilos (24 hrs).

Temple of Athene Lindia, the Acropolis, Lindos

CRETE

Crete (Kriti) must be better known to the armchair traveller than any other Greek island. It is a happy hunting ground for would-be historians, biologists, geologists, and for simple sun worshippers. Halfway between the mainland and Egypt, it is the largest Greek island (8620 sq km/3189 sq mi).

It is an island of forests, wild mountains, still lonely beaches (Christmas swimming on the south coast), riotous festivals, and Cretan music and dance. There are 500,000 inhabitants, 3200 caves, 250 species of vegetation unknown elsewhere, six rivers, one lake and no railway.

There are excellent roads between main centres, with a good bus service – local buses are half as expensive as tourist buses, but may leave while tourists are asleep! Minor roads through the mountains can be very minor indeed.

The ruins of the past are the first stop for visitors. In Crete there was an organized, cultivated empire, 2000 years before civilization appeared anywhere else in Europe. It reached its height just after 2000 BC and the name of one legendary king of the period, Minos, is used today to denote the whole culture, Minoan. The ruins of Minoan palaces attract visitors to Festos and especially to Knossos, where the palace was so complex it resembled a labyrinth. The Minoans, under a palace-centred bureaucracy, led a peaceful, self-sufficient life, producing bronzes, jewellery, and works of art that you can admire today. Presumably they controlled the seas, since they had no need of great fortifications.

Earthquakes in 1700 BC and 1550 BC weakened the Minoans, and allowed Greeks to impose themselves at least on the Palace of Knossos. The palace was reconstructed by Mycenaean Greeks (see page 8) and it is the remains of the Mycenaean palace which you visit today. Around 1450 some bigger natural disaster, probably associated with the volcanic eruption on Santorini (Thira), destroyed the Mycenaean culture in Crete.

After the Dorian invasions, the island had almost 1500 stable years. Then, in AD 823, the Saracens captured and held it for 100 years until the Byzantine reconquest. The Genoese ruled the island initially, but in 1210 it was bought by the Venetians. Crete was the last Greek speaking territory to fall to the Turks (1669, when Iraklio was taken) and nearly the last to be freed.

This history has affected the Cretan people; they are 'different' from other Greeks. There seems to be no substance to the legend that they are bigger and stronger, showing direct descent from the Dorians (many Cretan girls could have stepped straight off a Minoan fresco), but there is a distinct Cretan facial expression – tougher, more grizzled, not so inquisitive as mainland Greeks but more knowing. There is a difference in the music too. The traditional Greek song, soulful and falling, is not part of Cretan tradition, and the *bouzouki* that has swept over the rest of Greece has less place here. Instead, the traditional instrument, still played by shepherds in the mountains, is a type of lyre, and the music has, for western ears, a wailing, oriental melody and Arab rhythm.

As a holiday centre Crete successfully absorbs its thousands of visitors. There is plenty of organized activity with snorkelling, waterskiing, climbing and dancing, a surfeit of sightseeing, and desolate empty areas defiantly inaccessible to motorists. Weather varies from tropically hot along the south coast, with a dusty summer haze blown from the Sahara, to perpetual winter snows on the peaks of some of the mountains.

The island is divided into four nomes, each separated from its neighbour by a mountain range. To the west of the White Mountains (Lefka Ori) is Hania, between the White Mountains and Mt Idi is Rethimno, between Mt Idi and the Lassithi mountains is Iraklio, and in the east is Lassithi county.

Iraklio is the obvious centre for exploring Crete, especially for newcomers who have not yet discovered a favourite hideaway. Here are the major Minoan sites – the fertile Mesara plain between

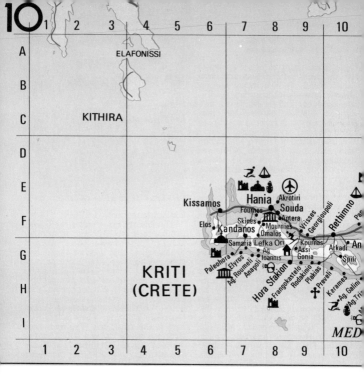

1 2 3 4 5 6 7 8 9 10

A ELAFONISSI

B

C KITHIRA

D

E Kissamos Hania Akrotiri
Souda

F Fournes Aptera
Elos Skines Mournies Georgioupoli Rethimno
Kandanos Omalos Vrisses
Samaria Lefka Ori Kournas

G Paleohora Ag Assi Arkadi An
Ioannis Gonia
Elyros Spili
Ag Roumeli Aradoli
KRITI Hora Stakion Rodakino
(CRETE) Frangokastelo Plakias
Prevelli
Karames
Ag Galini
Ag Tri
MED

1 2 3 4 5 6 7 8 9 10

Knossos and the southern shores has been densely populated since Minoan times. It is a region of music and dance, with vineyards and, near Iraklio itself, some intensive industrial growth.

Lassithi is the most varied region within this island. Its western border is a high plain marked like a chessboard by furrowed emerald-and-brown potato and bean fields, irrigated by 6000 whirling, white cloth-sailed windmills. Its north coast has seen the most tourist development.

Rethimno is the most rugged and least visited part of Crete, the birthplace of many well known artists and writers. The nome is dominated by Mt Idi (2452m/8058ft) with its harsh, precipitous gorges and caves. The south coast has sheltered but rather inaccessible beaches.

Hania is the land of the wild white mountains and lush green woodland – the last place where the Cretan wild goat (*kri kri*) lives in its natural state. The people of Hania have long been famed as warriors. Much of the countryside is almost inaccessible, in many ways reminiscent of the southern Peloponnese.

Agia Galini H11
(ΑΓΙΑ ΓΑΛΗΝΗ)
Rethimno A fishing hamlet which was not on the map until a few years ago. Now it is a very popular holiday village with *taverna* tables straddling the main street, safe deep bathing, waterskiing and wind-surfing. The beach is a mixture of coarse sand and shingle. Mopeds and scooters may be hired here to explore the arid mountains inland. Many rooms to let. *Rethimno 45km/28mi.*

Agios Ioannis G7
(ΑΓΙΟΣ ΙΩΑΝΝΗΣ)
Hania Three hours by mule south east of Ag. Roumeli is Ag. Ioannis, and a region of labyrinths and caves. If you have a taste for exploration, take a string and torch to look at the **Drakolakki Cave** with its bottomless lake.

Agios Nikolaos G15
(ΑΓΙΟΣ ΝΙΚΟΛΑΟΣ)
Lassithi (pop. 5000) On the Gulf of

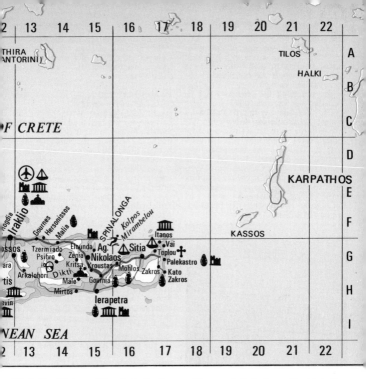

Mirabello (Kolpos Mirambelou), the capital of Lassithi is a lively, cosmopolitan seaside town built round an inner harbour, like a lake. In summer its population swells to 10,000 and it is the main resort catering for international tourists; the atmosphere remains happy and carefree. There are scooters for hire and all kinds of sporting activities.

East of Ag. Nikolaos is a string of beaches with *tavernas*, and coastal villages with Turkish and Byzantine remains. *Iraklio 64km/40mi.*

Anogia (ΑΝΩΓΕΙΑ)   G11
Rethimno Anogia was burnt down by both Turks and Germans. Today it is the centre for Crete's finest woven cloth. There are 700 traditional weaves and you can buy straight from the loom. From Anogia the ascent to the summit of Mt Idi takes 12 hours. *Iraklio 31km/19mi.*

Aptera (ΑΠΤΕΡΑ)   F8
Hania Site of the music contest between the Sirens and Muses in mythical times. The Muses won and the Sirens,

pulling out their feathers, dived into the sea to form the small white Lukai Islands in Souda Bay. The huge walls and many ruins of the ancient city remain. *Hania 16km/10mi.*

Arkadi (ΑΡΚΑΔΙ)   G10
Rethimno At the head of a steep gorge is a 17th-century monastery (Moni Arkadiou), guarded by a handful of monks and a few dogs. It resembles a small fort and in the past has been used more for defence than religion. In 1866 it was blown up by the Abbot, killing 829 people, rather than surrender to the Turks. This event is still celebrated every year on November 8 and 9. There is a small hotel at Arkadi. *Rethimno 79km/49mi.*

Elounda (ΕΛΟΥΝΔΑ)   G15
Lassithi This fishing village is fast becoming a holiday centre with many small hotels. There is an excellent beach on a calm lagoon, formed by the nearby island of Spinalonga (an artificial island which was a leper colony until 1952). *Ag. Nikolaos 11km/7mi.*

Elyros (ΕΛΥΡΟΣ)   G7

Hania Elyros was one of the most important ancient cities of south-west Crete, flourishing under the Romans and Byzantines. It was destroyed by the Saracens and though there is little left of the old town the region is rich in Venetian and Turkish ruins.

The Venetian castle of **Paleohora** (Castel Selino) looks down onto the village of the same name and a beautiful sandy beach. From here you can get a boat to **Gaudos**, the triangular islet south of Ag. Roumeli. It is believed to be the island where Calypso kept Odysseus for seven years before sending him back to Ithaki. It has no accommodation, being inhabited only by shepherds. The beaches are beautiful. *Hania 48km/30mi.*

Mt Idi from Festos

Festos (ΦΑΙΣΤΟΣ)   H11

Iraklio Festos (Phaistos) flourished about the same time as Knossos. The great three-storeyed palace on the hilltop dominated the villages below, where 30,000 people once lived and worked for the king. The site was excavated by the Italian School of Archaeology. Of special interest is the impressive grand staircase in the palace, carved with sacred snakes. Inside there are the royal rooms, bathrooms and rainwater cisterns, and one of the oldest metal forges in the world. Visit the picturesque tourist pavilion and restaurant.

Agia Triada (4km/2mi west of Festos) supplied much of the alabaster and gypsum for the building of the Palace of Festos and is a Minoan site in its own right with the ruins of a small summer palace overlooking the sea. *Iraklio 55km/34mi.*

Frangokastelo   G9
(ΦΡΑΓΚΟΚΑΣΤΕΛΛΟ)

Hania At the foot of the mountains between Ag. Roumeli and Plakias is the massive fort of Frangokastelo, set on a fine sandy beach. A massacre took place here in 1828; 650 Cretans were slain by the Turks and it is said that on May 17, the anniversary of the massacre, the Cretan dead rise up and silently march into the sea. The sight is seen when the weather is completely calm and warm – the conditions for a mirage. *Rethimno 42km/26mi.*

Gortis (ΓΟΡΤΥΣ)   G12

Iraklio This was the Roman capital of Crete and today there are extensive remains of the ancient city. Most remarkable of the discoveries at Gortis was the law code, which was laid down in the 5th century BC and built into the Roman Odion in AD 100. Written on stone in an archaic Doric dialect, and in the boustrofedon or ox-plough style (alternate lines reading from left to right and then right to left), it was a model for the laws of Athens and Sparta, for Roman law and our own present day law. *Iraklio 35km/22mi.*

Gournia (ΓΟΥΡΝΙΑ)   G15

Lassithi On the hillside overlooking the Gulf of Mirabello (Kolpos Mirambelou), Gournia is the best preserved Minoan town on Crete. There are many little streets of workshops, storerooms and houses leading to a small palace. *Ag. Nikolaos 16km/10mi.*

Hania (ΧΑΝΙΑ)   E8

Hania (pop. 40,000) Hania is an elegant, restful town built on the site of ancient Kidonia. After the disaster of 1450 BC it became one of Crete's most important cities until it was abandoned in Byzantine times. It was rebuilt in 1252 AD by the Venetians who constructed magnificent homes for themselves inside a fortress on the site of the acropolis. Many years later in 1537, when the pirate Barbarossa threatened the town, a 30ft-deep moat (9m) was constructed around the walls.

The centre of everyday life is the cruciform covered market from where all parts of the town are easily located. To the north is the old Venetian walled town in the Torpana quarter – a tangle of crumbling streets – and a harbour with its graceful lighthouse. To the south east is the fashionable 19th-century district where the historical museum on Sfakianaki Street houses the Archives of Crete, second only to the national archives in Athens.

It is possible to swim at Hania but better to take the bus from the centre of the town to **Neo Hora** (5 mins away, west), where the sea and the sand are clean. The **Akrotiri Peninsula**, dominated by a hill where Crete's favourite son El Venizelos is buried, offers peace near Hania (north east). Good swimming on its west coast, but its east and south coasts are close to the airport and the naval base of Souda Bay.

Nightlife is lively and noisy especially down by the harbour where young Greeks meet in the cafés for a glass of Cretan *raki*. The main festival of Hania is from mid-May to mid-June and on August 15 the town hosts the Pan-Cretan festival.

Buses for the surrounding countryside start from Platia 1866, while for Rethimno and Iraklio they start from the market place. *Iraklio 116km/72mi.*

Hora Sfakion   G8
(ΧΩΡΑ ΣΨΑΚΙΩΝ)
Hania This is the centre of the Sfakatia region, isolated by mountains, and probably the most individual area in Crete. The people have retained their independence throughout the centuries. The older people still wear national costume. Some accommodation can be arranged, and there are excursions by boat to villages along the coast (inaccessible by road). *Rethimno 47km/29mi.*

Ierapetra (ΙΕΡΑΠΕΤΡΑ)   H15
Lassithi (pop. 9000) This is the most southerly town in Greece, the nearest to Africa (370km/230mi). It is a lovely winter resort with a Venetian fortress, vestiges of a Roman theatre and an interesting museum.

Mirtos, accessible by bus from Ierapetra or along the riverbed from **Male**, was an early Minoan weaving centre. *Sitia 64km/40mi.*

Iraklio (ΗΡΑΚΛΕΙΟΝ)   F12
Iraklio (pop. 77,000) Iraklio (Herakleion) is the largest city in Crete and originally the port for Knossos; today it has Crete's main airport, where most tourist flights from Greece and all international flights arrive.

Iraklio is cosmopolitan but it is not a particularly attractive town. There are many hotels, shops, an excellent market, a youth hostel, and transport to every part of the island. It is the nearest centre for the archaeological site of Knossos, and boasts two really important museums – any sightseeing will be better rewarded after an initial fact-finding visit.

The Archaeological Museum in the main square, Platia Elevtherias, contains the most fabulous collection of Minoan art treasures in the world. The Historical Museum on Akti Makariou contains many Venetian relics and much from the early Christian, Byzantine and Turkish periods.

There is a 16th-century-BC villa with a shrine, weaving room and a wine press at **Rodia** (west, along the road to Rethimno), and a Venetian fort on the shore. *Hania 116km/72mi, Sitia 137/85.*

Knossos (ΚΝΩΣΟΣ)   G12
Iraklio A visitor to Iraklio town will want to visit the remains of the Minoan-Mycenaean palace at Knossos, as much as the visitor to Athens will want to see the Parthenon. You will need the guide-book available at the site to fully describe the complex labyrinth of over 1000 rooms, courts and passages, decorated with brightly coloured frescos (not originals). However, if you like just to wander round, it may help to know the history of the palace.

The Minoan rulers at Knossos flourished for nearly a thousand years until they were displaced by early Greeks. The labyrinth of rooms was probably built for defensive purposes or security, to confuse raiders as they now confuse the visitor; another theory is that they were tombs. The Minoans' great sport was bull jumping, a civilized version of Spanish bullfighting, as can be seen on the frescos (and on the pottery in Iraklio); the bull was almost worshipped.

The following is a brief outline of the legend which grew to explain Knossos' existence. The Queen of King Minos had a child by a bull and this monstrous creature was called the Minotaur. Daedalus designed the labyrinth (Knossos) as a home for the Minotaur which demanded an annual tribute of youths and girls, sent from Athens at the request of King Minos. The Queen of Athens had a son by Poseidon (who visited her in the form of a bull) and this son, Theseus, killed the Minotaur, and eventually became King of Athens.

The labyrinth at Knossos is Minoan but the palace itself was probably a Mycenaean construction. However, all the buildings were destroyed in some natural disaster and the site was lost before 1000 BC. Sir Arthur Evans discovered it just before AD 1900 and devoted his life to excavation and reconstruction. His reconstruction was – shall we say – imaginative, and bent to fit his theory that the whole site was Minoan. The decipherment of Linear B and realization that there was Greek building on top of pre-Greek, took place only after his death. As a result, what you see today above ground is not necessarily authentic, but it should still be seen. *Iraklio 7km/3½mi.*

Kritsa (ΚΡΙΤΣΑ)   G15

Lassithi   Kritsa is a time-forgotten mountain village. Being known as 'authentic' it has, in fact, become rather synthetic but is remarkable for its vivid 14th-century frescos in the church of Panayia Kera. On the last Sunday of August there is a festival at the church, including a mock wedding in traditional style; around this time local weddings are often celebrated and visitors are welcome.

Kroustas (south west) is an unspoilt village with more frescoed churches and a huge bonfire festival on June 25. There is an occasional bus between Kritsa and Kroustas. *Ag. Nikolaos 11km/7mi.*

Malia (ΜΑΛΙΑ)   G14

Iraklio   East along the main road from Iraklio the coast is fast developing. Past the American air-force base at **Gournes** and the ancient site of **Heronissos** (now a minor holiday resort) is the vast seaside palace of Malia, which was built by the Minoans in 1900 BC but was devastated by earthquakes 200 years later. A second palace was built over it and this was ruined in the 15th-century-BC disaster. This site is third in importance after Knossos and Festos.

The nearby village of Malia is profiting from tourist interest in its heritage. There is a youth hostel and plenty of sleeping and eating-places. *Iraklio 37km/23mi.*

Matala (ΜΑΤΑΛΑ)   H11

Iraklio   Matala was one of the first south coast resorts to be developed, largely because of its beautiful safe beach. It is flanked by high cliffs pitted with caves which have been used as dwellings or churches for thousands of years, and now provide shelter for homeless travellers. It is still a small village, but teeming with cafés and restaurants.

To the north east is the town of **Mires** which has a large market on Saturday mornings. Handy for **Festos**. *Gortis 69km/43mi.*

Plakias (ΠΛΑΚΙΑΣ)   G9

Rethimno   Plakias has a lovely beach and a few rooms to let but it is extremely isolated and a car is really essential, especially to reach the Preveli Monastery between the coast and the Kouraliotiko ravine. *Rethimno 29km/18mi.*

Rethimno (ΡΕΘΥΜΝΟ)   F10

Rethimno (pop. 15,000) The town is a mediaeval throwback with crumbling Venetian houses and narrow dark streets overhung by wooden balconies. At night the fish restaurants along the harbour are buzzing with activity. There is a long sandy beach. The Fortezza (old Venetian fortifications, open daily from 0700 to 1500) which includes the well-preserved mosque, and the Loggia which is now a museum (closed from 1300 to 1700, and on Mondays), are amongst the best Venetian buildings in Greece.

Travel from Rethimno to other parts of the region is not always easy although

Matala beach

the roads are being improved. To the west lies **Georgioupoli** (20km/12mi) with its unending beaches and the occasional holiday hotel; inland, at **Kournas**, is Crete's only lake, known for its eels. *Iraklio 69km/43mi.*

Samaria (ΣAMAPIA)　　　G7
Hania The *Xiloscala* (wooden staircase) marks the 760m/2500ft descent from **Omalos** to Europe's longest gorge – the Gorge of Samaria – which runs for 11 spectacular miles (18km) to the sea. With preparation it is possible to make this excursion into a splendid expedition.

The walk itself, between 300m/1000ft walls of rock in places a few feet apart, takes about seven hours and is comfortingly patrolled by guards. It is not difficult though sometimes hard on the feet and not for the claustrophobic. There is always the hope of seeing the last remaining wild goats in Crete perched on the cliff face. Take your own food and drink, and check all boat and bus times in Hania before you leave.

The gorge ends at the village of **Agia Roumeli**. There is an evening boat to **Hora Sfakion** (see page 123) which is supposed to connect with a bus to Hania. If you miss either connection there is overnight accommodation in both villages, and a morning bus back to Hania from Hora Sfakion. *Hania 35km/22mi.*

Sitia (ΣHTEIA)　　　G16
Lassithi (pop. 6000)) A pretty unspoilt resort, popular with Cretans from Iraklio. The seafront is lined with cafés and restaurants and there is a dark sandy beach. In mid-July a lively three-day wine festival is celebrated. There is a good round-the-region bus service and the Karpathos/Rodos ship stops here on its way from Ag. Nikolaos.

Toplou Monastery (14km/9mi east) is an isolated three-storey fortress built in the late 15th century. A 'must' for monastery goers. Above the monastery gate is a hole through which the besieged monks used to pour oil on their attackers. It has a history of siege and resistance. At the beginning of the War of Independence (1821) the Turks captured it and hung the bodies of 12 monks on the gates. *Iraklio 137km/85mi.*

Zakros (ZAKPOΣ)　　　G17
Lassithi This tiny hamlet has important Minoan archaeological remains. A huge gorge leads from Zakros to **Kato Zakros** at the sea. Some of the buildings here can be seen under the water because this side of Crete is sinking. The palace itself was only found in 1962. There are a few rooms to let in the village and a good pebbley beach to swim from.

A lonely dramatic drive from Zakros through **Palekastro**, set high in an olive grove above the sea, brings you to the palm fringed beaches of **Vai** where the only wild date palms in Europe grow. There is a beach *taverna* open in summer.

Further north, **Itanos** was used by Ptolemy as a naval station; the city thrived on a trade of glass and dyes. Today, there are prehistoric, Hellenistic and early Christian ruins to be seen. *Sitia 39km/24mi.*

Communications: There are direct scheduled flights from London (Heathrow) to Iraklio, otherwise Crete has to be reached via Athens: Athens to Iraklio (45 mins), and in the summer there are flights from Athens to Hania.

There are many car ferries from European ports such as Marseille, Genova (Genoa) and Venezia (Venice), and from Pireas on the mainland to Iraklio (12 hrs). During the summer season there are frequent passenger sailings for both Iraklio and Hania from Pireas, and rather fewer services to Kissamos from Githio and Pireas.

Festivals: January 6 the waters are blessed throughout Greece – a cross is thrown into the sea and the young man who retrieves it is honoured, Lent – during the previous two weeks there is a carnival atmosphere. Clean Monday – the first day of Lent is kite flying day all over Crete, Good Friday – candlelight funeral processions with fireworks and feasting everywhere, April Orange Festival at Skines and Sheep Shearing Festival at Assi Gonia, May 21–24 International Dance Festival at Hania, June 24 bonfires are lit everywhere and young boys leap through them, July 15 Wine Festival with music and dancing at Rethimno, August 15 Assumption Day at Mohlos with fireworks and dancing, August 31 The Holy Sash of the Virgin at Psihro with local dances and feasting, October Chestnut Festival at Elos, November 7–9 Anniversary of the 1866 Explosion – holiday with special festivities at Arkadi and Rethimno.

Specialities: doughnuts, *bougatsa* (custard pies), fish (especially from the Bay of Souda), oranges. *Raki* is a stronger version of *ouzo* and commands respect. The wine is unexceptional and unresinated.

INDEX

All main entries are printed in heavy type. Map references are also printed in heavy
type. The map page number precedes the grid reference.